MW00658012

PRAISE FOR *HUSKY FOOTBALL IN THE DON JAMES ERA*

"Don James is a Hall of Fame coach who I loved competing with during my coaching career at the University of Louisville and Indiana University. I know that not only Washington fans but all college football fans will enjoy this book. It's a great read. I loved it!"

—Lee Corso, *ESPN College Gameday*

"Derek Johnson's book is an essential addition to the library of any Husky fan. It chronicles an unforgettable, championship chapter in the history of Northwest sports—much of it in the words and recollections of the people who made history."

—Sam Farmer, *Los Angeles Times*

"The most electrifying modern era of Washington football, from exhilarating highs to exasperating lows, is well chronicled by Derek Johnson, who draws insights on the tumult from those who made the Don James era so memorable."

—Art Thiel, *Seattle Post Intelligencer*

"Any Husky fan is sure to find much to learn and enjoy in this exhaustively detailed account of the Don James era. The interviews with many of the key participants, including James himself, are particularly revelatory and Johnson doesn't shy away from delving deep into the controversial end of that era."

—Bob Condotta, *Seattle Times*

"Every Husky diehard needs this book... The strongest parts are the intermittent chapters that are Q&As with former Huskies. The subjects, which include Joe Steele, Chuck Nelson, former WSU coach Jim Walden and Bob Rondeau among others, are clearly at ease with Johnson. These interviews offer the readers "inside" views of what was going on at that time—Huskies fans will get frothy over these."

—Molly Yanity, *Seattle Post-Intelligencer*

"I know the book took me back to some of the most exciting times of a 40-year career in sports journalism. While it is predictable because the Washington teams of Don James were predictable—playing with unprecedented passion and precision—the book's conclusion is shocking. Has Derek Johnson unlocked the mystery surrounding Don James' resignation? Could it have been political?"

—Blaine Newnham, *Seattle Times*

HUSKY FOOTBALL
IN THE
DON JAMES ERA

DEREK JOHNSON

INTRODUCTION BY DON JAMES
FOREWORDS BY LINCOLN KENNEDY
AND DAVE HOFFMANN

Most of the images in this book are licensed by Collegiate Images.

Visit us online at www.derekjohnsonbooks.com

ISBN 13: 978-0-9793271-0-0
ISBN 10: 0-9793271-0-5

Printed in the United States of America

For my Father

Contents

Foreword by Lincoln Kennedy ... xi

Foreword by Dave Hoffmann ... xiv

Introduction by Don James ... xvi

Acknowledgements ... xix

Chapter 1 – December 1974
Don James comes to Washington ... 3

Chapter 2 — October 11, 1975
Humiliation Down in Dixie ... 8

Chapter 3 — November 22, 1975
Miracle in a Monsoon ... 11

Chapter 4 — November 20, 1976
Breaking the 1,000-yard Barrier ... 15

Chapter 5 — September 24 & October 1, 1977
Dreary Days ... 18

Chapter 6 — October 8, 1977
"We Came Together As A Team" ... 22

Chapter 7 — November 12, 1977
Winds of Change ... 26

Chapter 8 — January 2, 1978
"It was a Tremendous Moment" ... 31

Chapter 9
A Visit with Joe Steele ... 36

Chapter 10 — October 7, 1978
A Sense of Redemption ... 44

Chapter 11 — October 29, 1978
A Tale of Revenge ... 49

Chapter 12 — September 21, 1979
Mark Lee's Miracle Punt Return ... 53

Chapter 13
A visit with Tom Flick ... 56

Chapter 14
A Visit with Chuck Nelson ... 77

Chapter 15 — January 1, 1982
"Who's Jacque Robinson?" ... 84

Chapter 16 — November 6, 1982
Fourth Quarter Epic ... 90

Chapter 17 — November 13, 1982
Desert Rose ... 92

Chapter 18 — November 20, 1982
What Might Have Been ... 96

Chapter 19
A Visit with Former WSU Coach Jim Walden ... 101

Chapter 20 — September 17, 1983
A Fourth Quarter to Remember ... 111

Chapter 21— September 15, 1984
Hugh Millen's Homecoming ... 115

Chapter 22 — January 1, 1985
Purple Reigns Supreme ... 120

Chapter 23
A Visit with Ron Holmes ... 127

Chapter 24
A Visit with Husky Radio Announcer Bob Rondeau ... 136

Chapter 25 — October 19, 1985
Pride Goes Before a Fall ... 144

Chapter 26 — September 20, 1986
Payback ... 148

Chapter 27
A Visit with Chris Chandler ... 152

Chapter 28
A visit with Former UW Athletic Director Mike Lude ... 159

Chapter 29 — November 19, 1988
The Darkness Before the Dawn ... 182

Chapter 30 — September 9, 1989
"I Sense a Chemistry Developing" ... 185

Chapter 31 — September 30, 1989
Death of a Quarterback ... 189

Chapter 32
A visit with Dave "Hammer" Hoffmann ... 193

Chapter 33
A Visit with Steve Emtman ... 204

Chapter 34
A Visit with Dana Hall ... 213

Chapter 35 — September 22, 1990
"All I Saw was Purple" ... 224

Chapter 36 — November 3, 1990
Nothin' But Roses ... 228

Chapter 37- January 1, 1991
Pasadena Onslaught... 231

Chapter 38 — September 21, 1991
Slaying Big Red ... 235

Chapter 39 — October 19, 1991
"Wow... Now This is College Football!" 240

Chapter 40 — November 23, 1991
Perfection 244

Chapter 41 — January 1, 1992
"A Great Day in the Life of a Football Coach" 247

Chapter 42
What the Nation was saying about the Huskies... 253

Chapter 43
A Visit with Napoleon Kaufman... 255

Chapter 44 — September 19, 1992
"One of those Nights to Remember" 262

Chapter 45, October 31, 1992
Dissolution 266

Chapter 46
The Past is not Dead 277

Chapter 47
The Roses of Wrath 284

Chapter 48
A Letter from former UW President, Dr. William Gerberding 292

Chapter 49
Saying Goodbye 296

Husky Football in the Don James Era
18 Seasons (153-57-2) (.726) 305

Foreword by Lincoln Kennedy

WHILE GROWING UP, I was well aware of the importance of sports to the American culture, especially football. But I didn't appreciate its full effect until I came to UW as a freshman in the fall of 1988. The day I donned the Husky uniform in front of a capacity crowd was the day I suddenly comprehended the magnitude college football has on our society. To imagine a kid from San Diego who played in the band for most of his life to suddenly be in front of 72,000 frenzied fans and have them cheer with just the raising of his helmet was something I never thought would happen to me. It was like a dream, exhilarating yet surreal. I cannot explain how it feels to be seventeen years old running into Husky Stadium for the very first time. It was one of the greatest moments of my life.

One of the greatest games I was a part of was the 1992 Nebraska game at Husky Stadium. There's a chapter in this book featuring it, along with my commentary. I remember this game especially because it took place in the evening, unlike most of our college games that usually started around noon. With the nighttime setting and a raucous Husky crowd, we played one of our best games as a team. If the prior year had left any doubt if we could beat a nationally recognized program, we quickly squashed it by beating Nebraska again. Most of our big name players had great games (including yours truly) mainly because we knew we had a national audience and that there were pro scouts watching us. But to be completely honest, we wanted the respect other schools were getting. And we were determined to take it from anyone on our schedule.

I don't remember a lot of the details of my last game in Husky Stadium, in November 1992. But I do remember while we were crushing Oregon State, I had a lot of conflicting feelings. I looked into the eyes of the juniors and sophomores, the future of Husky football, and thinking that I was leaving my Alma Mater in good hands. I felt relief that the tradition that was handed down to me would continue through them. And I remember looking around Husky Stadium at our faithful fans and feeling pride that while I was there we had achieved more than any previous Husky team ever. My teammates and I had brought this worthy city and university long overdue respect and acknowledgment. But along with the satisfaction, came an overwhelming feeling of sadness. I was sad because I was about to start a new life, and my college years were almost over forever.

Looking back, I still haven't forgotten my college experience. Despite the bitterness from the sanctions period of 1992-93, I still cherish my time at Washington. I still revere Coach Don James—a man of profound integrity. And the city and the people of Seattle will forever share a special place in my heart.

When Derek asked me to be a part of this book, I jumped at the challenge. It is my hope that after you read *Husky Football in the Don James Era,* you will be able to imagine yourself either in the stands or on the field. Or maybe you'll relive some of your own memories from actually being at the games. Either way, always remember: "Mighty are the men and women who wear the Purple & Gold."

Lincoln Kennedy
All-American and All-Pro Offensive Tackle
Washington Huskies 1988-1992
Atlanta Falcons 1993-1995, Oakland Raiders 1996-2004

Foreword by Dave Hoffmann

DEREK JOHNSON IS A skilled writer who has become my friend over the last few years, after multiple interviews and personal conversations. He has a lifetime of experience watching and covering the Dawgs. Like many I have met in Seattle, Husky football was an important part of his life growing up. The combination of his writing skill, experience and good heartedness, have allowed him special access to former players and coaches.

Derek is enjoyable to speak with, as noted by the depth of his interviews in *Husky Football in the Don James Era.* I thoroughly loved reading the great stories of players who came before me. The players' insights in the pages of historic game sketches are special. These are memories the fans and players will carry for a lifetime.

I also enjoyed reading about our fearless leader, Don James. After reliving the Pac-10 sanctions time and remembering the disrespect and cowardice shown to him in 1993, I am reminded that no one could take away what we did in the preceding three years. Nobody can ever take away the national title won by the man with the most honesty and integrity in America. All of my teammates and I are proud to have been the Dawgfather's men. Coach didn't call us "boys," he called us "men." He led by example and expected us to follow. We did, and became men.

Derek's book reminds me of the excitement of game day and how much I loved running out the Husky tunnel and onto the field with Coach James and my teammates. Everyone knows that Coach was always meticulously prepared. But what I loved was that when I looked into his eyes right before kickoff and saw his posture, I knew he was ready for a fight. Whether from the stands or the turf of Husky Stadium, we are all better for having been around him.

Dave Hoffmann
All-American Linebacker
Washington Huskies 1988-1992
Chicago Bears 1993, Pittsburgh Steelers 1994-1995

Introduction by Don James

SINCE MY RETIREMENT IN 1993, I have had the pleasure of getting to know Derek. He and his family have had and still have a great interest and love for Husky athletics, especially the sport of football. His Dad, Ron Johnson, is a tremendous supporter of Husky football, having only missed one home football game since 1957.

Derek began attending Husky games at the age of five, when I was starting my second year as head coach at the University of Washington. He witnessed many memorable games from my eighteen-year career with the Huskies. My first two and a half years at Washington were very difficult, but our 1978 Rose Bowl championship put us on the map. Overall, we went to six Rose Bowls, one Orange Bowl, and experienced many other wonderful moments and victories. My retirement was also a difficult time for everyone involved. *Husky Football in the Don James Era* captures many of those moments, with commentaries from several of my former players.

During the past few years, I have done a number of interviews with Derek and have enjoyed reading his many articles. From the very beginning I have been impressed with his method of research, his questions and more importantly his writing skills.

You will enjoy what Derek and the Husky players have to say about their experiences and the inner workings of the Husky football program.

One of the chapters features a game against eleventh-ranked BYU in 1986. I remember standing on the sidelines at Husky Stadium and watching BYU's Robert Parker return the opening kickoff for a touchdown. After that, we really got after them. We scored 52 straight points to put the game out of reach. Our defense was outstanding. We had 10 quarterback sacks and held BYU to -45 yards rushing. I also remember being discouraged when we gave up two touchdowns late in the fourth quarter. However, we still won 52-21.

That BYU game sums up my career at Washington. I told the media afterwards that "I didn't like the start and I didn't like the finish, but in between it was pretty good."

Don James
Head Football Coach, University of Washington 1975-1992
Member, College Football Hall of Fame

Acknowledgements

FOR REASONS SUFFICIENT TO the writer, several games, players, observations and experiences have been left out of this book. There is little detail of USC stonewalling Washington at the goal line, in the fourth quarter of their 1979 showdown at Husky Stadium. There is no mention of the interesting recruiting stories from the late 1980s and early 1990s from former UW Recruiting Coordinator Dick Baird. There is no mention of the two hundred Husky fans that crammed into Longview's Triangle Tavern that night in 1982 to listen to the radio call of the victory over undefeated Arizona State. There are no depictions of the delightful antics of The Husky Marching Band, aka *A Touch of Class*, led by the late Bill Bissell.

Also left out were many precious memories from my childhood, such as Dad and I tailgating in Husky Stadium's north parking lot... eating turkey sandwiches and potato chips, sipping hot chocolate from plastic cups, and listening to Larry Nelson's old Tailgate Show on KOMO radio, often while rain pattered upon the windshield. Dad always refused to leave the car until Don James' pre-game interview was finished.

Special thanks go to the following people: Dawn Cahoon, for her invaluable and tireless editing suggestions, Greg Lewis, Dave "Hammer" Hoffmann, Lincoln Kennedy, O.B.J., Ed Cunningham, Kim Grinolds, Dave Samek and Don and Carol James.

Thanks to the following people, who in various ways, contributed their time, insight or support: Steve Emtman, Napoleon Kaufman, Jennifer Johnson, Ron and Margaret Johnson, Joe Steele, Stephen Hoffmann, Dan Eernissee, Dave and Karen Torrell, Amy Hollibaugh, Reem Hamadeh (for her relentless encouragement of my writing back in the day); David Handy, Warren Moon, Pat Thrapp, Mike Lude, Brian Tom, Jeff Bechtold, Sana Shabazz, Chris Fetters and everyone at Dawgman.com, Rick and Penny Soderberg, Mike Rohrbach, Spider Gaines, Ronnie Rowland, Tom Flick, Antowaine Richardson, Jacque Robinson, Steve Pelluer, Chuck Nelson, Bob Rondeau, Mark Stewart, Joe Krakoski, Dick Baird, Scott Hammond, Chris Chandler, Jim Lambright, Dawn and Craig Cahoon (and their adorable little future Husky, Maddie Cahoon); Ink Aleaga, Dana Hall, Beno Bryant, Mike Roberts, Tom and Sherry DeSanto, Jim Walden, Dennis Brown, Ron Holmes, Stafford Mays, Mark Lee, Joe Kelly, Spider Gaines, Jimmy Rodgers, Tim Peoples, Hugh Millen; and WBGO's John J. Cooper—my buddy back in New Jersey—for keeping me company with his jazz show while I worked deep into many a night.

"The past is not dead. In fact, it's not even past."

—William Faulkner

HUSKY FOOTBALL
IN THE
DON JAMES ERA

Chapter 1 – December 1974

Don James comes to Washington

DON AND CAROL JAMES, walking side-by-side, were being led by athletic department officials down the shadowy corridor of the Husky Stadium tunnel, toward the vivid patch of daylight up ahead. The stadium was empty and quiet. It was an overcast day in December 1974, and Don James had just been hired as the new football coach for the University of Washington. Being from Kent State University in Ohio, James possessed little familiarity with the details of Washington's storied football history. But that tunnel had been the thoroughfare to thousands of Husky players for decades. Players like Consensus All-American tailback George Wilson in the 1920s; tailback Hugh McElhenny and quarterback Don Heinrich of the early 1950s; the legendarily tough Don McKeta and linebacker Rick Redman in the 1960s; and of course, Sonny Sixkiller, the electrifying Cherokee quarterback who achieved folk hero status in the early 70s.

As Don and Carol James emerged from the mouth of the tunnel, they found themselves near the corner of the west end zone. They looked across at the vast steep tier of the south side upper deck. They saw the weather-beaten seats which nearly encircled the field and comprised the stadium's lower bowl. They spied the old scoreboard at a distance, and beautiful Lake Washington just beyond that. And they wandered out upon the dark green Astroturf. Don's "new office" looked great. The only part that seemed surreal was when they stepped out in front of the stadium, adjacent to the rushing traffic of Montlake Boulevard. It was there, as they gazed up at the reader board in disbelief, that they saw the pronouncement in giant letters: "WELCOME COACH JONES."

In Washington's previous two seasons of 1973 and 1974, the Huskies had struggled mightily-- compiling records of 2-9 and 5-6. The previous coach was Jim Owens, and he had stepped down after eighteen years that witnessed both glory and tumult. Now, as word of James's hiring spread through Western Washington, many Husky fans and sportswriters expressed disappointment. People had hoped for a big-time name like Dan Devine from the Green Bay Packers or Mike White from the California Golden Bears. The reality was that Don James was the UW's fourth choice. *The Seattle P-I's* Phil Taylor tried to provide solace to his readers: "While James may be something less than a household word around Seattle and the Pacific Eight, he is regarded with considerable respect back in the tough Mid-American Conference."

The next day, Washington Athletic Director Joe Kearney introduced Don James to the assembled Seattle-area media. James didn't intimidate anyone with his size, standing at just 5'8". He was methodical in manner and seemingly slow to smile-- and just four days shy of his forty-second birthday. At that first press conference, one beat writer noted that James comported himself with "stern sincerity." James went on to describe himself as being "more of an organized guy than emotional guy." When asked of his thoughts on the Washington job, he said: "There are eight or ten teams with an opportunity to be a national champion. Obviously, there are eighteen teams with an opportunity to get into the Rose Bowl. In the Big Ten there are probably two or three with a real chance, maybe the same way in the Pac-8. I think we're one of them. I think we have a great university and a great facility and we've been there before. People in my profession think that this is a school where you can accomplish anything you want in coaching, that you can become a national champion."

James indicated that a whole new system was going into place, and concluded the press conference by saying: "With the schedule we've got, we're going to have to be dog-gone good. The season starts in nine months, against a very good Arizona State team. We've got to get good in a hurry." Upon meeting the players, he set about improving the culture at Washington. He implemented a strenuous off-season conditioning program. Some players resented the change. Other players, like linebacker Dan Lloyd, expressed enthusiasm, after witnessing measurable improvements in their own speed, strength and agility.

When it came to recruiting, James told his newly-assembled staff of assistant coaches that they needed to "Build a fence around the state of Washington." James showed his staff film of USC playing and pointed to the screen. "These are the type of players we need to locate and recruit if we're ever going to win a conference championship." He employed a unique system for evaluating recruits. It involved numbers ranging from 1.1 – 4.10. The first number reflected the anticipated year that the recruit would become a starter, and the second would be the game number. Thus, a recruit with a 2.3 rating, was anticipated to become a starter by the third game of his second season. The tracking of players was conducted manually upon note cards. James insisted his incoming recruits possess five key components: (1) They must give 100%; (2) Have courage on and off the field; (3) Have the ability to master their position, and not hurt the team with mistakes; (4) Care about their teammates; and (5) Have great loyalty, which is invariably tested with adversity.

As winter turned to spring in early 1975, practices began at Husky Stadium. It was an adjustment for the players, as they were used to the more hands-on ways of Jim Owens. For one, a tower had now been placed along the south sideline at midfield. Every day, as practice began, Don James would ascend that tower. There he would stand taking notes, mostly in silence, save for an occasional comment spoken into a bullhorn toward an assistant coach. Otherwise, he remained above the fray, surveying the scene, in a perpetual pose of solitary sufficiency. Scattered below were his assistant coaches, yelling orders and encouraging players through the strenuous drills. Every Husky, at some point during his time at Washington, cast an anxious glance up toward the tower, wondering how they rated. "Every single minute of every single practice was accounted for," recalled former Assistant Coach Skip Hall years later to writer Steve Rudman. "The one thing Don would do before each practice was listen to each assistant. He'd go right down the line and fill in a chart showing who would be doing what during each segment. Every minute was utilized to the fullest. I think Don's organizational ability was one of his real strengths. I remember that every minute seemed carefully laid out with each coach deciding what the need for the day was. And then everything was written up. And he was very efficient with time. We had meticulous organization and planning. We critiqued everything, and we used those critiques to get better. The thoroughness was incredible at times. Some of the coaches who had been on Jim Owens' staff would get into some of Don's meetings and they'd come out with their heads spinning. Everything was played out ahead of time. The other thing is that Don hired good people. He had a good plan and he managed people well. He had the ability to motivate and get the most out of his people."

By early September 1975, Don James's debut at Arizona State was less than a week away. He was irked with some of his players. "I am not satisfied," stated James to the media. "The offense looked like it was going through popcorn drills. We weren't aggressive. We were sluggish." A reporter cited to him a handful of players that were publicly upset from being named to the scout team, when previously they had been starters under Jim Owens. James acknowledged this. "Yes, those guys on the scout teams are down," he said. "And we understand their plight, their position. But a mature competitor goes all out every day."

It wasn't until Friday night that James named a junior college transfer named Harold (Warren) Moon as his starting quarterback. Raised eyebrows and even muted anger emanated from some Husky fans as the news broke. It had been largely assumed that the previous year's starter, Chris Rowland, would continue to lead the way. Moon would be making a start despite not yet having attended a class at Washington.

On the humid evening of September 13, 1975, in Tempe, Arizona, Don James led his first Husky team running onto the grass at Sun Devil Stadium. Throughout the game, rain squalls and swirling winds would inundate the field. Flashes of lightning were sighted in the distance, out in the barren desert. On Washington's first play from scrimmage, Moon fumbled the snap and Arizona State recovered. This quickly led to a Sun Devil touchdown, which set the game's tone. By late in the fourth quarter, the Sun Devils led 28-12 and possessed the ball inside the Husky five-yard line. Arizona State Head Coach Frank Kush called time out with just three seconds left, in order to get in a final play. Along the opposing sideline, Don James outwardly remained stoic. But in reality, he churned with indignation. Moments later, the Sun Devils lined up and executed an end run to perfection, to tally their fifth touchdown and finish off the Huskies 35-12. The UW players trudged toward the locker room, enduring the screaming taunts from ASU fans. Washington's unknown new coach now had an 0-1 record. Don James would have to wait three years before attempting revenge on Arizona State and its coach, Frank Kush.

Chapter 2 — October 11, 1975

Humiliation Down in Dixie

Washington at Alabama

THOUGH THE DEEP SOUTH is known for its hospitality, you couldn't tell that to the 2-2 Washington Huskies. From the moment their plane landed, the visitors from Seattle were beset by Tuscaloosa's 80-degree heat, 90-percent humidity, and 100-percent fanaticism for football. Washington stayed at a hotel owned by legendary Alabama coach Bear Byrant. When they went downstairs for breakfast, greeting them was a giant mural of Crimson Tide players running full-speed ahead. As the Huskies were bussed to the stadium, they were wide-eyed as the Alabama State Patrol shut down the freeway and escorted them with multiple squad cars and frenetically flashing lights. Inside the stadium, the scene was every bit as impressive. Noted *the P-I's* Phil Taylor: "Hell, the size of the band that Alabama put on the field would have frightened John Phillip Sousa."

In Bear Bryant's decade as Alabama coach, he boasted a home-field record of 49-1. Don James felt, however, that his Huskies were prepared sufficiently to compete. James told reporters that Washington would have to play faultlessly to have a chance. "Alabama is the kind of team that doesn't need any help," said James. "We just can't afford to make any mistakes."

Washington's Pedro Hawkins promptly fumbled away possession of the opening kickoff. Soon after, Alabama QB Richard Todd rolled outside on a keeper, and waltzed untouched into the end zone for the first touchdown. Washington got the ball back, but was quickly forced to punt. Crimson Tide return man Willie Shelby jogged onto the field, and the home fans adorned him with their usual affectionate chant: RUN, WILLIE RUN! RUN, WILLIE RUN! As the kick sailed through the air, Shelby camped under it at his own 16-yard line. He caught it and was hit by Washington's Stan Wilson—but Wilson failed to wrap up. Shelby kept his balance, wriggled free of tacklers, cut down the left sideline behind an entourage of crimson jerseys, before swerving back into the middle of the field at the Husky forty-yard line. From there he glided into the end zone beneath waves of frenzied cheering.

By the second quarter, with the sweltering heat radiating off the field, Alabama's third and fourth string players were already funneling into the game. Just before halftime, a backup running back named Tony Nathan plunged into the end zone, to extend Bama's lead to 38-0.

Throughout the second half, Bear Bryant kept sending waves of backups into the game, with no apparent drop-off in talent. When the Husky defense attempted to shut down the middle, the Crimson Tide simply went outside. For Washington, the casualty list began to mount like something from a Civil War battlefield. Linebacker Michael Jackson broke his ankle. Tackle Bob Graves sprained his knee. Linebacker Dan Lloyd banged up his knee. Bear Bryant could have scored 80 points had he stayed with his starters. But the clock expired with Alabama triumphing 52-0.

In the locker room, Husky linebacker Paul Strohmeier slowly shook his full head of red hair and spoke in a hush. "When a team like that builds up momentum, it's awfully hard to stop them. And they have *so many* players. I went against four different tight ends, and each was as good as the last. And their running backs are so quick and powerful as runners."

After the game, reporters took stock of an extremely bitter Don James. "We didn't play well at all today," he said. "Not to take anything away from Alabama, which is a superior team, but you can't help them with fumbling and ineptness." A Tuscaloosa reporter asked James if the oppressive heat was the primary reason for Washington's struggles. "We didn't lose it in the fourth quarter," James snapped. "We lost it in the first quarter." A Seattle-area reporter asked how the Huskies would handle this humiliation. "It will be interesting to see," said James. "It may take a week or so to tell. Those injuries, of course, are going to hurt us. But you can get up off the ground and do something about it, or you can wallow around in the mud and slop. It's a matter of pride."

Back at the University of Washington on Sunday night, the assistant coaches began leaving the Tubby Graves building to head to their homes. Assistant Coach Skip Hall emerged into the hallway and was startled by what he saw.

"Don James was in his pajamas," said Hall. "Here he's coming down the hall in his pajamas carrying his toothbrush. I think he spent that week living in his office determined that we were going to get better. As assistants, we worked very long hours to build the program. But we never worked harder or cared more than Don James. He always set the pace."

Years later, Don James recalled that 1975 Alabama game played in the land of Dixie. "When you're coming down the tunnel, and your starting linebacker grabs your hand, you know you're in trouble."

Chapter 3 — November 22, 1975

Miracle in a Monsoon

Husky Stadium — Washington vs. Washington State

IT WAS ALMOST TIME for Tuesday's practice, in preparation for Saturday's battle against the Washington State Cougars. This would be Don James's first Apple Cup, and to this point his first UW team was 5-5. The Washington players were still inside their warm locker room. Outside, it was near-freezing and the Husky Stadium turf possessed a thin sheen of frost. Several beat writers were hanging around, and quickly they fixed their attention on the stadium field manager. He was busy hosing down a large section of the Astroturf. The reporters' curiosity was piqued, and they started speculating amongst themselves. Finally, one of the reporters went over and asked the field manager why he was spraying water on the turf. "Because Don James told me to," was the terse response.

The players and coaches emerged from the tunnel and took to the field. Don James climbed up into his tower and jotted notes as the team began practicing. In the portion of the field that was saturated, the water had frozen over. The players kept skidding and falling. Frustration was evident, as the players' shouts and curses got louder. The reporters looked on, knowing there was a good reason for hosing the field down. Over the past few months, they had learned that

James' practices were immensely structured. Absolutely every detail was planned for in advance. As long-time followers of Husky football knew, the stadium's south upper deck shielded the sun from a large portion of the field at that time of year. So by the end of this practice, the reporters theorized that James was anticipating icy conditions against WSU and was forcing his players to adapt.

When practice ended, James climbed down from the tower and met with reporters. He was immediately asked, "Why was the field watered down?"

"I made a mistake," said James. "I was hoping that by spraying the area where there was frost that it would disappear. I didn't realize it was as cold as it was."

Wrote Dick Rockne in the next day's *Seattle Times*: "James dispelled completely the football coaching mystique that every move is calculated to defeat an opponent. The man who coached the team that beat UCLA and Southern Cal this season erred yesterday. And what's more, he admitted it."

By late Saturday afternoon, Don James was standing along the sideline in a Husky Stadium besieged by winds and drenching rain. The stadium was half-empty, as thousands of fans had fled for someplace else warm and dry. Said Georg N. Meyers of *The Seattle Times*: "The sub-arctic gloom was soon penetrated by the overhead lights. The inundated Astroturf looked like moonlight on the Ganges."

There were 2 minutes and 47 seconds left in the game. The Cougars were leading the Huskies 27-14, and had the ball 4th and one from the Washington fourteen yard line. A timeout was called. The Huskies assumed that WSU would kick a field goal. The Cougar players, however, wanted to rub the Huskies' faces in it. Wanting another touchdown, they began pleading with their Head Coach Jim Sweeney to throw for the end zone. Sweeney resisted for a moment, before relenting.

Standing in the shadow of his team's end zone, Husky safety Al Burleson watched as Washington State broke huddle and approached the line of scrimmage. The Cougars weren't kicking. They were lining up to run a scrimmage play! Burleson saw Cougar QB John Hopkins take the snap and look for a quick pass to tight end Carl Barschig. And Burleson made a perfect break on the throw. He intercepted it cleanly at the 7-yard line and sprinted untouched 93 yards up the sideline. The Washington bench was a scene of bedlam. Steve Robbins's extra point cut the deficit to 27-21.

Washington kicked off and then stuffed the shell-shocked Cougars into punting four plays later. WSU punter Gavin Hedrick booted the ball 45 yards to Washington's Pedro Hawkins, who was immediately dropped for a one-yard loss at his own 22-yard line. The Huskies now had less than two minutes remaining and no timeouts.

Quarterback Warren Moon, having a wretched day, jogged onto the field and joined the huddle. He was a paltry 3 of 21 for 73 yards, and had been booed throughout the game. In the rain, Moon took the snap and dropped straight back in the pocket. He wound up and tried to throw deep down the center of the field to the speedy Spider Gaines. But the pass was badly under-thrown, and two Cougars converged on it. "The ball hit one defender's hands," recalled Gaines. "The other defender crashed into him and the ball fell into my hands. I knew nobody was going to catch me."

Gaines turned and sprinted untouched into the end zone. The roar from the remaining 25,000 fans reached several miles in all directions. The Husky players were diving and jumping all over each other. The normally ultra-stoic Don James was jumping up and down like a game show contestant. Kicker Steve Robbins booted the extra point, and the Huskies beat the Cougars 28-27. Soon after, the players carried James off the field and then fully-clothed into the showers to drench him further. He wore sopping clothes as he was presented the Apple

Cup Trophy, after which he addressed reporters. "No, I've never seen anything quite like that," he said. "I had to admit to the players that things looked a little dim at one point. But that was the most bizarre finish of my coaching career. It certainly was exciting. I still can't believe it. I guess I'll have to watch it on TV."

A reporter asked James if he would have authorized a pass in the same manner the Cougars did down near the goal line. "Oh, no, I'm not going to ding Jim Sweeney," said James. "I've seen a lot of coaches criticized for sitting on a lead."

Having just played his final collegiate game, Al Burleson was asked to describe his 93-yard interception for a touchdown. "I didn't think there was anybody out there quick enough to catch me," he said. "We were practicing all week against their 'fire' pass, that quick pass to the tight end. Just as (the QB) got ready to throw, Paul Strohmeier hit him. I cut underneath the tight end.

"And what a way to end the season," said Burleson. "I'm very happy for Coach James. I think he has a good system. Not taking anything away from J.O. (former Husky Coach Jim Owens), but I've never seen a staff that knows so much about the game."

Senior Husky Linebacker Dan Lloyd was asked about the Cougars. "They had a good offense," he said. "But I don't care how much they marched down the field, they only got three points in the second half. They missed those three field goals in the second half, but those are the breaks of the game. But it's just nice to get those Cougars. You know how bad they feel over there. That's what makes it so nice."

Chapter 4 — November 20, 1976

Breaking the 1,000-yard Barrier

Washington at Washington State

THE HUSKIES HAD A 4-6 record as they arrived in Spokane that Friday afternoon, for the Apple Cup battle against WSU the next day. In recent weeks, Washington battled tough but succumbed in losses to USC and UCLA (each ranked among the nation's top five.) Meanwhile, the Cougars had been riding the lively arm of quarterback Jack Thompson, known as "The Throwin' Samoan." WSU was fired up and ready to exact revenge for their humiliating Apple Cup collapse the year before.

As the Husky players retired to their hotel rooms, running back Ronnie Rowland climbed into bed and looked up at the ceiling. Both he and his teammate Robin Earl possessed the slight possibility of reaching a rushing milestone. Rowland couldn't wait for kickoff.

"I was in my room the night before," said Rowland years later, with a chuckle. "I needed to get 195 yards in order to get to 1,000 yards, to become the first and only Husky player to get to 1,000 since Hugh McElhenny in 1950. So I was in my room, calculating and visualizing me getting it."

As the Huskies and Cougars ran onto the field at Joe Albi Stadium, the air was cold but the sunshine was out—a far cry from the monsoon conditions in Seattle the year before. 35,800 fans loaded up the bleachers and greeted the opening kickoff with a festive atmosphere.

On Washington's opening drive, Moon dropped back as if to pass, then handed the ball off to Rowland on a draw play. The play was well-blocked, and Rowland scooted through the hole then burst downfield for a 59-yard touchdown. The scoreboard read: Washington 7, Washington State 0.

Two and a half hours later, early in the fourth quarter, UW's Warren Moon dropped back seven steps in the pocket, and threw a picture-perfect spiral to receiver Spider Gaines for a 39-yard touchdown— to make the score 42-14. The two teams exchanged possessions of the football, before WSU return man Don Swartz fumbled a punt, which was recovered by Washington's Stan Wilson at the Cougar 26-yard line. On the very next play, Rowland took a toss sweep and proceeded to juke and gallop through the Cougar secondary for the touchdown, to increase the Husky lead to 49-14.

With less than a minute remaining in the game, Rowland was standing on the sideline with his helmet off. The Huskies were leading 49-32, and Rowland had exited the game with 193 yards and two touchdowns. Years later, Rowland recalled what occurred at that next moment.

"There were only a few seconds left," said Rowland. "The stadium announcer says RONNIE ROWLAND HAS 999 YARDS FOR THE SEASON. I am standing there thinking, 'I can't believe this! How can it end like this?' The Cougars had the ball and were backed up at their own goal line. There were less than twenty seconds left. There's nothing our defense can do. Suddenly their QB Jack Thompson gets sacked (by UW's Kevin Richardson) in the end zone for a safety! They had to punt to us. Nesby Glasgow made a fair catch with three seconds left! Coach James called time out. I put on my helmet and ran back out there for one more carry."

As wrote *The Tacoma News Tribune's* Mike Jordan: "The UW fans (in the corner of the end zone) began yelling 'Ronnie! Ronnie!' in unison. When the Huskies lined up, everybody except 700 million Chinese knew who was going to get the ball."

"So I get the football on a dive play, and I ran as hard as I could through the right side, right up (lineman) Jeff Toews' back," recalled Rowland. "I picked up three yards, so I finished with 1,002 yards for the season. It was like a storybook finish there for me. Jeff Toews, who is just a great human being, he and I both came from San Jose. He came up to me afterward and said, 'I never blocked so hard in my life!' And I finished 2nd in the Pac-8 Conference in rushing, behind USC's Ricky Bell. Of course, I was a distant second, as Bell had something like 1,600 or 1,700 yards!"

In the victorious locker room, reporters were taken aback by Washington's Robin Earl. The mammoth fullback had rushed for 121 yards and two touchdowns, finishing the season with 963 yards rushing. He began choking back tears, when a reporter asked him what it felt like to have just played his final game wearing the purple and gold.

"I've got a big lump in my throat," said Earl. "I don't know if I want to smile or cry." After being asked about the 1,000 yard barrier, Earl concluded: "I was glad to see Ronnie get a thousand yards. I guess it wasn't in the cards for me."

Chapter 5 — September 24 & October 1, 1977

Dreary Days

Washington at Syracuse and Washington at Minnesota

UPON A COLD, MUDDY field in upstate New York, Syracuse had driven all the way down to the Washington 14-yard line—by way of elusive running from their quarterback named Hurley. Now, with just 0:23 left in the game, the Orangemen's diminutive David Jacobs trotted onto the field. He lined up, waited for the snap, and stepped forward to boot a 31-yard field goal through the uprights. An anemic crowd of 12,839 fans cheered in surprised, and perhaps tipsy, glee. Not only had they been able to buy beer at a Syracuse game for the first time ever, they had also just witnessed their pitiful team upset the west coast's Washington Huskies 22-20.

After the game, Washington quarterback Warren Moon sat slumped for a long time at his locker, his head buried in his hands. The Husky record was now 1 win and 2 losses. Reporters waited and waited for him to compose himself. They were cutting him some slack, for Moon had been a target of vilification for two years back in Seattle. The fans at home actually booed him every time he ran onto the field. However, he had actually played pretty well this day, completing 16 of 25 passes for 257 yards and two touchdowns. This obviously was providing him little solace. Finally, he slowly looked up and began fielding questions.

He spoke with such a low voice that some reporters were unable to understand him.

"The elements hurt us a lot," he said. "It was hard for the backs to get a quick start. I know I slipped a lot. (Syracuse) was stunting almost every other play and our lines didn't pick it up at first. A couple of fumbles hurt us, then we couldn't wrap up the quarterback in that last drive."

Moon's head slumped back into his hands, and he fell silent again.

Don James, meanwhile, was being asked if his team had taken Syracuse lightly.

"I've been around football long enough to know that you can't take any football team lightly," he said. "Syracuse was hungry after losing six straight games over the past two seasons. But I guess our kids didn't have the proper respect for them... And we are not a very good football team at this point."

The Huskies flew home to tend to their wounds and prepare for a trip to the Midwest to play struggling Minnesota. The weather in Seattle was cloudy and gloomy all week, befitting the team's mood. During practice drills, two assistant coaches cast furtive glances at each other, wondering through facial pantomime if things could be any worse. Don James stood silently up in his tower at mid-field, taking notes as he surveyed the field. The grunts from players, the smacking of colliding shoulder pads, the whistles and yelling from assistant coaches, echoed throughout the otherwise empty stadium. For several players, it felt like militaristic drudgery with no reward. Still, they kept going. At week's end, the team packed up and boarded a plane bound for Minneapolis, for a game with the Minnesota Gophers.

In the first quarter, from UW's 46-yard line, Moon noticed that Minnesota was loaded to the strong side. He checked off in order to have speedster Spider Gaines run a crossing route against the grain.

This decision proved astute, as Moon hooked up with Gaines— running left-to-right across the middle— at the Minnesota 30-yard line. Gaines then turned on the jets, running around three defenders, and utilizing a superb block from teammate Joe Steele at the 10-yard line, to sneak into the right corner of the end zone. By the second quarter, the Huskies would score again on a Moon keeper, to build their lead to 17-7; but then things got tough.

With 4:44 left in the game, Washington was clinging to a 17-16 lead. Warren Moon had completed 10 of 16 passes for 151 yards, but could only stand on the sidelines and watch, as Minnesota started their final drive from the Husky 47-yard line. Two minutes later, on a fourth-and-one from the UW 25-yad line, running back Marion Barber plunged through the left side for a first down. Then the Golden Gophers milked the clock to just five seconds remaining, and brought out their strong-legged kicker, Paul Rogind. And Rogind was clutch, perfectly dissecting the uprights with a 32-yard kick as time expired. Minnesota players rushed the field in a mob scene, in celebration of their 19-17 upset win.

It was déjà vu in the Washington locker room. Moon moved about his locker slowly, speaking in a nearly inaudible whisper. "I'm tired of losing this way," he said. "I'd rather lose 50-0. I said before the season started that if I played well the team would do well. I think I'm playing pretty well, but I guess it isn't good enough for us to win. I'm beginning to wonder what it takes from my position to win."

Don James praised Warren Moon's performance, defending his quarterback from speculation that he should be replaced; but James lamented everything else. "We didn't get much established," he said. "No, we didn't throw much, and it's easy to second-guess yourself. But when you have a lead, you don't know whether to protect it, or try to get more."

As the Washington Huskies flew back to Seattle, their record was now 1-3. Don James, in his third season, was 12-14. Many Husky fans were furious. Numerous letters to the Seattle newspapers decried the "boring offense" and "lousy coaching." Worse yet, a handful of seniors on the team, holdovers from the Jim Owens era, became bolder in their public criticisms of Don James. Sophomore running back Joe Steele later recalled, "I remember we were 1-3 and were going down to play Oregon. And there was an article in the paper, in the *UW Daily*. *The Daily* was asking Blair Bush what the problems on the team were and he was saying that it seemed like there was a communications problem."

As the Huskies prepared to play Oregon, UW's junior linebacker Michael Jackson was asked his thoughts. "It's just that we've been dead so far," he said. "We make some good sticks but nobody seems to get very excited about it. It's like we're dead. We don't know what to do about it. I've been trying to figure it out."

Jackson was asked what would help get the Huskies back on track.

"The fans can stop booing Warren Moon," he said. "If they did that, it would help a lot. He's a good quarterback. He's the best quarterback we've got. It's really stupid what a lot of fans think about him. You know, it's like the whole city is against him. Sometimes we will go downtown wearing our Husky letter jackets and when people find out we play football the first thing they ask is 'Why does Don James keep playing Warren Moon?' The players on the team like him as the quarterback. I've never heard any of them say anything bad about him. They believe he should be in there. I think if people stopped getting on Warren and got behind him—like the players are behind him—things would be a lot better."

Chapter 6 — October 8, 1977

"We Came Together As A Team"

Washington at Oregon

AN ALREADY GLOOMY WEEK was about to deteriorate further for the 1-3 Washington Huskies. The two team busses glided southbound along I-5— headed for Oregon. Like everything else in Don James' program, the manner of road trips followed a strict plan. Busses one and two were to proceed uniformly no matter the situation, unless James dictated otherwise. On this day, as usual, James sat at the front of the lead bus, studying down and distance charts, preparing for the Ducks, when something outside caught his eye. The second bus had changed lanes and was motoring past the first bus. The assistant coaches riding in the passing bus felt pangs of alarm. They knew that James would be furious.

Don James instructed his driver to accelerate to get back in front of the other bus, but the driver declined. By the time the two busses reached the Portland Red Lion Hotel, James was fit to be tied. He and his driver argued, before James fired him on the spot. The Huskies would have to wait for a replacement driver to usher them later to Eugene's Autzen Stadium.

Some Washington players, primarily from the remaining Jim Owens holdovers, privately wondered if and when their coach would be fired.

Some felt that James was too militaristic and dictatorial. Everything was falling apart with the terrible start to the season. Speculation raged. "Coach Owens was a much more personable guy," recalled center and Captain Blair Bush. "He knew your name and would say hi, maybe ask you how your classes were going. He was friendly, and Don was just the opposite. We didn't know if he knew our names. And he wasn't going to stop and say hi or anything like that."

The next day, upon entering the visitor's locker room at Autzen Stadium, the Husky players grew stunned. Don James was going around to every single player and personally wishing them good luck. This simple act sent a jolt of energy throughout the room. A change came over the team—the players could feel it happening—and momentum began to rise as the players donned their helmets and exited for the field. "Something happened there in the locker room," recalled Joe Steele. "We came together as a team."

Current Husky Hall of Fame Curator Dave Torrell was standing just outside the tunnel in a roped-off area as the Huskies ran onto the field. He was startled by the intensity in the players' faces as they passed by. "I went back up to our seats where (Husky booster) Don Barnard was seated, and I told him that I hadn't seen us look that intense in forever. I told him this game had the makings of a slaughter."

The Huskies kickoff coverage team took to the field, with a group of players known to teammates as "Rohrbach's Trained Killers." They received that nickname due to their aggressive play, as led by the leadership and maniacal style of backup linebacker and team captain Mike Rohrbach. Husky placekicker Steve Robbins approached the football and booted it deep. The Duck return man caught it at the goal line and ran forward. Rohrbach busted the wedge at breakneck speed then nearly broke the Duck ball carrier in half with a vicious hit. The ball was fumbled but Oregon managed to recover.

Two plays later, Husky linebacker Antowaine Richardson recovered a Duck fumble at the Oregon 38-yard line, and three plays later UW running back Joe Steele scored on a 3-yard run. Another monster hit separated a Duck running back from the ball and Husky Kyle Heinrich recovered at Oregon's 25-yard line. Six plays later, Steele scored again on a six-yard run. A few minutes later, UW running back Kyle Stevens scored around right end. Soon after that, Husky linebacker Bruce Harrell blocked a punt out of the end zone for a safety. The rout was on.

Late in the second quarter, the Huskies led 26-0 when Warren Moon spied a blitz coming as he dropped back to pass. He waited as tight end Scott Greenwood got behind two Duck defenders then tossed an easy throw to him for the touchdown. This gave Washington a halftime lead of 33-0, while having out-gained Oregon in total yardage, 270-18. The late Greenwood would finish the day with 7 catches for 120 yards and two touchdowns. "The strong safety was blitzing a lot, so I would just go to the area he left," he said afterwards. "And Warren was really sharp today."

With less than two minutes left in the game, Washington led Oregon 54-0—and had the ball at the Duck 2-yard line. Don James ordered backup quarterback Duane Akina to twice take a knee and run the clock out without scoring again.

In the aftermath, Oregon Coach Rich Brooks looked catatonic. "I anticipated this might happen," he said. "But not that it would happen against Washington. We never quit, we just never got started. They controlled us on offense and defense. They did whatever they wanted. I'd never been previously in a game in which we were thoroughly embarrassed as we were today. We made every mistake a team could make. It was a helpless feeling... like trying to swim through the water after a dam has broken."

Don James's face was a portrait of relief. "I finally got rid of a two-week headache," he joked with reporters. "We played well, but we had some good things happen to us today. The guys came out hitting and forced those early turnovers. There was really some excellent hitting." A reporter asked James what had gotten into his team after the lousy 1-3 start. "If I knew that, I'd be the world's greatest coach," said James. "But who knows what happens in college football."

Linebacker Michael Jackson fielded questions from reporters with enthusiasm and a smile. "We had a good week of practice before the Syracuse game, then couldn't seem to do anything right," he said. "We had a good week of practice this past week and now we have it together. Losing those early games rules out the other bowl games for us. Now we want to go to the Rose Bowl. We realize the need for us to win is now."

Chapter 7 — November 12, 1977

Winds of Change

Husky Stadium - Washington vs. USC

EARLIER IN THE DAY, USC Head Coach John Robinson had said to reporters, "Washington has an environmental advantage tomorrow to a degree in that our kids just aren't used to playing in the rain. Some of our kids have *never* played in the rain." As the powerhouse Trojans sat down for their Friday night dinner, most table talk focused on the weather. As players and coaches later retired to their rooms at the Edgewater Inn in downtown Seattle, countless glances went out toward the white-caps upon the rollicking waters of Puget Sound. Winds carrying cold rain lashed all night against their windows. Several players struggled to sleep.

The Seattle-area newspapers trumpeted the first sellout crowd in Husky Stadium in over five years. Starting with the Oregon game from five weeks earlier, the Huskies had gone 4-1 in conference play. Now only USC, UCLA and Washington were left in the Rose Bowl race. Washington had not been to the Rose Bowl in fourteen years. On the other hand, USC had gone eight times in the past eleven seasons, and were fully expecting to go again.

Just prior to kickoff, the clustered USC team made its way down the dimly-lit tunnel toward the field, while the converging Huskies trailed right behind them. The testosterone-charged chants of the Husky players clamored and echoed off the concrete walls.

The Trojans were log-jammed at the mouth of the tunnel, awaiting the signal from the officials to run onto the field. Up ahead, the nasty weather and rowdy crowd awaited them. Right behind them, the Washington Huskies continued their frenzied chant. Several Huskies, including defensive lineman Doug Martin, sensed that the Trojans were intimidated. USC got the signal and exited onto the field, making their way toward the far sideline on the stadium's south side, under a hail of boos.

As this occurred, the Huskies stepped forth, waiting to emerge. The 59,541 fans looked to the mouth of the tunnel and saw the first wave of assembled gold helmets and purple jerseys, and roared to further heights. A moment passed before the signal was given, then the Washington Huskies began their advance. Don James led the way, jogging forward with his head slightly bowed; his face deadpan and confident. The air siren blared throughout the stadium. The Huskies poured forth from the tunnel—a vast battalion of purple and gold, comprised of one hundred and fifty players. They gathered along the sideline at midfield, merged together in an energized cluster, jumping up and down, chanting, barking, energized for battle.

Moments later, Washington's Steve Robbins kicked off, sending the football airborne into the elements. USC failed to secure it, and Washington recovered at the Trojan 18-yard line. Though Husky kicker Steve Robbins would subsequently miss a chip-shot 29-yard field goal attempt, a tone had been set. Players on both sides felt it. In the early going, USC's eventual Heisman Trophy-winner Charles White found little space in which to run. The Husky defense pounded the point of attack and swarmed to White each time he touched the football.

As the game progressed, spectators felt staggered to see Washington bottle up USC's feared rushing attack.

The score remained 0-0 until 4:08 left in the second quarter, when the Huskies had the ball fourth and goal at the Trojan 2-yard line. In what quarterback Warren Moon would later call "The biggest play I ever made in my career," Moon took the snap and faked a handoff to tailback Joe Steele, which drew in the linebackers, before sliding around end for the touchdown.

USC promptly drove down the field, and had a chance to tie the game. Wide receiver Randy Simmrin got wide open in the end zone, but John Hertl's pass was behind his helmet and out of reach—sailing onto the stadium track. The Trojans settled for a field goal. The Huskies led 7-3 going into halftime.

Just before the start of the third quarter, an inveterate rain maker named Chief Antelope trod out into the east end zone sporting full-on head feathers and battle attire. Chief Antelope was a Native American, who loved the Huskies because he was under the erroneous impression that Don James was part Indian. To the roaring delight of 59,541 fans, with his arms fully extended and waving wildly, the Chief began a gyrating rain dance. Just minutes after he finished, the crowd couldn't believe it, as the skies darkened further and promptly unloaded another downpour.

The relentless Husky defense, weather conditions and raucous crowd crippled USC's psyche in the second half. The Trojan offense would go on to fumble six times for the day, losing three. They would also suffer three interceptions as well having two punts blocked. Quarterback John Hertl overthrew his receivers continuously, as a bundled-up John Robinson stood watching his team and thought: "We seem bent on self-destruction. Hell, every time I look up, Washington is on our twenty-yard line!"

Husky tailback Joe Steele capitalized on one turnover, plunging in from a yard out to give Washington a 14-3 advantage. Then quarterback Warren Moon, who would only throw thirteen passes the entire game, found Spider Gaines through the rain for a 19-yard strike, to push the lead to 21-3.

Conditions became even more miserable in the fourth quarter. The hovering clouds seemed to verge on touching the upper deck. The wind increased and swirled throughout the stadium, dispatching pieces of small trash everywhere and carrying a cardboard carton the length of the field. The stadium's feeble light standards provided a sepia-colored gloaming to the field. It was amid this setting, as Washington merely attempted to run the clock out, that Warren Moon brought the offense to the line of scrimmage. It was third down and five from the Husky 29-yard line. Moon took the snap and rolled around right end, veering left to avoid going out of bounds, before accelerating through a crease and suddenly seeing nothing between him and the end zone. He pushed his fatigued legs to keep churning, as his sodden uniform felt heavy. He crossed the goal line with a 71-yard touchdown scamper. This pushed Washington's lead to 28-10. Moon looked around him and for the first time noticed that the fans were cheering *him.*

The closing minutes were surreal to watch. In desperation, USC's Hertl handed off to Charles White, who reversed to receiver Howard Studdard, who in turn threw downfield to Randy Simmrin. But this ball, too, was wildly overthrown. In the game's final thirty seconds, USC was flagged for unsportsmanlike conduct stemming from a cheap shot to a Husky's facemask.

As Washington celebrated in the rain with their home crowd, USC hustled off the field, suffering torrents of verbal abuse from fans hanging over the edge of the tunnel. Tailback Charles White hollered profanity at the game officials, protesting the nature of several calls. Minutes later, as Washington went up the tunnel and reached their locker room, they encountered a sign on the door reading: HUSKIES WILL COME OUT SMELLING LIKE ROSES! Inside the locker room, they found a bouquet of one dozen roses that had been smuggled in by a sorority. However, there was to be no talk of the Rose Bowl, per Don James's edict to his team. After all, the Huskies still needed to beat Washington State and have USC knock off UCLA. But James didn't seem upset by the smuggled roses. In fact, reporters noticed that he couldn't stop smiling. But first, the team paused to kneel in silent prayer— before erupting into climactic whoops of joy.

"I was delighted to see the rain fall when they were playing catch-up," said James. "That front moved in right on time. Weather would hurt any team coming out of Southern California. Everyone wanted rain all week... And by the way," added James, to the throng of reporters, "We gave the game ball to Moon."

Several feet away, a drenched Warren Moon stood at his locker with microphones thrust toward his face. Much-maligned during his career at Washington, he now spoke in a low voice while clutching a single rose. "This is my rose," he said with a beaming smile. "I am not supposed to talk about it, but I think you know what it signifies."

Meanwhile, in USC's somber locker room, All-American safety Dennis Thurman addressed reporters. "We'll be all out against UCLA," he said quietly. "We have too much pride on the line in that game for us to take it lightly." Then he added: "It looks like Washington will take our place this year."

Chapter 8 — January 2, 1978

"It was a Tremendous Moment"

Washington vs. Michigan (Rose Bowl)

YEARS AFTER THE FACT, former Husky quarterback Warren Moon looked back at his college career that culminated with the 1978 Rose Bowl. "At times it was real tough," he said. "I could hear the booing, but because of the track at Husky Stadium, I couldn't hear specific things that were being said. What bothered me the most was in knowing that my girlfriend and friends were in the stands and they were hearing some of the things that were being yelled at me. There were some times where they almost got into fistfights in their defense of me. It was real tough.

"I talked with Coach James many times about what was happening, regarding the pressure from fans and media. He told me that he was getting pressured by Alumni to make a change at quarterback. But he told me that he felt I was the best at that position and he was going to continue to give me his full support... I owe a lot of my success to Don James."

Moon's voice grew heavier with emphasis as he added, "I guarantee you that going through that difficult experience helped make me a better quarterback later on in my career. It also made me a stronger person. And going into the Rose Bowl in my senior season, we really felt like we could compete with anybody in the country, especially after the way we handled USC."

The rest of the country didn't feel that way. Washington's opponent was to be the Michigan Wolverines, who were ranked third in the nation. When the odds-makers contrasted Michigan's 10-1 record with Washington's mark of 7-4, the Wolverines were made a staggering 14-point favorite. In betting terms, that meant Washington had no chance. The Michigan team itself demonstrated disdain for the Huskies, as Moon vividly recalled.

"When both teams were at Disneyland, they made it clear that they wanted to have very little to do with us," said Moon. "Rick Leach (UM's quarterback) refused to pose with me along with Mickey and Minnie Mouse, as was the tradition for the quarterbacks. I found out later that he had done that once or twice before, because he thought it distracted him from concentrating on the upcoming game... But especially at the time, it all served as extra motivation for us to prove ourselves."

To start the game, Michigan drove to the Husky 38, but then was forced to punt. A bad snap resulted in the downing of the punter at the Husky 49, and the Dawgs took over. With a balanced offensive game plan, Washington drove right down the field and scored on a Moon rollout around left end, to open up a 7-0 lead. This set the tone.

In the second quarter, Michigan stopped the Huskies and forced them to punt. Warren Moon and the offense came off the field. Husky punter Aaron Wilson stood in position at his own 20-yard line. He caught the long snap, paused momentarily as Michigan's powerful rush drew toward him, before stepping forward to fling a perfect pass to a wide-open Kyle Stevens. Stevens set off to zipping and darting through traffic before finally being corralled after a 60-yard gain. This play exasperated TV commentators and millions of fans. "Who fakes a punt that deep in their own territory?" wrote one national columnist.

However, in film study the Husky coaches had seen a weakness in Michigan's punt return team, and Don James choreographed this play to exploit it. Its timing surprised even Moon. "I didn't even know the fake was on at the time," he said. "I had just come off the field and was drinking a cup of water and suddenly I'm back in the game again."

Moon tallied his second rushing touchdown of the game, and soon after he and his teammates jogged toward the locker room for halftime. The Huskies stunned the nation with their first half performance, rolling up a 17-0 lead and out-gaining Michigan 246-111 in total yards.

In second half, Washington drove once again into Michigan territory. With 5:21 left in the third quarter, Moon dropped back to pass and hit Spider Gaines on a perfectly-timed corner route in the back of the end zone to increase the lead to 24-0. Moon recalled that play as being a near disaster. "Spider slammed into the wall and was down for a minute. I was more concerned for his well being than anything else, until I saw that he was OK."

It seemed now that Washington would cruise to victory—but Michigan struck like lightening. Exploiting confusion amongst the Husky secondary, Michigan's Rick Leach hit receiver Curt Stephenson for a 76-yard strike, cutting the deficit to 24-7. Washington's offensive game plan grew conservative, and Michigan quickly reclaimed possession and scored again. Then with 4:00 left in the game, Leach scrambled to avoid pressure and threw a 32-yard TD strike to running back Stanley Edwards. The Huskies blocked the extra point attempt, but the lead was trimmed to a harrowing 27-20.

Michigan stuffed the Huskies again and got the ball back. With little resistance they drove to the Washington 8-yard line. It was 1st and goal, with 1:29 remaining. It was now nightfall at the Rose Bowl. The stadium lights glowed upon the green grass, as national-TV cameras and 105,312 frenzied fans looked on. Leach took the snap and rolled right. He dumped a pass into the flat to Stanley Edwards. The running back's momentum was carrying him toward the orange pylon of the end zone. But as Edwards reached back and grappled for possession of the ball, Husky linebacker Michael Jackson came over top of Edwards's shoulder pads. As they tumbled together, Jackson wrested the ball free and rolled to the ground with possession.

The Husky sideline erupted and half of the players ran onto the field. But there was still 1:21 left to play, and Washington coaches frantically corralled everyone back to the sideline. Michigan wasn't yet dead. The Wolverine defense stymied the Huskies and forced Washington to punt. Rick Leach and Michigan assumed possession at the Husky 48-yard line with no timeouts and thirty-eight seconds to play.

Leach rolled out and heaved the ball deep down the right side. As defensive back Nesby Glasgow ran stride-for-stride with the receiver, he dove and picked off the pass. The Husky sideline again charged onto the field—as now all that was left was for Warren Moon to take a snap and kneel down to run out the clock. With the game over, it was a scene of happy chaos. Humanity swarmed in all directions. Warren Moon searched for particular faces.

"I was looking for my family, they were hard to find at first," he said laughing. "But I did find them. It was very, very special that they could be a part of that with me. They had been so supportive throughout everything I had been through. I also looked for the guys I was close to— Michael Jackson, Nesby Glasgow, Antowaine Richardson, Ronnie Rowland... It was a tremendous moment."

In the locker room, a surprise greeted Warren Moon. "Don James came over to my locker, hugged me and said 'Good job,'" said Moon. "He was the main reason I went to Washington. He seemed really down to earth, and like someone whom I could trust. He really went to bat for me. He always felt I was the best at that position and stuck by me."

Nearly thirty years later, people constantly remind Warren Moon what that game meant to them. "When I travel around the country, I still have people come up to me," he said. "They tell me that that Rose Bowl was one of the best games they ever saw. It was the type of game a Rose Bowl should be."

Chapter 9

A Visit with Joe Steele

BISHOP BLANCHET HIGH'S JOE Steele was the first premier prep player that Don James recruited to Washington. Steele was a powerful running back with great vision and good speed. He played at Washington from 1976-1979. Despite suffering a devastating knee injury half-way through his senior season that cost him a NFL career, Steele left Washington as its all-time leading rusher with 3,091 yards.

Derek Johnson: It was back in December 1974 that Washington hired Don James as their new football coach. The following year James made it clear to his assistant coaches that you were the #1 priority as far as recruiting. James told them that they were going to build a fence around the state of Washington, and top local recruits like Joe Steele had to be kept home to be Huskies. Can you describe what that whole recruiting process was like for you?

Joe Steele: I started being recruited by the Owens group. Jim Owens' last years there were in 1973 and 1974. When Don James came in, it was a big deal for Seattle. There was change. They did a national search and brought in somebody completely new from outside the area. When Don did come to town, I had heard that they considered me one of the top prospects in the community. Don came to my house prior to my senior year in high school and visited with my Mom and Dad, and he met some of my brothers and sisters. Jim

Lambright was actually the guy that recruited this community, so he was part of it also. But you could tell that there was something special there with Don. He was very organized and had a real nice approach. He had a nice style in his recruiting. Then Jim Lambright stayed in touch, and I got to know him very well, and got to appreciate his style very much.

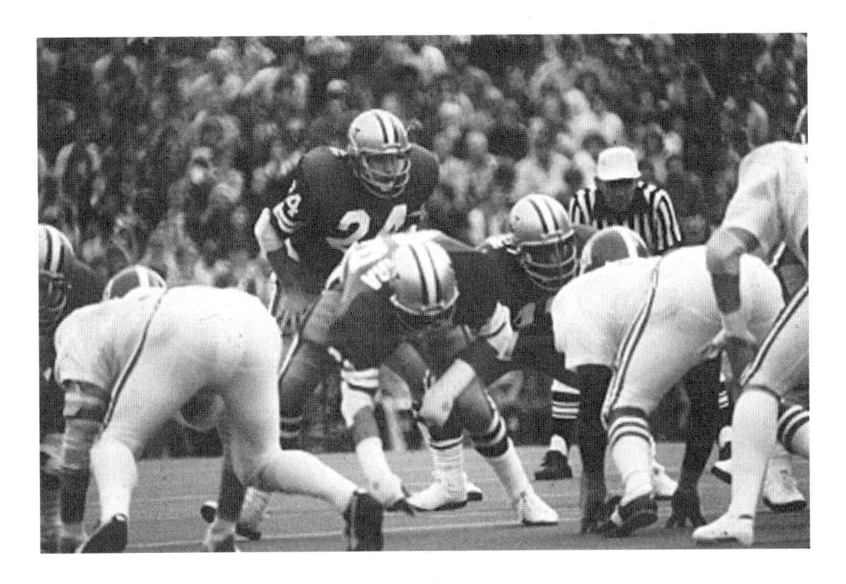

So I went through my high school senior year, and some of the national teams started showing up in town. I heard from Nebraska, Oklahoma, Notre Dame as well as all the Pac-8 schools. I took a trip to Nebraska. After playing a high school basketball game for Blanchet on a Friday night, I headed to the airport. I arrived in Lincoln, Nebraska at about five in the morning. They put me in a hotel and I slept for three or four hours, and then I met with Coach Tom Osborne. They paired me with another recruit who was from northern California, thinking that I would have something in common with someone else from the west coast.

I got done with that trip and got back on a plane on Monday. My Blanchet teammate Trip Rumberger took a trip to Wyoming that weekend, and I saw him at the Denver airport. I told him, "I'm done with this. I'm going to the University of Washington."

Trip made the same commitment, as did Ken Gardner, who was also a teammate of ours at Blanchet. I got a hold of Jim Lambright, and he showed up at our practice that afternoon, and we shook hands and all that. It was a pretty exciting situation. And Don James was such a part of that. You could see that the program was going in the right direction, and that he was bringing in talent.

Johnson: Was there something specific about Coach James that you liked?

Steele: I was the kind of player that if I liked and respected the head coach, I would do whatever it took to succeed there. I just really liked his leadership skills. You could just see it, it was very natural. I could see he was just a tremendous leader. In Jim Owens' final years, the program was down. But Don James told me, "If you come to Washington, you will play in two bowl games." And we did. We played in the Rose Bowl and then the Sun Bowl my senior year—even though I was hurt at that time.

Coach James had a plan. He knew it wouldn't be done overnight. But you could see him adding the building blocks and improving everything. Don James coached the assistant coaches and they coached the players. He coached from the tower. His program was very disciplined and detail-oriented.

Johnson: The first splash you made as a freshman in 1976 was a 72-yard touchdown run to beat Oregon.

Steele: My freshman year was interesting. Ronnie Rowland had come in and he was a very good JC transfer out of San Jose. He was very good. And Robin Earl was the fullback, and a very big man. I was the guy that got chances here and there. That Oregon game was about the fifth or sixth game of the year, and at Husky Stadium. It was a 7-7 tie, and I took a toss sweep around the right end. There was very good blocking, and I found daylight. I put my sights on the end zone. Oregon had a very quick defensive back trying to catch me from the left-hand side. I maneuvered toward the center of the field, and got to the end zone. I later saw a quote in the newspaper from Coach James, saying that no matter how far I had to run, that guy wasn't going to catch me. That was kind of my deal. There was regular speed and football speed, and I had football speed. That was an exciting time, and a great day.

Johnson: Don James says that he will never forget the game that saved his job, and that was the 54-0 win over Oregon in 1977 in Eugene. The interesting thing was that James had backup quarterback Duane Akina take a knee at Oregon's two yard line in the final minute to run the clock out, so as to not go over sixty points.

Steele: Well, I think that Don was a smart character in that regard. He trained us to be that way too. He was always very careful not to attack other coaches, other players and other fans—knowing that they would be able to use that against us in the future. You know, that kind of leadership is incredible. He knew that every year he was at Washington he was going to play UCLA, Cal, and Oregon and Oregon State. He was always careful not to give the other team any fodder to use against us. I'll tell you that he used that against other teams. He would take quotes from the paper, other teams saying "Washington isn't good," or "We're not concerned about Washington." Well, during those Thursday afternoon talks, he would use those quotes, and he would get us frothing at the mouth. He had a Monday afternoon transition meeting about the previous game, then on those Thursday afternoon meetings, he brought the troops together.

Johnson: Describe those Thursday meetings.

Steele: Everybody was sure to be on time, and we would be in the room talking. When Coach James entered, the entire room would fall silent. He would start in and get intense and get after whatever he was talking about. There was always a good story, something different each time, with good meaning behind it.

Johnson: He would use anecdotes?

Steele: Yea, he would. He would take stories out of the past, or articles that had been written. Or the opposing coaches who would blame us for something. For example, UCLA would play little tricks, little games, like spreading false rumors that our punter Rich Camarillo was ineligible when he was eligible. Coach James would bring these to our attention to get us cranked up.

Johnson: Against Alabama in Husky Stadium in 1978, the Huskies were driving for what would have been the winning touchdown, when you fumbled at about the thirty yard line. The Crimson Tide recovered, and hung on to win 20-17. Coach James told me that the '78 Alabama game was the best he had ever felt after a loss. It was an epic. Please describe your perspective and the play where you fumbled.

Steele: Well, it's interesting that Coach James said that. Bear Bryant was in town, and Alabama was a great team. I believe they won the national championship that year. There was an aura that you could feel with Alabama arriving in Seattle. It was a hard-fought game. I carried the ball about 35 times and had 82 yards, so I got pretty beat up. Those guys were very, very physical from the Southeast. It was late (in the game) and we had a chance to tie the game with a field goal or win it with a touchdown. I fumbled twice in that game. Once was from a real tough hit, and the other was a flukey deal late in the fourth quarter, where I was reaching for the extra yard and someone's foot came down and knocked the ball loose.

But you know, you're playing Alabama, you're carrying the football 35 times and getting the hell beat out of you, and it was really unfortunate that it came down to that. It was one of the first challenges in my career that I had coughed it up. In my career I didn't cough it up much. Our field goal kicker was Mike Lansford—a phenomenal kicker. A 47-yarder would have been nothing for him. Had I not fumbled, we would have at least tied it up. One of the things about fumbles, that ball is gold, you just can't fumble. We worked on that a lot. James pushed that down through the assistants to us. Those that don't fumble will play. If you fumble, you won't play.

I tell you something, I took that one hard. It was one of the first times that my mistakes had severely impacted the outcome of a football game. But all you can do is learn from it and grow from it and carry on and try to get better. That's what I did.

Johnson: Later that year in the season finale against the Cougars, you ran for a career-high 193 yards. You also broke Hugh McElhenny's single season rushing record of 1,107 yards. Describe that game.

Steele: Two years earlier, Ronnie Rowland had gone over 1,000 yards against the Cougars, and now I had a chance to do the same thing. It was pretty exciting. It was one of those cold afternoon Apple Cup games in Joe Albi Stadium in Spokane. It was late in the game and we were leading 31-8. We had put the second and third team players in. I was just shy of Hugh McElhenny's single season rushing record that had stood from the early 1950s. That was pretty exciting that we could be a part of trying to break that. The whole offensive line was pretty cranked up about it. The whole team was cranked up about it.

Well, it came down from the press box that I was twenty-five yards away from getting the record. I remember assistant coach Ray Dorr, who was a gentleman and great man who passed away awhile back, he came over and said "You've got one chance to do this." I will never forget getting the handoff with great blocks in front of me, and breaking about a 28-yard run into the end zone. It was like one of those magical moments that felt like it was meant to be. The offensive linemen buried me in the end zone with a pig pile. They were all piled on top of me in the snow. It was a pretty exciting time for everybody. The neat thing about it was that Coach James allowed it to happen. Even though he was pretty stoic and focused, he let us have fun too.

Johnson: After you broke McElhenny's career rushing record against Wyoming in 1979, did you have any contact with him— the man they called "The King"?

Steele: I met him a couple of times. After that, *the P-I* had their banquet the following January and he was there and he presented me a football. He was a gentleman and he was always very nice. I appreciated that. When I arrived at Washington as a freshman, even though it had been twenty-five years since McElhenny had played there, I heard the stories and knew what he had meant to the football program. He's still the guy. I have some records and Napoleon Kaufman has some records, but he is still one of the premier running backs Washington ever had. He still has that single game record—he had 296 rushing yards in one game against the Cougars in 1950. That's a pretty special number.

Johnson: Likewise, years later when Napoleon Kaufman broke your career rushing record, did you have any contact with him? He told me what an important achievement breaking your record was for him.

Steele: It was a similar situation in that the University of Washington had a banquet and the University asked me to come out and present Napoleon with the ball that he had broken the record with. I had been around the program a little bit and had met Napoleon. He was a nice young man and I was happy for him. He had some big stats. He came in early and played early. He had three seasons of gaining 1,000 yards. He was fun to watch. That era was something special, with guys like Napoleon and Steve Emtman around.

Johnson: Lastly, what was the most special memory you have of your time at Washington, particularly relating to Coach James?

Steele: (Pauses several moments in silence, before speaking softly.) My senior year I was severely injured against UCLA in Los Angeles. I tore three ligaments in my right knee. I had my full weight planted on that knee and got a helmet hit squarely on the inside of the knee and completely blew it out. It was a very severe injury. I still have four screws in there to this day. That following week I was in the hospital, and Coach James was there and I could see that he was very caring. Even though football is a tough game and a game of injuries, Coach James really cared. Not only him but the entire program cared.

It was a challenging time for me, with that kind of injury, and not knowing what kind of impact it was going to have on my career and my life. Even though football is a brutal game of hard hits, there's a soft side and a caring side, and I really saw that from Don in his repeated visits to the hospital. Don was special and his wife Carol was special and I appreciated that. There were teammates and others from the University who visited and showed they cared, people like my position coach Al Roberts and Jim Lambright. So my fondest memory is from my final weeks around the program, in going through that challenging time, and being surrounded by people like Coach James who cared about me and about my well-being.

Chapter 10 — October 7, 1978

A Sense of Redemption

Husky Stadium — Washington vs. Alabama

IT WAS AT THE Hyatt Hotel near Sea-Tac airport, that the nervous young waitress approached the most famous coach in the history of college football. Paul "Bear" Bryant had just arrived into town with his legendary Alabama squad. This was to be the first and last time the Bear would bring a team into Seattle. Once again, his Crimson Tide was a contender for the national championship. "Excuse me Mr. Bryant," cooed the waitress. "There's a gentleman over there who considers you a living legend. Would you give him your autograph?" Bear Bryant smiled and reached into his plaid sports jacket for a pen. "It would be my pleasure," he said, in a growling southern drawl. "You tell him I am just not sure whether I am living or not." When she blinked, he added, "I'm just an ordinary worn-out old football coach."

With thinning hair, craggy face and a rumbling voice, the 65-year old Bryant was winding down his career. He arrived in the Pacific Northwest with a staggering career record of 276-77-16. And he would coach another five years, to break the all-time victory record with 315. Now he was in Seattle, finding himself in an unfamiliar environment— but within a familiar ritual: Awe-struck reporters were gathered around him the day before a game, to feverishly transcribe every word he uttered. Or at least, every word that was intelligible. Northwest reporters weren't used to the southern drawl, nor the sentences that would start out loud and clear, and diminish to a monotone growl. As *Seattle Times* Sports Editor Georg N. Meyers described, it was "like listening to a tape recorder whose dying battery is coughing up its final volt."

Bryant was asked what the chances were of his team repeating the 52-0 rout of the Huskies, as occurred three years earlier in Tuscaloosa—in Don James' first season at Washington. "We don't anticipate anything like that, I hope," said Bryant. "It was a warm day, and it seemed like the more people we played, the more we'd score." Then he quickly added: "Any team that's in Don James' hands will be a good football team. He's an excellent football coach."

A record 60,975 fans crammed into Husky Stadium under overcast skies and moderate temperatures. Several hundred fans had purchased standing-room only tickets. At 1:30 PM, the appointed time of kickoff, the Crimson Tide were intentionally delaying entering the tunnel, and still holed up in the visitors' locker room. Washington's opponent *always* ran out of the tunnel first. This infuriated Don James. His team was forced to run out first, and then James made his way over to official Charlie Moffett and protested what Bear Bryant was doing. Moffett agreed to have a word with Bryant but refused to take any action against Alabama. The crowd began growing restless as the minutes passed, before Alabama finally appeared. They ran out of the tunnel in their all-white uniforms, with crimson helmets and crimson trim. Husky fans reacted with a sense of awe in seeing the visitors from Dixie pour onto field and reach the south sideline. The solidly-built 65-year old legend ambled behind them, wearing his trademark saw tooth hat and a gray sports jacket. Alabama's intimidating wishbone offense was to be led by quarterback Jeff Rutledge, and All-American running back Tony Nathan (8.5 yards per carry) and backup Major Ogilvie (6.5 yards per carry).

From film study and scouting, Bear Bryant had instructed his defensive coaches to key on Husky running back Joe Steele. By now, Warren Moon was gone to the CFL, and Tom Porras was in his place as the Washington quarterback. Porras didn't possess the same commanding presence as Moon. He often stammered in the huddle when calling plays, and struggled with accuracy on his throws.

But Porras looked improved against Alabama. Late in the first quarter, he dropped back to pass, launching a throw to speed burner Spider Gaines, who had gotten behind Alabama's double-coverage with startling ease. The result was a 74-yard touchdown. It was Washington 7, Alabama 0. Bedlam prevailed at Husky Stadium.

The two teams battled to a near-standoff in the first half. Mid-way through the third quarter, Washington was clinging to a 10-7 lead, when a critical special teams error spelled doom. On 4th down from its own 26-yard line, Husky punter Aaron Wilson took the snap, but in seeing the rush, decided to take off running instead of kicking the football. Alabama defenders buried him at the 16-yard line. Three plays later, Alabama broke huddle and approached the line of scrimmage. The Husky Stadium crowd was on its feet roaring in desperate support, but Rutledge quick-snapped and pitched the ball to the trailing Tony Nathan, who plunged across the goal line—to give the Crimson Tide the lead at 13-10. Alabama would soon add another touchdown, startling the Huskies by lining up in the I-formation, with Rutledge connecting with a wide-open Rick Neal in the east end zone.

In the fourth quarter, trailing 20-10, Husky receiver Spider Gaines waited for the snap of the ball, then went out for a pass route. Gaines made a move to the inside— fooling Alabama cornerback Murray Legg— before turning on the afterburners to catch the pass that resulted in a crowd-electrifying touchdown. It was now Alabama 20, Washington 17.

The Husky defense tightened, and promptly forced Alabama to punt. Washington took control of the football and began a determined-looking drive. But a long pass to a wide-open Spider Gaines bounced off his facemask. Gaines heard Murray Legg behind him, shout "Whew! That was close!" A few plays later, Washington had driven the ball to Alabama's 30-yard line with 1:41 left. Porras took the snap and handed off to running back Joe Steele. Steele ran up through a hole in the line, and got hit. While attempting to stretch his arm for an extra yard, a defender stepped on the ball, popping it loose. A mad scramble ensued—and suddenly white jerseys and crimson helmets were leaping up and down in jubilation, as the home crowd fell mute.

Alabama ran the clock out to preserve the win. Players from both teams advanced onto the field and toward each other. Husky wide receiver Spider Gaines immediately tracked down Coach Bryant to shake his hand. Then Don James met the Bear at midfield and offered congratulations. Bear Bryant told Don James that since the 1975 rout that occurred the last time they squared off, Washington had made the biggest three-year improvement of any team he had ever seen.

In the locker room, addressing the media, James sadly shook his head each time he began to answer a question. "(Alabama) has been an explosive team this year," he said. "But I felt we took it away from them. We made them work for everything except when we mishandled punts. The thought is that I've done a poor job of coaching. We haven't had good kicks all year. When somebody rattles you and you don't kick good, then everybody is going to come at you. I'm the coach so it's up to me in the end."

In the Alabama locker room, the Crimson Tide players were whooping it up louder than Seattle reporters had seen a Husky opponent do in some time. Meanwhile, Bear Bryant was down the hallway, seated and sipping a can of soda. A cluster of reporters and microphones hovered near. He spoke slowly in his southern drawl.

"Well, I don't really have a great deal to say other than Ah'm very happy we came out a winnah," he said. "I think our players really won the hard way. (The Huskies) really made us look bad on some plays. They're a good, sound football team. They made that one defensive mistake."

Years later, Don James reflected upon this epic. "It was everything you would want in a college football game," he said. "It was very competitive, with some great hitting by both sides. It was a great opportunity to coach against a legend like Bear Bryant. The fans had a great time. There was mutual respect from each team to the other. In my entire career, it was probably the best I ever felt after a loss."

Chapter 11 — October 29, 1978

A Tale of Revenge

Husky Stadium — Washington vs. Arizona State

DON JAMES VIVIDLY REMEMBERED the last time his Huskies played Arizona State. It had been three years earlier in 1975, in his first game at Washington. The Sun Devils, led by their combative coach Frank Kush, had called timeout with three seconds left in order to run up the score. Arizona State prevailed over Washington 35-12. James later recollected, "Frank Kush said after the game that he blamed the players for doing that. My argument to that is, well fine, have your quarterback take a knee."

Come October 1978, Arizona State was coming to Seattle. The Sun Devils boasted the Pac-10's #1 defense and #2 offense and were ranked #12 in the country. Their previous win was a monumental 20-7 upset over powerhouse USC. All week along, Washington practiced with ferocious intensity. The seniors, who were the only ones to have experienced the '75 contest, exerted much effort retelling that experience to their younger teammates. Up in his tower, James himself was stoic as always. After a practice, a reporter pressed him as to whether he believed ASU had run up the score. James sidestepped the question. He chose instead to quote Bill Peterson, his former boss at Florida State, from many years earlier.

"Bill Peterson used to say, 'I take those things with a salt of grain,'" said James. The inquiring reporter noted that he thought he detected a smirk on James' face.

Come Saturday's kickoff, a brisk wind was coming off adjacent Lake Washington and chilling the 47,389 fans in Husky Stadium. The Huskies exploded out of the tunnel. They head-butted each other, slammed shoulder pads, barked, shouted and clapped. Washington's front line of Stafford Mays, Chris Linnin and Doug Martin, along with linebacker Michael Jackson, immediately began an all-out assault upon ASU's offensive line. In the first quarter, the Sun Devils ran the ball nine times, gaining a mere 11 yards.

In the first half, each time that ASU quarterback Mark Malone dropped back in the pocket to throw the ball, the Huskies repeatedly tipped and batted his passes into the air. Three of them were picked off. Said Husky linebacker Michael Jackson: "They throw the quick pass to try to catch you off guard. And when you throw it that quick you almost have to throw it low. They've hurt every team that they've played with this. We knew that if we let 'em do it to us, they'd pick us apart. So we came in there with our hands up."

The most dramatic of these batted passes came from Husky defensive lineman Chris Linnin. He rushed in with his hands up, tipped a Mark Malone pass into the air, then caught it and rumbled 45 yards to the Sun Devil 9-yard line. Husky fans exploded with joy. "All I did was go up to block it and then I kept my eye on it," said Linnin. "Malone is 6'4" and doesn't throw with an arc. A smaller quarterback will put more arc on the ball and it's harder to block a pass with an arc."

Each Husky touchdown, forced turnover, interception, pancake block or bone-crunching tackle brought exuberance from the Washington players. "We were up," said Porras. "We just couldn't wait to play ASU to show what we could do."

Trailing 20-0 right before halftime, the Sun Devils pinned themselves deep in their own territory due to a personal foul. ASU's Henry Pollard started jawing with Washington linebacker Greg Grimes, and then started throwing punches. "He told me I was playing too aggressively," said Grimes. "I told him that was what the game was about. He said he was going to get me. He threw a couple of blows. I just held him up."

The second half featured more of the same. Washington's defense swarmed to the football and punished Sun Devil ball carriers. Washington won the football game 41-7. Had James decided to run up the score, it would have been worse. After the game, the Huskies reveled in happiness. Reporters brought up the revenge factor from three years earlier. "The players mentioned that '75 game a lot more than I did," insisted Don James. Said Husky QB Tom Porras— with a grin— "Yeah, I've heard about that '75 game a few times from the seniors."

Sherry Stripling of *The Seattle Times* noted that Don James was answering questions after the game with noticeable "rapid-fire answers" along with "dashes of pride."

"For the first time, this is what I expected the 1978 Husky football team would be," said James. "I've never been around a team that was more ready to play. We put guys in there who had never played before and they ran around wildly doing crazy things. It was dangerous to be on the field."

Meanwhile, Sun Devil coach Frank Kush was fuming. "Up front on our offensive line, if you'll pardon the expression, Washington kicked the hell out of our offensive line," he said. "Offensively we were just very inept, and their defense, which is about the best defense we've played against all year, just came out and took it to us. And we're looking for people who have the courage to run the ball back," he said. "We couldn't return anything today... And we just don't have a punter. That one kid who kicked for us was a pretty good high school kicker. He kicked for a 41-yard average in high school. But he hasn't done anything for us this year. I don't think we can kick the ball over 26 yards. We need to do something about that. Our kicks gave Washington good field position all day."

"It took us three years to get back at them," recalled James years later, while being interviewed in an empty Husky Stadium. "We got 'em out here, and it was *the most* prepared football team I think I ever had. We kicked their butts, and that game was the beginning of Frank Kush's downfall. He punched his punter during our game and got sued, and was fired a year later. You asked me which game of my career was the most fulfilling— well that one would be right up there."

Chapter 12 — September 21, 1979

Mark Lee's Miracle Punt Return

Washington at Oregon

BAD THINGS WERE HAPPENING for the undefeated Huskies against the Oregon Ducks. The Autzen Stadium sell-out crowd of 42,500 was raucous, due to their Ducks whipping Washington 17-0 in the second quarter. There would be no repeat of the disaster they experienced the last time the Huskies visited back in 1977, when Washington had won 54-0 and Oregon couldn't do anything right. On this day however, the Oregon offense motored up and down the field, led by their elusive quarterback Reggie Ogburn. The Duck defense, meanwhile, stifled the Huskies on every possession. As the third quarter drew toward a close, a victory over hated Washington seemed assured. That was when, without warning, Ogburn went down with an injury and left the game. Wariness emanated from the crowd.

With thirty seconds left in the quarter, Washington tailback Joe Steele plunged into the end zone on an off-tackle, to finally put the Huskies on the board. Then with 3:33 left in the game, the Huskies pushed the ball over the goal line again to pull to within 17-14.

Now the Oregon fans panicked; they were haunted by the ghosts of countless failures against Washington in the past.

Husky coach Don James consulted his notes then elected to boot the ball deep instead of attempting an on-side kick. He risked that Oregon would run the clock out and that the Washington offense would never see the ball again. But James rolled the dice that his defense could stop Oregon. The defense proved James right, limiting Oregon to a three-and-out. There was 1:58 left. James sent senior defensive back Mark Lee into the game to return the punt - for the first time in Lee's career. The previous returner, Freshman Paul Skansi, had fumbled away two punts earlier in the game. James tersely addressed Lee before sending his new return man onto the field.

"Don James pulled me aside", recalled Mark Lee years later. "He told me to just CATCH THE BALL and then RUN OUT BOUNDS. He didn't want any more turnovers. But then the Duck punter (Mike Babb) out-kicked the coverage. Now all bets are off if the punter out-kicks the coverage, alright? Well, I go to track down the ball, and I catch it one step from the sideline and right in front of Don James. After catching it I started to run backwards about 10 yards and I see my teammates Bruce Harrell, Jim Pence, Antowaine Richardson, and others creating a wall for me. And when I turned the corner I was gone!"

In scampering his way around the wall, Lee saw that there was only one remaining Duck who stood a chance of tracking him down. "One guy got his hands on me," said Lee. "But it wasn't enough. Once I got around him things just opened up." Lee raced 58 yards and crossed the goal line, stunning the Oregon crowd into muffled despair. The primary epicenter of substantial noise sounded from the eight thousand Husky fans going crazy in the back of the end zone. On the field, the white-shirted Huskies mobbed Mark Lee in the end zone and danced along the sidelines. The Duck players trudged back toward their bench— save for the player who had the final shot at Lee but missed. He was laying face-down and spread-eagled in the middle of the field. Reporters watched, waiting to see when he would get up. The player remained motionless for full minute, before slowly rising to his feet and jogging dejectedly back to Oregon's bench.

The Washington Huskies went on to conclude the 1979 season with a 14-7 victory over sixth-ranked Texas in the Sun Bowl, to finish at 10-2.

Chapter 13

A visit with Tom Flick

TOM FLICK WAS A quarterback at Washington from 1976-1980. In December 1979, he led the way to a 14-7 upset over sixth-ranked Texas in the Sun Bowl. The following season, he quarterbacked the team to a 20-10 victory over USC in Los Angeles, snapping the Trojans' 28-game unbeaten string. Flick subsequently led Washington to the 1981 Rose Bowl, where they lost to Bo Schembechler's Michigan Wolverines 23-6.

Derek Johnson: Awhile back I interviewed Don James, and I asked him which Husky player got the most out of his program in his eighteen years at Washington. He mentioned two names—Greg Lewis and Tom Flick.

Tom Flick: Really? (Sounding pleasantly surprised)

Johnson: Can you go into detail about what he was talking about?

Flick: I think the reason we had such a great line of quarterbacks come through Washington was that we had a phenomenal position coach. His name was Ray Dorr. You can ask Warren Moon, Steve Pelluer or myself, and most anyone that was coached by Ray, that was probably our favorite coach in all of our careers—be it the NFL or any other place we went. He got us so fundamentally ready to play, from a physical standpoint and a mental standpoint, that when we got on the field it was such an enjoyable experience to react and not have to think your way through a game. I thrived under that, as Warren did, and everyone else.

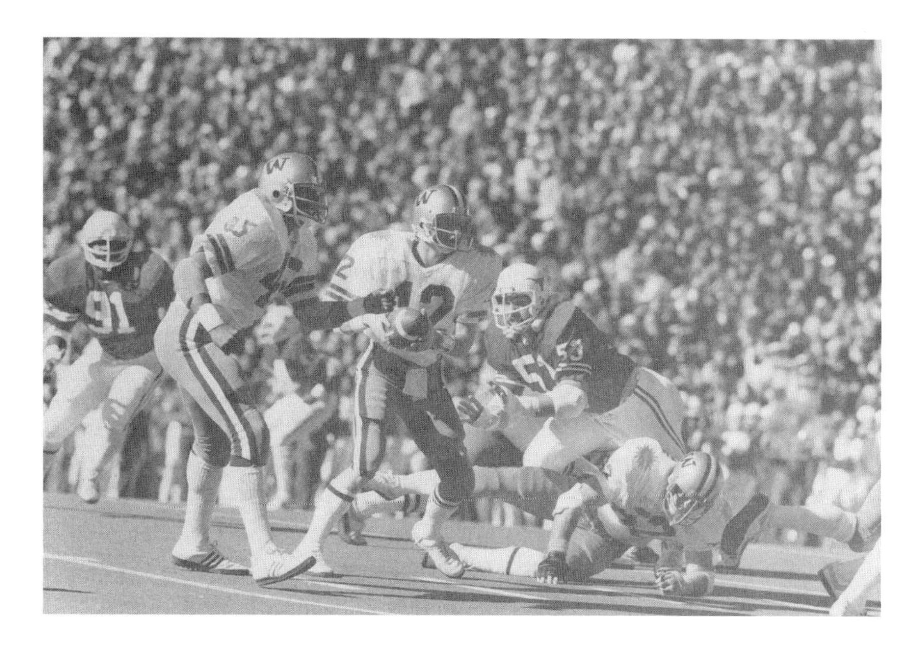

I remember my first practice at Washington in 1976, I was overwhelmed by the speed that everybody moved and how big everybody was. At that point, you find many freshmen realize whether they can stay and make it or whether they should have gone to a smaller-sized school. We had had a tremendous recruiting class, with the likes of Joe Steele and Doug Martin, who went on to become great players. We bonded together and knew that this was the start of something big. I loved it. I loved the competition. I became acclimated to the speed of the game, and realized as a freshman that I belonged there. Yet, for awhile I played behind Warren Moon and some others and I watched how they prepared and whatnot. It was a natural progression. I had a long-term mindset, that it mattered most where I was as a junior and a senior, because ultimately it was my goal to play in the NFL, which I did. Ray Dorr was just a huge impact.

Johnson: You sound surprised to hear that Don James said that about you.

Flick: Yes, I am surprised a little bit. If you asked Coach James additional questions he would go on to tell you that I wasn't the greatest practice player. By no means does that refer to effort. For some reason, when you put folks in the stands, something changed in me. I always worked hard—that was kind of my thing, I had the philosophy to work harder than everybody else. You go put 60,000 fans in Husky Stadium, and it negatively affects some players. But for me, I loved it; I would always think, "This is so great, where else would you want to be?" I actually felt more comfortable and free when I had ownership of the game. In practice, I always had a coach standing outside the huddle and correcting me. I loved to be able to get my imagination and personality involved, and I loved the role of leadership, I really did. I had so many great guys on my team. But I loved that role of serving, challenging, encouraging and inspiring. I loved creating the belief system in my teammates that we can move down the field through obstacles of the defense and be successful. I think I enjoyed that part more than anything else.

Johnson: Let's talk about the 1980 showdown with undefeated and second-ranked USC at the Los Angeles Coliseum. The Huskies hadn't won down in Los Angeles since 1964. Now this might be the stuff of urban legend, I don't know. But the story I heard was that prior to the 1980 game, defensive coordinator Jim Lambright stood before his players and pulled his teeth out of his mouth and held them up for all to see. He went on to say that they had been knocked out the last time the Huskies won down in Los Angeles back in 1964, and it was high time for payback. Have you any knowledge of that story?

Flick: (Laughing heartily) That's a great story! It may be true, I'm not sure— but that's just a great story. I love Jim, and I'm going to bring that up the next time I see him.

Johnson: I also read a quote from a player on that team say that knowing Lambright, he probably knocked his teeth out himself that day, just to invent the story and get everybody fired up.

Flick: (Laughing) That sounds more realistic! Oh, gosh, our defenses were great. I loved Coach Lambright's defensive style. We used to be so aggressive and attack. He was great on that side of the ball.

Johnson: But tell me what you recall from the game against USC in 1980.

Flick: USC was under a violations code that year, yet they still had the #2 ranking in the country. They had a 28-game unbeaten streak. But I remember at the beginning of the year, the (Pac-10) media had their annual gathering. As a captain, I went to the luncheon with Coach James. A reporter asked, "Well Tom, where do you think the Huskies will finish?" I made a comment about winning the Pac-10 Championship, and this caused some snickers. After the season, I was at a NFL combine and was talking with California Bear quarterback Rich Campbell, who was drafted by the Green Bay Packers. We became good friends. But he said to me, "Tom, I couldn't believe it when you made that statement! We were all just laughing at you down in California."

But the reason I made that statement was that our team had such a strong camaraderie amongst each other. We really cared for each other and liked each other. We desired to never let each other down, and we believed completely in our coaches and our system. We were what I called a "legacy team." We had no sub-groups or cliques. We were all together.

Johnson: What memories do you have from being on the field that day against USC?

Flick: I had a placid calmness come over me when we took the field. USC had a tremendous number of athletes. Reads were occurring faster. But we were united in our purpose. It was a beautiful sunny day in the Los Angeles Coliseum—I mean where else would I want to play? It was a perfect setting.

Johnson: And in the 3rd quarter, Ray Horton broke free for a 73-yard punt return for a touchdown.

Flick: I remember that it was a collective effort. Ray had the great punt return. (Defensive lineman) Rusty Olsen stripped the ball from the QB late in the game. We scored enough points on offense. I threw a touchdown pass to Paul Skansi. I threw it up there and he elevated way up and caught it. I didn't know he could jump that high.

I remember something that happened late in the fourth quarter, with about a minute to go. We were leading 20-10 and were running the clock out. We were standing in the huddle, and I told the guys, "Hey fellas, let's turn around and wave to all the Husky fans in the corner of the stadium." So we disbanded the huddle and all turned and waved, and the fans went ballistic.

I also remember when we were leaving the locker room, heading to the busses, the USC alumni and fans were heckling us. Comments like, "You didn't really win." It was a crack-up. It was like they were in denial, this air of supremacy. I thought it was interesting.

Johnson: After the game, USC Coach John Robinson came into the Husky locker room and shook Coach James' hand again. Then Robinson tracked you down and shook your hand.

Flick: He did. Coach Robinson was a good man. The year before up in Husky Stadium, we had another thrilling game with USC. It was essentially a winner-to-the-Rose Bowl kind of game. They had Charles White and Marcus Allen, two future Heisman Trophy winners there. Late in the game we drove down to their goal line, but couldn't punch it in. USC won 24-17. It was a great game, but a heartbreaking loss. Coach Robinson made a beeline for me and found me amid a group of players. He made a point to say, "Boy that was a great game you played. No reason to be ashamed of that performance." And I really appreciated that. That was a great game. I still reflect on that one. It was one of the most exciting games I ever played in.

Later in my pro career I was with the New England Patriots, and my agent Leigh Steinberg told me that Coach Robinson, who by then was with the Los Angeles Rams, was trying to create a trade for me. I would have loved that, but I injured my elbow. I had really wanted to get back to the west coast.

Johnson: What would surprise people to know about Coach James?

Flick: People didn't have a complete picture of Don James as a coach. Certainly he's known as a great organizer and tactician of the game, that's all true. But people fail to give him credit for being a great motivator. He is a *tremendous* motivator. Goodness sakes, those Thursday meetings, he would give his overview of the opponent and his perspective. His speeches were mesmerizing. That guy could motivate. People don't ascribe that to him. I also found him to be very calming. He was intense, but I never felt like he was out of control. Another thing I loved about him was that he allowed his coaches to coach. He coached the coaches, and they coached us. If you look at his coaching style, look at what all the assistants have done. Jim Mora went off to be a head coach, as did Bob Stull, Gary Pinkel and Skip Hall. Coach Harris is currently in the NFL. And there are others.

Johnson: What specifically made Coach James such an effective motivator?

Flick: He was a former athlete himself, and a very good one. He had a very competitive streak in him. He was emotionally engaging. He didn't step out of his persona much. I know that you have talked to many of his former players. If you talk to anybody who played for him, from first stringers to scout team guys, you will see the respect that we had for him was unparalleled. The respect everyone had for him was immense.

Johnson: Dave Hoffmann told me that what he loved most about Coach James was that when Coach addressed the team right before kickoff, Hoffmann got a sense that James was ready for a fistfight. It was under control, but that intensity was imparted to everybody in the room.

Flick: No question about it. You knew that he was deeply involved, and that if he was able he would go compete on the field himself. He was a competitor, and had a sense about himself that I loved. He was focused, tough, ready, informed and very competitive. We always felt he was a phenomenal leader.

There were several difficult moments and defeats in the first two and a half years of the Don James era at Washington. Here, the late Ray Dorr and Chick Harris look on as their frustrated head coach walks the sideline.

Defensive lineman, Stafford Mays

Running back Joe Steele takes a swing pass during 24-3 win over San Jose State in 1977.

Don James addresses the media in the 1970s

Receiver Spider Gaines and linebacker Michael Jackson

Don James and booster Dave Torrell enjoying a round of golf in the 1970s

Eventual NFL Hall-of-Famer Warren Moon
hands off during the 1977 season.

A soaked and happy Don James receives the Apple Cup Trophy from
Governor Dixy Lee Ray, following UW's 35-15 win over the Cougars in
1977. The victory helped send the Huskies to the Rose Bowl.

All-American linebacker Michael Jackson stands proudly outside Pasadena's Rose Bowl in December 1977.

Doug Martin pursues Alabama quarterback Jeff Rutledge during the epic battle in Husky Stadium in 1978. Legendary Coach Paul "Bear" Bryant can be seen in the background. The Crimson Tide prevailed with a 20-17 win over the Huskies.

Injured running back Joe Steele stands with the other Husky captains, prior to the epic showdown with USC in 1979. Linebacker Antowaine Richardson provides Steele a pat on the back.

Receiver Anthony Allen celebrates a touchdown catch in 1981, with teammate Aaron Williams providing a hug.

MVP Jacque Robinson plows across the goal line during Washington's 28-0 victory over Iowa in 1982 Rose Bowl.

Linebacker Stewart Hill and All-American defensive tackle Ronnie Holmes pursue the ball carrier during Washington's 32-15 win over Stanford in 1983.

All-American linebacker Mark Stewart collects one of his five quarterback sacks in Washington's 10-7 win over UCLA in 1982.

Cornerback Tony Alvarado and safety Jim Rodgers celebrate.

Quarterback Steve Pelluer looks to hand off during the 1983 season

As millions of Americans watch on NBC, Don James receives congratulations for Washington's 28-17 win over #2 Oklahoma in the 1985 Orange Bowl.

Center and captain Dan Eernissee takes a breather during UW's 28-17 win over Oklahoma in 1985 Orange Bowl.

Quarterback Hugh Millen surveys the defense during the 1985 season

Oregon State fans celebrate in Husky Stadium following their team's historic 21-20 upset over the 37-point favorite Huskies in 1985. (Photo courtesy of Oregon State University)

All-American safety Tim Peoples blocks an Ohio State punt during Washington's 40-7 win in 1986.

All-American placekicker Jeff Jeager set a NCAA record
by kicking 80 career field goals.

All Pac-10 linebacker Joe Kelly in action in 1985

All-American defensive end Reggie Rogers pursues the UCLA quarterback.

Linebacker Joe Kelly writhing in pain on Husky Stadium turf, during Washington's 31-17 loss to Oklahoma State in 1985.

Lonzell (Mo) Hill and Chris Chandler

Don James gets support from his wife, Carol.

Chapter 14

A Visit with Chuck Nelson

CHUCK NELSON WAS A consensus All-American who kicked for the Washington Huskies from 1980-1982. He set an NCAA record by connecting on thirty consecutive field goals. The Husky Stadium scoreboard would refer to him as "Auto", which stood for "Automatic." Nelson kicked dramatic last-second game winners against Stanford in 1980 and California in 1981. He also has a singularly painful miss in the 1982 Apple Cup, when the Cougars knocked the Huskies out of the Rose Bowl.

After a long NFL career, Nelson returned to Seattle to become the radio color commentator for Husky football, partnering with play-by-play announcer Bob Rondeau.

Derek Johnson: When I think about the 1981 game against USC in November at Husky Stadium, I think about that horrible wind and rain storm that was hammering the Puget Sound area. Personally, as an eleven year old, I was up the night before until 2 AM looking out the window wondering if the trees were going to fall over, and if we were going to go to the game. Needless to say, my Dad knocked on my bedroom door at 7 AM and told me to get ready to leave early. For yourself as a player, can you describe what the night before that game was like for you and your teammates?

Chuck Nelson: Well, it was obviously a game of huge magnitude playing an opponent like USC, with all the great players they had. We were working our way back into contention toward the Rose Bowl, after a loss to UCLA. That Friday night we were staying at the old Greenwood Inn over in Bellevue, which has undergone numerous name changes in the twenty-five years since that time... Good gracious! Has it been twenty-five years? Wow. Just thinking about that, it's kind of a lightning bolt.

Anyway, the first hint that the weather was going to really be a problem was Saturday morning after our meetings. They told us that the busses were leaving earlier than scheduled, because the 520 bridge was closed, and we would have to go across the I-90 Bridge. So that added fifteen to twenty minutes to our commute time. But you know, as a kicker, the first thing you do in the morning is open the blinds and start looking for flags and trees.

Johnson: When the game got underway, with the weather combined with two tough teams, it quickly turned into an epic defensive battle. Do you remember the moment in the second quarter when USC's

Marcus Allen took the ball around left end for twelve yards to become the first player in NCAA history to gain 2,000 yards in a season?

Nelson: Oh, sure. Marcus Allen was obviously as high a profile a player that there was in college football. The 2,000 yard milestone was something that we were very aware of. It also wasn't the type of day to throw the football, so we figured he would gain a lot of yards, and he did (Allen gained 155 yards on 38 carries). As a football fan, as most players are, we were very respectful of that type of accomplishment. From that aspect, it was special to have witnessed that moment in history. Our feeling was, "OK, good for him... Now let's go win the football game."

Johnson: Moving into the fourth quarter, the Huskies and Trojans were locked at 3-3. I remember casting my gaze toward the scoreboard and thinking, "This game is gonna end in a tie." But then Husky QB Steve Pelluer began leading a drive down the field. There was a pass interference penalty and two completions of about 15-20 yards each. Can you describe what ensued from that point?

Nelson: I remember thinking the same thing. I was seeing that scoring opportunities were very few. I was thinking that three points may be all we were going to get. But then we got the ball back and were going away from the lake, and into the strong wind. I recall one ball that Steve threw that couldn't have been more than 15-20 yards in the air, and yet it had about a seven-second hang-time, and seemed to take forever to get there. We got it down there with a chance at a 47-yard field goal. It was physically the best kick I ever hit in my entire career. In terms of just hitting the ball solid and given the conditions. I managed to hit it hard enough and straight enough for it to fight through everything and get through the uprights. I'm sure the USC players knew that was probably the ball game.

Johnson: So now the fans are going bonkers and the Dawgs are up 6-3. What followed after that was one of the great moments in Husky football history.

Nelson: I certainly remember thinking that field goal ought to do it, with the way our defense was playing. We stood out there in the huddle waiting to kickoff, and that's when the parade of garbage bags began. Hundreds of people had cut holes into garbage bags for rain protection, and they all decided it was a good moment to let them go. With the general whirlpool activity of the strong wind at Husky Stadium, just having that five minutes of standing around watching those garbage bags flying all over, whirl-pooling around the track, and cart-wheeling from one end of the field to the other, and staff people running around trying to pick them up, and the Husky fans roaring and doing The Wave around the stadium… I was thinking to myself, "This is pretty cool!"

It had been just a couple weeks earlier that The Wave had been born in Husky Stadium, against Stanford on Halloween. So between the garbage bags and The Wave, that was quite a five minutes. Then we got the signal to kickoff, and it was from the right hash down the right side of the field. After I kicked it I remember being fascinated, because the ball was accelerating and decelerating as it was going. It would shoot forward, and stop, then shoot forward—and kept changing pace. Ultimately it lands on the fifteen yard line and bounces over the head of USC's Fred Crutcher. He misplayed it, and there was a big dog-pile in the end zone. I remember sprinting down there as fast as I could. And my teammate Fred Small pops out of the back of the pile with the football. And I was thinking, as kickers like to say in those rare circumstances, "I kicked a touchdown!" We knew the game was over then. We were back in position for the Rose Bowl, and it was quite satisfying—a good day.

Johnson: You can decline answering this question if you wish, regarding the late Fred Small. I was talking awhile back with your former teammate Dan Eernissee. Dan said that back in '83 when the unknown Larry Michael caught the two-point conversion to beat Michigan, the Husky players felt happy for Larry to see him get lots of media attention throughout the nation. But Dan said in the case of Fred Small recovering the kickoff to beat USC, the general consensus among the Huskies was that Freddie's ego didn't need any additional encouragement.

Nelson: (Laughing) Well, Fred was a good guy. I liked Fred. I remember the next day watching the Husky Highlight Show, (uses official-sounding voice) "With Bruce King and Don James—five o'clock on channel 4." Fred Small was being interviewed after the game, and he said he didn't know how he was going to respond to this. He was from Los Angeles and for him to be able to score this TD against the LA guys, and to be able to talk smack with his friends back home was pretty significant for Fred. He was a young, aggressive linebacker, and just the kind of guy you needed on a kickoff team.

Johnson: USC's All-American lineman Roy Foster commented after the game that for USC to lose to Washington two years in a row was an embarrassment. Of course, you guys had also beaten USC in Los Angeles the year before. I was talking with former Husky QB Tom Flick about that 1980 game, and he said that the Trojans were in denial that they got beat by the Huskies. Did you get that feeling from USC after beating them again in 1981?

Nelson: Oh, absolutely. They were still very much USC. I mean, think about it, the two names you've brought up have been Marcus Allen and Roy Foster—two pretty good football players. They had that competitive arrogance, that competitor in them wouldn't allow themselves to admit that we had beaten them. I'm sure they thought the weather took it away from them, or whatever.

Johnson: In regards to Coach James, do you remember anything relating to him in that 1981 USC game?

Nelson: He was the same as he always was. Don was even-keeled all along. You could tell when he'd get a little puckered up, but his interactions with the team were pretty even all week. Don could get you going, but he was interesting. His Thursday talks would be twenty to thirty minutes. And it was the same thing for pre-game and halftime speeches— he would be very calm and very factual. Then he'd go along, get up on his toes, and get red in the face, and get loud for just two sentences, and then he'd calm back down again.

It was classic stuff. He never said anything to me during the games, regardless of the magnitude of a kick, even if it was a potential game-winner. He would never say anything on the way out, just saying FIELD GOAL! FIELD GOAL! And the field goal team would go out, and then we would come back, and he would tell me where he wanted me to kickoff from—right hash down the right, or left hash down the left. But he never made reference to anything going on in the game. No matter how dramatic the situation may have been.

Johnson: Well, I read you being quoted that after you kicked the field goal to break the NCAA record for consecutive field goals made, you ran over to get your instructions for the kickoff, and Don James shook your hand and said "Right hash—get it out of here."

Nelson: (Chuckling) Yes, same thing as always, except he shook my hand that time. In all my time there, that was the only thing that was ever different from the norm.

Johnson: That season was an exciting time.

Nelson: I look back at that time as the glory days of Husky football, to be honest with you. Expectations weren't as high. Certainly the teams from 1990-1992 were spectacular, and those teams were better than ours were. But in our time, the success was still so new and fresh. With that Rose Bowl win with Warren Moon, we had come out of nowhere. Then we beat Texas in the Sun Bowl, went to two more Rose Bowls, and there was a lot of new excitement over Husky football.

Johnson: Yes.

Nelson: We hadn't become the big monolith yet. Those were fun days.

Chapter 15 — January 1, 1982

"Who's Jacque Robinson?"

Washington vs. Iowa (Rose Bowl)

UNDERNEATH A CHILLY GRAY November sky, Don James stood silently up in his tower at midfield and scanned the practice drills below. The intensity of his players was ratcheted up a notch—no doubt because legendary running back Marcus Allen and his third-ranked USC Trojans were coming to town that Saturday. As always, James surveyed the various drills and scribbled meticulous notes. As the scout team began scrimmaging against the first team defense, something caught James' eye. A vivacious and burly freshman scout team tailback was playing the role of Marcus Allen, and was constantly juking Washington's heralded defenders right out of their shoes. From high above, James noted: "Our scout team tailback is looking better than anyone we're putting on the field in games. We've got to get this guy some playing time."

Robinson got into the game in the 4th quarter against USC, and despite a fumble, he contributed some yards in Washington's monumental 13-3 victory. The following week, the Huskies were in Husky Stadium, squaring off against Washington State with a Rose Bowl berth on the line. By late in the second quarter, Robinson had an impressive 75 yards rushing . . . and 2 fumbles. As Washington began its final drive before halftime, Robinson entered the huddle, only to have Husky captain and huge offensive lineman James "Boots" Carter glowering at him.

'Hold onto the ball, freshman!' barked Carter.

Robinson looked back wide-eyed, and replied with a sincere, "Yes, sir!"

Don James kept Robinson on the bench much of the second half, relying instead on the sure-handed Cookie Jackson to play tailback. It was a prudent move, as Jackson tallied 103 yards on the day, including a nifty 23-yard scoring scamper around left end to seal the Cougars' fate in the fourth quarter. Around that time, stadium announcer Wendell Broyles spoke into his microphone that USC had just beaten UCLA— which meant that the Huskies were going to the Rose Bowl if they held on to beat the Cougars. The Husky Stadium crowd let loose a frenzied roar, and chanted ROSE BOWL! ROSE BOWL! Washington indeed closed out the Cougars to return to Pasadena for the second straight year— and the third time in five seasons. The Huskies were upsetting the long-standing balance of power and tradition of the Pac-10.

As nation-wide traditions go, Thanksgiving is a time for turkey and cranberries; Christmas a time for presents and caroling; and the Rose Bowl on New Year's Day was supposed to feature a match-up between USC or UCLA vs. Michigan or Ohio State. Sportswriters and pundits, however, were yawning in late December, as the Washington Huskies and Iowa Hawkeyes arrived in Southern California for the 68th Rose Bowl. At a press conference, a reporter from back east posed a question to Don James: "The Fiesta Bowl has Marcus Allen, the Sugar Bowl has Herschel Walker, the Cotton Bowl has Bear Bryant and the Orange Bowl has No. 1 Clemson. What exactly does the Rose Bowl have to offer to millions of television viewers?"

With no hesitation, the Husky coach quipped: "Don James and Hayden Fry."

Across the board, the national media saw nothing appealing about this match-up. Nobody knew too much about the 9-2 Huskies who hailed from the most remote part of the continental United States. And the Hawkeyes, led by Coach Hayden Fry, had achieved their first winning season in twenty-one years, with a hum-drum record of 8 wins and 3 losses. The media widely referred to this game as the "Doze Bowl." Or that these teams were the "Odd Couple" or the "Ugly Ducklings" of college football. Even legendary comedian Bob Hope got into the act, when he publicly joked: "Iowa is an Indian name meaning, 'Where in the hell are Michigan and Ohio State?'"

"We were all kind of overwhelmed to be there," recalled Jacque Robinson about his team's trip to Southern California. "There was this steak restaurant that Rose Bowl teams went to every year called Lowry's Beef Bowl, and we were looking on the walls at all of the great teams that had been through there. It gave us a sense of how big a game this was to be. Then on Christmas day, we had a team dinner and that was where we all got our Rose Bowl watches. Coach Lambright and another assistant coach were the ones handing out the watches. That assistant coach said to me, 'You're gonna be the difference in this ballgame.' I was like, 'Ok, sure'. Then Lambright says to me, 'Jacque, you're gonna be the difference in this ballgame.' He said the exact same thing! And I was like, 'Yea, OK Coach, whatever, just give me my watch!'"

On New Year's Day it was a mild and cool afternoon at the Rose Bowl, with thin clouds wrapped around the San Gabriel Mountains in the distance. 105,611 fans filled the stadium—Iowa fans on one side wearing black and yellow, and Husky fans on the other side wearing purple and gold. At the point of kickoff, the odds-makers in Las Vegas had the Hawkeyes as 3 ½ point favorites.

As a scoreless first quarter gave way to the second, Jacque Robinson stood on the sidelines, awaiting his chance to give starting tailback

Cookie Jackson a breather. Robinson's white jersey and gold pants were still gleaming and clean, and he began to fuss with his uniform. Attached to his belt was a little white towel with roses on it. Robinson began straightening it out to make it look good, when suddenly in his peripheral vision, he saw assistant coach Al Roberts charging toward him. Roberts tore the towel from his uniform and tossed it away.

"ROBINSON! THE PRETTY BOYS ARE OVER THERE PLAYING WIDE RECEIVER! YOU'RE HERE TO PLAY FOOTBALL!"

A few minutes later, Roberts again got into Robinson's face.

"WAKE THE HELL UP! I SEE A FRESHMAN IN YOUR FACE! I DON'T WANT TO SEE A FRESHMAN IN YOUR FACE!"

Halfway through the second quarter, the Huskies took possession of the football and Robinson was shuttled onto the field. Washington proceeded to drive inside the Iowa 10-yard line. A couple of attempted rushes were smashed down by linebacker Andre Tippett and the Hawkeye defense. It was now 4th and goal-to-go at the one yard line. In the tense huddle, the call was a toss sweep to the tailback. As they headed for the line of scrimmage, the Husky players knew to be on the look out for Tippett slicing in. As the ball was snapped and pitched back to Robinson, the Husky linemen dominated their blocks. Robinson waltzed into the end zone untouched. Millions of television viewers across America and around the world had just witnessed Washington take a 7-0 lead.

At halftime, the Huskies had expanded that lead to 13-0. By early in the fourth quarter, Washington was knocking on the door again with the ball at Iowa's 3-yard line. The Huskies huddled and QB Tim Cowan announced the play.

"They called my number again and I was freakin' out", recalled Robinson. "I was like, 'OK! I gotta pound it in there!' But then Tim faked the handoff, but I didn't know it, I'm reaching for the ball and it's not there. And my first thought was OH NO! DID WE FUMBLE?

But Tim had kept the ball and ran around end for a touchdown. He came back to me and said, 'Sorry Jacque, but they had two big guys in the middle just waiting for you.' And when Tim had faked the handoff those two big guys from Iowa WERE charging in to get me. I told Tim, 'Hey don't worry about it, you did me a favor!'"

Now trailing 21-0 and time running out, Iowa mounted a last-gasp drive deep into Husky territory; but a Gordy Bohannon pass was intercepted in the end zone by Washington's Derek Harvey. The Huskies marched right back down the field, finding themselves at the Iowa 34-yard line with less than four minutes to play. With the sun setting in the partially cloudy sky, the Rose Bowl's perimeter lights were taking effect upon the field. Jacque Robinson took a delayed handoff, weaving through a hole on the right side, before bounding 34 yards down the right sideline. Iowa's Andre Tippett made a desperate lunge toward him at about the 10-yard line. Robinson glided into the end zone, before a myriad of flashing camera bulbs. He was immediately mobbed by adoring teammates, as Tippett lay prone near the 10-yard line, pounding at the muddy turf with his fist.

Robinson finished the day with 142 yards rushing and 2 TDS on 20 carries—sufficient to become the first freshman ever named the M.V.P. of the Rose Bowl. All the Huskies' faces beamed with joy, as several of them hoisted a grinning Don James atop their shoulders to carry him off the field.

In the locker room, Robinson was oblivious that the media was waiting for him, and was in the showers and dressing area for a full hour. Impatient Rose Bowl officials finally ventured in to retrieve the youngster and present him to the vast array of microphones, TV cameras and popping flashbulbs. Robinson was dressed in a double-breasted suit of Oxford gray, with a miniature adhesive rose upon each lapel. In the first moments, he exhibited a startled expression standing before the onslaught of attention.

"Every week we have to practice against the best defense in the Pac-10," he said. "I feel our defense is the best. When you get that kind of experience in practice, it is easier to come out and play in games." As he continued to answer questions, Robinson's smile grew wider and he became more relaxed and jocular. "I was shooting for M.V.P," he said as he surveyed the room. "And by the time I'm a senior, I want to win a Heisman Trophy for Washington!"

Meanwhile, about all that Iowa's Hayden Fry had to say was: "Jacque Robinson? Who's he?"

National reporters were also bombarding a jovial Don James with the same question. "I just introduced myself," quipped James. "I'm glad he's a freshman. I just checked the program."

Chapter 16 — November 6, 1982

Fourth Quarter Epic

Husky Stadium — Washington vs. UCLA

WASHINGTON HAD CARRIED THE mantel as the country's #1 team for seven weeks, before losing to John Elway and Stanford 43-31. The goal of a national championship all but vanished, but the Rose Bowl remained a possibility. The following weekend, Coach Terry Donahue led his ninth ranked UCLA Bruins into Husky Stadium with a 7-0-1 record. Their quarterback was Tom Ramsey and his backup a walk-on named Rick Neuheisel.

"I enjoyed that kind of game," recalled Husky All-American linebacker Mark Stewart, who had five sacks that day. "Rolling up the sleeves and saying 'OK here we go—we're gonna battle here.' UCLA's tight end, he was a good player; I believe he played in the pros for a couple of years. But I basically beat the crap out of him all day long. He was more graceful and more of a route runner. He wanted to run routes and catch the ball. Basically blocking wasn't his thing. I was manhandling him, and the tackle that they had out there wasn't able to block me that day either. They were not physically strong enough. I really brought my game on that day."

With the Huskies hanging on to a 10-7 lead, the contest came down to one last defensive stand. With one minute left, UCLA faced a 4th down and 6 yards to go from the Husky 40-yard line. "All of us in the huddle were just going, 'we gotta stop them, and we're not going to let them score!' said Stewart. Ramsey dropped back in a seven-step drop and threw an arcing spiral down the middle of the field. For a brief moment, it appeared UCLA receiver Jo Jo Townsell was going to easily catch the ball. As it descended into his waiting arms, the stadium crowd gasped. But cornerback Bill Stapleton closed in. His wallop reverberated throughout Townsell's body. The ball popped loose and bounced incomplete. Townsell crumpled into a heap, his facemask buried into the Astroturf. After a moment, he slapped the ground in frustration.

Washington defenders jumped up and down all over each other. Bill Stapleton especially, a skilled and tough all Pac-10 defender, flopped around the field with unabashed joy, seemingly devoid of coordination.

"I do remember seeing the ball go downfield and seeing Stapleton hit that guy," said Stewart. 'He hits him and the ball comes out, and that was big! That game was such a slugfest. All the guys we had back there in the secondary— Ray Horton, Vince Newsome, Bill Stapleton, Vince Albritton, Chris O' Connor— all of the guys, were just big-time hitters."

Chapter 17 — November 13, 1982

Desert Rose

Washington at Arizona State

FRESH OFF THEIR HUGE win over UCLA, the 8-1 Washington Huskies boarded a plane heading south, to take on the undefeated and third-ranked Arizona State Sun Devils that Saturday night. Arizona State needed only to beat Washington, to secure it's first ever trip to the Rose Bowl. There was great delight among Sun Devil fans as a prominent Tempe psychic predicted that Arizona State would destroy the Huskies. Area merchants peddled shirts and hats with roses on them. All week long, several Sun Devil players made derogatory remarks about the Washington players. To boot, Al Luginbill, the defensive coordinator of ASU's #1 ranked rushing defense, stated: "Our defense could go down in history as one of the best defensive units to ever play the game."

Husky fans back in Seattle, however, had bigger fish to fry. They were faced with one gigantic problem—this game wasn't going to be televised. After receiving a deluge of panicked phone calls, the University of Washington did what it could, in securing the rights to broadcast the match-up on closed-circuit TV. Giant viewing screens were set up in Hec Ed Pavilion. When those tickets sold out in mere hours, Athletic Director Mike Lude arranged to place additional viewing screens inside of Husky Stadium.

Come Saturday night, the desert city of Tempe crackled with energy, as 72,021 fans — a record for a sporting event in the state of Arizona—crammed into Sun Devil Stadium. Many thousands of them clutched roses that they had bought outside the stadium entrances. As the first quarter concluded with a 0-0 tie, the Arizona State coaching staff was concerned. Normally, the Sun Devils liked to blitz 1/3 of the time, usually sending their kamikaze safeties and linebackers up the middle and right atop quarterbacks before plays could develop. In this game, however, they were holding off. Washington's offense was implementing things that Arizona State hadn't seen in the scouting films. For starters, there were no gaps to run through, thanks to the Husky offensive linemen narrowing their splits to the point that their cleats were almost touching their teammates'; and the Husky line was firing off the ball rapidly, thanks to their quarterback Tim Cowan using a quick count on virtually every play. There were also changes in blocking schemes. Said offensive tackle Don Dow, "For example, if I saw the free safety coming in from real deep, I'd nail him."

Washington was first to draw blood in the second quarter. Husky punter Jeff Partridge took a snap and drilled a punt deep into the Tempe night, which the ASU return man promptly fumbled. The ball was recovered by Husky Scott Fausset. A moment later, at the ASU 20-yard line, Tim Cowan huddled the team and called for a draw play to running back Jacque Robinson. As Cowan approached the line of scrimmage, he saw that the Sun Devils were in bump-and-run coverage on the outside. Cowan called an audible, deciding instead to take a shot into the end zone. He took the snap and dropped straight back into the pocket, set his feet, then launched a throw down the right side. For a moment, it appeared he had over-thrown receiver Aaron Williams; but Williams had beaten cornerback Mario Montgomery by a step, and he leaped and extended himself so that his body was parallel with the ground. To those who witnessed it, Williams seemed to levitate as he drifted across the goal line. With his right arm extended outward as completely as possible, he snared Cowan's pass with one hand, landing in the end zone with a touchdown. A groan of dismay emanated from the stadium crowd. After Chuck Nelson's PAT, the Huskies led 7-0.

To start the second half, Washington kicked off with a 10-3 lead. The Devil return man promptly bobbled the ball, and Husky Vince Albritton recovered deep in ASU territory. Moments later, Jacque Robinson took a pitch and plowed into the end zone, staking the Huskies to a startling 17-3 advantage. In time, Arizona State would claw back. ASU Running back Darryl Clack ripped off an electrifying 50-yard touchdown run, and the Devils followed that up with a field goal.

With just six minutes left in the game, Washington led 17-13 and took the ball over on their own 4-yard line. Pitting themselves against the nation's #1 ranked rushing defense, the Huskies went to the ground in an effort to drain the clock. Jacque Robinson gained several of his 124 yards, picking up three first downs, and utilizing more than five minutes, which secured the victory. Somber Sun Devil fans slowly filed out of the stadium, leaving behind thousands of scattered red roses for maintenance workers to throw away. Several Husky players threw their helmets into the air and caroused in triumph on the field. In the words of *The Seattle P-I's* Jack Smith, the Huskies had "torn the Devils down from the unbeaten, probably denying them their first Rose Bowl and generally laying waste to this desert community."

"All week they talked about how they were going to beat us," recalled Husky All-American linebacker Mark Stewart. "We didn't say anything. We kept quiet. We respected them, but they didn't respect us. And another thing was that they hadn't been in a pressure game like we had." Unbeknownst to Stewart and his teammates, at that moment back in Seattle, some of the 2,000 fans who had watched the game via closed-circuit TV were tearing down the goal posts in otherwise empty Husky Stadium. Washington was now just one win away from their third consecutive Rose Bowl.

In Tempe, after the media finished their interviews and the players had all showered, dressed and left the Husky locker room, only two people remained. Don James stood nearby, while his quarterback Tim Cowan was seated on a bench. Suddenly James broke the silence: "Tim that was a great job." Taken aback, Cowan glanced up; but before he could respond, Don James was already out the door, leaving Cowan behind in stunned solitude.

In Arizona State's locker room, Sun Devil Defensive Coordinator Al Luginbill was asked by a reporter whether he still stood by his quote from earlier in the week, when he said that the Sun Devil defense might go down as one of the best in college football history.

"This was vintage Don James," was all Luginbill said.

Chapter 18 — November 20, 1982

What Might Have Been

Washington at Washington State

THE TOUGHEST PART OF the schedule now seemed behind the Washington Huskies. In successive weeks, they had emerged victorious from two epics against undefeated teams. The Huskies were now 9-1 and ranked #6 in the nation. Only the lowly Washington State Cougars (2-7-1) stood in the way of a third straight trip to the Rose Bowl. Seattle-area travel agents were already advertising Rose Bowl packages in the local newspapers. The talk nationally was of how Washington and Michigan would be squaring off again in Pasadena. By midweek however, Don James was atop the midfield tower—and growing disgusted. Instead of maintaining their intensity, his players were letting up. He even spotted intermittent moments of discreet clowning taking place. Finally, James had seen enough of practice. With pursed lips and his notebook clutched in hand, he descended the ladder. The team's demeanor grew alarmed as James stepped onto the Astroturf and proceeded to kick them off the field. James then told his assistant coaches, "Our kids aren't taking the Cougars seriously. We've got to get through to them."

Normally when the Cougars hosted the Apple Cup, they did so in Joe Albi Stadium in Spokane—for the increased seating capacity.

This year, they would be playing the Huskies in Pullman's Martin Stadium, for the first time since 1950. Coach Jim Walden exhorted the public in his weekly press conference, pleading: "I want to hear and see nothing but wild-eyed screaming Cougar fans." He needn't have said anything. Cougar fans were already delirious with anticipation for the Apple Cup.

With the game underway, it was business as usual. Washington controlled the first half and took a 17-7 lead into the locker room. A third straight trip to Pasadena was now only thirty minutes away. The cocksure Huskies opened up the third quarter with the football. Quarterback Tim Cowan dropped back and threw a quick pass to Paul Skansi, who held the ball for only one second, before being smashed by a Cougar defender. The ball popped loose, and Washington State recovered at the 28-yard line. It was the only fumble on a scrimmage play in Skansi's collegiate career. Five plays later, the Cougars scored, trimming the deficit to 17-14.

On the ensuing kickoff, Washington's Dennis Brown was back at the goal line in replacement of Aaron Williams, who was nursing a broken finger. The kick sailed end-over-end through the air. Brown positioned himself under it, readying to jettison himself up-field with his world-class speed. As he attempted to catch the ball, however, he bobbled it to the turf. A Husky teammate recovered at the five yard line, but Washington was now in a tight spot. The crimson-clad fans (many of them drunk) sat in the nearby end-zone seats, and were giving the Huskies a hellish earful. In the next three plays, Washington couldn't get anything going, and had to punt.

After taking over the Husky 48-yard line, a defensive pass interference call and six consecutive running plays brought the Cougars to the Washington seven yard line. Quarterback Clete Casper stood over center and barked out signals, before handing the ball off to running back Tim Harris, who couldn't believe what he saw: Going up against one of the formidable defenses in the nation, the right side of the Cougar line had just blown open a hole of canyon proportions. Harris giddily zipped into the end zone untouched. The ensuing extra point sailed cleanly through the uprights, giving Washington State a staggering 21-17 lead over the sixth-ranked team in America. The 40,000 fans jammed into chilly Martin Stadium were electrified. News flashes were firing off in cities throughout the Pac-10 Conference—that the Washington State Cougars were on the brink of the unthinkable.

With less than six minutes left in the game, the Cougars had the ball and a 21-20 lead. Clete Casper dropped back under pressure and attempted to throw the ball away. Casper's wounded duck floated toward the sidelines, but Washington defensive back Ray Horton made a spectacular leaping snare of the ball before it touched the ground. All of Martin Stadium groaned. Casper returned to the sideline looking into the facemasks of his dejected Cougar teammates—including one who was openly sobbing.

Fate seemed to be smiling upon Washington, as the Huskies zipped straight down the field on six Tim Cowan completions, three of them to receiver Anthony Allen. On third down and five from the WSU 18-yard line, Cowan handed off to Jacque Robinson. The Huskies interior line dominated their blocks, and Robinson seemed to have an inside pathway to the end zone. Mysteriously, Robinson decided to cut outside, and Cougar cornerback Mark Blocker managed to grab Robinson's foot and bring him down for a two-yard gain. This brought on fourth down and three.

Washington's Chuck Nelson, the most accurate place kicker in NCAA history, trotted onto the field. Nelson had made a NCAA-record thirty consecutive field goals. He lined up, and the snap back to holder Steve Pelluer was caught and hurriedly placed upon the tee. But Nelson's kick sailed wide of the goal post by a mere foot. The fans in Martin Stadium burst into dumbfounded joy.

Washington's determined defense stopped the Cougars in three plays and got the ball back; but Cougar Coach Jim Walden knew the Huskies were desperate and had to throw on every play. He decided to sell out on the pass rush and send seven guys at the quarterback. When Cowan dropped back into the pocket on first down, he was promptly drilled in the back, coughing up the football in the process. It was recovered by Cougar Jerald Waters. Four plays later, place kicker John Traut booted a field goal, to extend Wazzu's lead to 24-20.

Washington's last gasp came from their own 25-yard line with fifty-six seconds left. But Cowan's first pass was errant, picked off by Cougar Mark Pleis, who, not wishing to risk a fumble, promptly dropped to the ground like he'd been shot. That was the ball game. When time expired, Cougar fans stormed the field and immediately got to work in tearing down the goalposts, which would ultimately be carried off and dumped into the frigid waters of the nearby Palouse River. Incredulous fans from around the Pac-10 Conference couldn't comprehend the news coming out of Pullman: Washington had been knocked out of the Rose Bowl.

"It's the greatest feeling of my career!" said Washington State's Clete Casper to reporters. Coach Jim Walden possessed an ecstatic satisfaction that was borderline tearful. "This is the biggest one for me," he said. "It's never too late to beat the Huskies... This one was obviously special for the pride of the Palouse after a series of frustrations this fall and such a long dry spell against Washington."

In the Washington locker room, late linebacker Fred Small sat by himself on the floor, his back supported by a cement wall, as he cradled his helmet in his lap and stared straight ahead in a daze. Don James spoke in private to his players, telling them that he didn't want to hear one negative comment about the Cougars when they spoke to the media. Soon after, the Huskies effused public praise for their cross-state rivals.

"The Cougars took the bad breaks and still played hard," said Husky fullback Chris James. "When things went their way, they were ready."

"The Cougars played well," said quarterback Tim Cowan. "They were due."

"They played well," said receiver Paul Skansi. "Give them the credit."

"We got where we wanted to be and it blew up in our face," said safety Chris O'Connor. "The Cougars were a lot more fired up than we were."

Instead of the honor of a third consecutive Rose Bowl, the Huskies found themselves in Hawaii on Christmas Day— playing in the inaugural Aloha Bowl. They won a thriller over Boomer Esiason's Maryland Teripans, finishing with a 10-2 record and the #7 national ranking. For the entire duration of the trip, however, the Huskies wondered why they weren't in Pasadena.

Years later, Don James lamented that cold day in Pullman. "That loss hurt me more than any other in my career," he said. "There was so much at stake. The players thought it was going to be easy, and I just couldn't get through to them. Oh… It took me weeks and weeks to get over that loss."

Backup Husky quarterback Steve Pelluer, who was the holder for Chuck Nelson's missed field goal attempt, reflected twenty-four years later upon that play. "I didn't think it was that particularly good of a hold," said Pelluer. "Chuck never said anything. When I looked at it on film over and over, I told him, 'Chuck, I don't know how good of a hold it was. It might have been my fault. I'm not sure I hit the spot exactly.'

"But Chuck always shouldered the blame himself," reflected Pelluer. "I don't know if we will ever know… until we get to heaven."

Chapter 19

A Visit with Former Washington State Cougar Coach Jim Walden

JIM WALDEN COACHED THE Washington State Cougars from 1978-86. With his ebullient personality and Southern accent (he hails from Mississippi) Walden was never at a loss for words. He once said, "Nothing in my job — not the Rose Bowls, not the Holiday Bowls, nothing — is more important than beating the University of Washington." He managed to beat the Huskies three times in his career, twice knocking Washington out of the Rose Bowl.

Derek Johnson: Don James once stated that each year when the Apple Cup rolled around, he was a 2,000 word underdog to you. What was your relationship with him like?

Jim Walden: Unbeknownst to a lot of people, we got along very well. Because you compete so hard as arch rivals, to the public it's important to think the worst. I competed hard against Don, and Don competed hard against me and USC and everybody else. But I think you always have to keep a cautious eye out for your chief rival in your state. Don did that better than most. But in the strange anatomy, off-the-field and behind the scenes, it was a good relationship. I was kind of out there and more flamboyant than him. I used to say that I'm like his wife Carol and Don is like my wife Janice. Janice was very reserved just like Don is. And Carol and I are very talkative. Like they say, opposites attract. I think that was where the quote of his came from, when Don said that he was a 2,000 word underdog to me—because I talked more. I didn't set out to be quotable, but people asked me questions and I answered them.

Photo courtesy of Washington State University

But getting back to the point, Don and I competed against each other for a long time. And then during the summers, we and our wives would take trips together with other coaches. So unbeknownst to our fans, the four of us were good friends behind the scenes. But somehow the public never wants to believe that you like one another—they want to think that you're like two pit bulls in a pen. But that was not the case.

I think Don and I kept it as professional as could be. You know, I look at the way some of the coaches are down south. You look at the coaches at Ole Miss and at Mississippi State—they don't even speak. They carry that into their own competition. Sometimes I don't know if (Alabama Coach) Mike Shula and (Auburn's) Tommy Tuberville even get along. I think they're scared to death to even be seen together! The

Alums down there get carried away in that sense. But none of that ever happened to Don James and Jim Walden. We never tried to present an image that we didn't like one another. But when you compete like we did, sometimes people get caught up in that and think that we didn't get along. But Don was, and is, a good friend. And it's a friendship that I treasure.

Johnson: Any interesting stories from the recruiting battles?

Walden: There's one story that illustrates the integrity of Don James, in regards to recruiting. It led me to believe, in later years, that the University of Washington did not step forward and defend one of the great coaches of our time. I will preface this by saying that all that Don James wanted from the Pac-10 and his own school was to say 'Don James has been here X number of years. The integrity he has shown in his capacity as leader, as coach, as friend and as a husband, is impeccable.' I believed in all my heart, when that problem came that one of his players (Billy Joe Hobert) had received money, to think that Don James knew about it was preposterous.

I will give you an example of how silly that sounded to me and how little some of the Washington people must have known about their own coach. One time we Pac-10 coaches had a meeting, as we often did. And what we discussed was the integrity of recruiting amongst ourselves. If there was cheating going on or shady things happening regarding kids we were recruiting on the west coast, we nevertheless felt we needed to bond together. We had enough problems fighting off the Michigans and Nebraskas, all the people coming into California, so we decided to at least have honor amongst ourselves. We decided that anytime we got a report from our assistant coaches saying that someone else's assistant coach was doing or saying something illegal, immoral or fattening, so to speak, then we would present that from one head coach to the other. Don't take it to the press. Just pick up the phone and call the other head coach and tell them what is happening.

Well, we had an occasion when one of my assistant coaches came and told me that one of Don James' assistant coaches was telling a kid that they could do something for him that was not legal. I said OK, and I went into my office and shut the door, and picked up the phone to call Don James. As a coach, you never want to have that kind of conversation with another coach, because it's uncomfortable as the devil. But I did it. I told him as delicately as I could what I was hearing about what his assistant coach was doing over a player that we were both recruiting. We had a brief, professional conversation. Don told me, "Jim, I will get back to you as soon as possible." Within thirty minutes, the phone rang and my secretary said it was Coach James. I went in my office and shut the door. He said, "Jim, your coach is correct. My assistant just admitted to me that he had done that thing. It is wrong, we will correct it, and we will no longer recruit that young man."

Don James said that he hoped we could move forward, but to show that it was in good faith, he wasn't going to recruit this player any further. And this was a high-profile recruit, and not some borderline player that maybe they just didn't want. This was a highly-recruited athlete, and Don James stopped recruiting him.

Mind you, we didn't get that player either! Don James told this young man no, and the young man told us no, and then the young man went to the Cal Bears. But that's a story that has always stuck with me that showed the integrity of Don James, the emphasis that he put on it, and the degrees to which he would follow through. Now you understand the import of that story. The University of Washington had a man that good, that honest, that respected, and they didn't stand behind him over one issue of which he had no control, and it blows my mind. It still does.

Johnson: One of the most exciting weeks I can remember was when I was eleven years old and experiencing the anticipation for the 1981 Apple Cup. For the only time in Apple Cup history, the winner of that game was going to the Rose Bowl. The Cougars were 8-1-1 and the Huskies were 8-2. The entire state of Washington was caught up in the excitement. What were your thoughts going into that game?

Walden: I remembering thinking, "Lord, what have I gotten myself into?" Don James had a great advantage over me in that ball game. He had already been to two Rose Bowls, and understood what was going on and what to expect in a game of that magnitude. For me, I knew we had to beat Washington to go to the Rose Bowl, but not much more than that.

There was a lot of emotion on both sides. But this was surreal to me. There was so much media coverage. I always thought I could handle the media pretty good. I'm over here at Washington State and maybe I could get two interviews a week. For Apple Cups, it was always more. But on that Monday before that Apple Cup, there were fifteen television cameras, and swarms of writers and reporters and I was like, "Whoa! What is this?" It was something!

As far as the game itself, the most vivid thing happened while we were leading 7-6. We knew it was going to be tough to beat Washington in Husky Stadium. We knew that the Huskies would play hard. But I thought that our quarterback Clete Casper gave us a good chance to win. Well, we're leading 7-6 halfway through the second quarter, and Clete spins around to give a simple handoff and snaps a hamstring. Can you believe that? He just did a basic handoff and he was gone for the day. Ricky Turner was our backup, and he just wasn't mature enough at that point. Clete Casper had the most commanding presence and leadership skills of any quarterback I ever had. He didn't have great athletic skills, but he was a great quarterback, a great leader. And when he went out, I knew we were in trouble.

Sure enough, we lost to the Huskies 23-10, and they got all the benefits that went with that victory. But I told Don later on, if he would have let me go to the Rose Bowl in 1981, I would have let him go in 1982. It would have been a lot more fun!

Johnson: Well, that leads me to my next question, which is really the elephant in the room. It was the loss that Don James said was by far the most painful in his eighteen years at Washington. It was the 1982 Apple Cup when your team beat the Huskies 24-20 to knock them out of the Rose Bowl. The goal posts ended up in the Palouse River. Tell me about that time.

Walden: Well, here we are, we have nothing on the line, and probably had a team that was better than Don realized. We came out of the 1981 season with an '82 team that could have been as good or better than the year before. But we started getting hurt early in the season, a rash of injuries. It took us forever to get those key people back to be the kind of team we could be. With about four games left in the season, our injured people started crawling back. By the Washington game, I felt like we had finally become the team we knew we could be. Did I think we could beat Washington? Well, they were the sixth-ranked team in the nation at that point, with a 9-1 record.

But I knew that it was the first time that the Huskies were coming to our campus in thirty-two years. We had always been playing the Huskies at Joe Albi Stadium in Spokane, but we were finally bringing them to Martin Stadium in Pullman. I'm telling you Derek, people in Pullman were so excited that week, they were almost hyperventilating at the thought that the Huskies were coming to their campus and stadium. Think about that, think about all of the senior classes at Wazzu who never got to see the Huskies come to their campus. It's mind-boggling, really.

We played a 4PM game, and there had been a lot of hoopla because Washington protested the game being moved to later in the day for

TV purposes. They were afraid it would be too cold. I thought heck, how much more colder could it be from Seattle to Pullman but ten degrees?

Nonetheless, Don brought his team in. We were down 17-7 at halftime but just hung in there. We were only 2-7-1, but they let us hang around too long. We got our offense going a bit. Then it was just one of those miracle things that happen. There was a lot of crowd noise, a lot of people on our side. And we just happened to play better than they did. A pretty good team beat a really good team that day. Of course, all hell broke loose when it was over. We had broken an 8-game losing streak to Washington. The fans tore down the goal posts. People everywhere. I never did see Don afterward. It was not a good feeling for him. He said once that when we had beat him in '82 and '83, that was the longest two years of his life.

It cost him the Rose Bowl. And I know that my Cougar friends will be mad at me, but to this day I would have much rather it not have cost him that. I didn't like the fact in knocking his team out that we helped put UCLA in the Rose Bowl. At the time I didn't care, of course. I was just so happy to break that losing streak to them and I was so proud of my players. But later I understood his feeling of not going to the Rose Bowl. I mean, there are losses and then there are killers. In that sense, we were tied. He had knocked me out, and I had knocked him out. It was a huge win for our program, and I can only imagine how devastating it was for Don.

Johnson: What has been the legacy of that game for you personally?

Walden: Well you know, from (coaches) Mike Price, Dennis Erickson and Bill Doba, great things have been done at Wazzu. Think about Bill Doba beating Texas in the Holiday Bowl! Mike Price getting the Cougars to the Rose Bowl twice. Dennis Erickson winning nine games and upsetting #1 UCLA. But of all the games, at that time in 1982, the Cougar Nation so desperately needed the validation that our football team was getting better and to know that we were no longer a laughingstock. The only way to prove that would be to beat somebody we shouldn't. And that year, our players and fans so desperately wanted to beat the Huskies. I later used a quote from a Husky player named Don Dow, and I have even told him about it since. The Huskies had so dominated our team over the years, not only was the Husky Nation thinking that a win over us was automatic, but the Cougar Nation was starting to wonder if we had sunk so far down that we were too far gone.

After we won, Don Dow said, "I never thought I would see this in my lifetime." Now THINK about that! The guy was probably twenty-two years at the time, and if he lives to be seventy, that's a lot of years! But what he expressed was an honest emotion. No one could remember the last time the Cougars beat the Huskies.

That's why the 1982 Apple Cup will always be remembered in two different ways. For you and Don James, it will be a horrible memory. And for me, it will be one of the best memories of my life! Such is life.

Johnson: If you were building a football team from scratch, and you could select one Husky from offense and one from defense from the years you were at WSU (1978-86) who would they be?

Walden: They had some really great defensive linemen in those days. But I would have to say Michael Jackson at linebacker. I always loved Michael Jackson. He was a forerunner to how linebackers play today. He was a standout and a dominant player. On offense, I think Joe Steele. As a running back, he just pounded you, a truly dominant player. I loved Joe Steele. But they had so many wonderful players, guys like Fletcher Jenkins and Doug Martin and Anthony Allen and Boots Carter. I would probably need to review my notes to make sure

I didn't miss anyone. I thought Jim Lambright was a great defensive coordinator. Don had a great staff around him.

Johnson: For my final question, I'm taking you to task on something from the 1984 Apple Cup. That was when Husky tailback Jacque Robinson played a key role in leading the Huskies to a 38-29 win that sent Washington to the Orange Bowl. In the week leading up to that Apple Cup, there were stories of Cougar players stuffing their pants during practice to look fat like Jacque Robinson.

Walden: Well Derek, as everybody knew, Jacque had a big ol' butt. We too had a kid here named Tim Harris and everybody called him "Big-Butt Harris." He just had a big lower body with a big butt. Well, so did Jacque Robinson! They can hide it all they want to, but Jacque was 5′8″ tall weighing 195 pounds with a big ol' butt.

Now, I didn't order this. But we get ready to go out for practice on Monday night, and one of our scout team backs—and it was a black kid, so it wasn't like white kids were making fun. But you know how scout team guys are— they're bored to death and looking for some fun. So one of our scout team running backs put on a gigantic pair of pants, and a bunch of teammates helped him stuff the back end with towels. He comes waddling out to practice with a gigantic butt and wearing #28 (Robinson's number). We just died laughing! It was just a great joke.

Well, word quickly got to Washington, and they got all bent out of shape. Of course, coaches are always looking for ways to get their players stirred up. But it became this big deal. But let me tell you, as bad as it was, it had nothing to do with us losing. In the fourth quarter we had a horrible call made on our Rico Tipton right over the middle. We would have won the game, but we had a horrible call of unnecessary roughness. Our middle backer and Washington's tight end's helmets stuck together. They're wrestling around trying to get separated, and the referee called it on us. I wanted to bite the referee's head off! How could they call it on us? The players had to remove their helmets just to get separated, and you're calling it on us? Washington had just thrown a third-down incompletion and that penalty gave them 15 yards and a first down. We lost our momentum and the Huskies went on to win the game. So it really had nothing to do with Jacque Robinson.

Johnson: I would say that Jacque's 160 yards rushing and 4 touchdowns had *something* to do with it.

Walden: Well, Jacque had a nice game, OK? But I will say, if we were doing it again, the kind of coach that I was, I always wanted my kids to have some fun. I thought it was funny, kids doing kids things. It was good for our team. If I had to do it over, I would do it again!

But I'm sure that Don James used that for some sort of emotional lift for his team. He had the reputation for doing that, and of being one of the most organized guys in the world. If it came down to how I organized a team and how he organized a team, I would never beat him. He was so organized he wanted to know exactly where his coaches were sitting up in the coaches' box. It was, "You sit in the third seat, you sit in the fourth seat, etc."

But that was Don James' way of keeping control of things. And so years later, when I heard that the Pac-10 said Washington was a program that needed control, I almost died laughing. It was Don James running that program! How could they even say that? To this day, it still blows my mind.

Chapter 20 — September 17, 1983

A Fourth Quarter to Remember

Husky Stadium — Washington vs. Michigan

THE FIRST PLAY OF the fourth quarter hit the Huskies with disaster. Washington Quarterback Steve Pelluer dropped back to pass and got hammered from his blind side. The ball flew out of his hands and rolled backwards for twenty yards into the end zone. Michigan's Mike Mallory pounced on it, giving the visiting eighth-ranked Wolverines a 24-10 lead. Despite the presence of over 60,000 fans, Husky Stadium was a murmur. A few thousands fans got up in unison and headed for the exits. Perhaps their surrender of faith stemmed from many of them having periodically booed Pelluer just a year before. As Washington resumed possession, the offense huddled and witnessed a commanding aura from their quarterback. "Steve Pelluer gave us all of his confidence," recalled center Dan Eernissee. "We just knew we were not going to be stopped."

"Generally speaking, we were pretty conservative offensively," said Pelluer years later. "We relied a lot on our defense. I used to get excited when we got into two-minute drills, because it was the only time the coaches would open it up and let us throw the ball. That first drive, we were in what we called a Sixty Protection. It wasn't a protection that we used a whole lot. My first read was to look at the inside linebacker on the side of the tight end, and if he rushed, it was a hot throw to the tight end. Our coaches called it at just the right time. On that first drive, we threw the hot throw twice. It's like they knew what was going to happen. I read it and the tight end read it, and everything just came together. It was amazing."

The Husky crowd roared back to life when Washington's Mark Pattison made a diving catch at the Michigan 3-yard line. Husky fullback Walt Hunt took the handoff on the following play and plowed across the goal line. This score trimmed the deficit to 24-17. Michigan subsequently drove the field and lined up to attempt a 32-yard field goal—but missed. That would have likely given the Wolverines the win. With less than three minutes remaining, the Huskies still clung to hope.

Washington mounted a drive to the Michigan ten-yard line, and the crowd was bursting with anticipation and tension. Pelluer was literally connecting on every pass attempt. He came up to the line with :34 left and the clock was running. He called an audible for an end zone corner route for receiver Mark Pattison, with the idea of putting the ball where only Pattison could catch it, otherwise rendering it incomplete to stop the clock. "It was a conversion route," said Pelluer. "If the defensive back is in bump and run, Pattison goes deep; if he's off, then Pattison runs a quick out. And the defender came up in bump and run, and I read it, and Pattison went deep and converted it. It's something we practiced all the time, and it unfolded perfectly because Coach James had us practice it so much."

After Pattison leaped high and hauled it in, it was suddenly Michigan 24, Washington 23. Husky Stadium thundered. Fans screamed for the two-point conversion. The Husky players hustled to the sideline for a conference with Coach James. This was 1983, when overtimes weren't yet a part of college football. On this day, there was no hesitation. "That was our philosophy," recalled James. "Against a non-conference team you go for the win; against a conference team, if you're still in the race, you go for a tie."

The Huskies ran back onto the field and huddled, before approaching the line of scrimmage and lining up in a double tight end set. It must have looked odd to Michigan, as skinny wide receiver Danny Greene was one of the tight ends— and backup Larry Michael was the other, substituting for the recently injured Leroy Lutu.

"As I took the snap I knew that the tight end was my first read," said Pelluer. "I didn't know that I was getting a rush from my back side. But (Michigan's Tom Hassel) was bearing down on me. Usually down at the goal line, you're supposed to have the blitzes picked up. The coaches call protections where you usually don't have to check to a hot receiver. That guy should have been picked up, but he must have come late from the secondary, and we just missed him. It was a look we weren't familiar with. Fortunately the first read was there and Larry Michael came across and was open. I laid it up, because people were all over him. I got hit as I released it."

As Michael came across the back of the end zone, he jumped high and caught the ball with two hands, before tumbling to the turf. The Huskies now led 25-24. Michael's teammates rushed to bury him in a pig pile. The goal posts literally swayed from the stadium's commotion. "It wasn't a spiral, but it was put right where it needed to be," said Pelluer of his throw. "Larry Michael went high for it. It was a timing play. I got hit as I released it. If Larry hadn't have been open, the play would have been dead, and we would have lost."

Steve Pelluer completed fifteen passes in a row in the fourth quarter, and was 27 of 33 for the day. "People bring this game up to me more than any other," he said. "Even more so than the Rose Bowl against Iowa."

"You had to love that Larry Michael, of all people, was the hero," recalled Eernissee. "He was one of those background guys that make up 90% of the team, and it was great for all of us to see his face and name splashed across the country."

Chapter 21— September 15, 1984

Hugh Millen's Homecoming

Washington at Michigan

TO UNDERSTAND THE SCOPE of what playing against Michigan meant to former Husky quarterback Hugh Millen, we go back to his formative years.

"My Dad went to Michigan, and was a huge Michigan fan," he said. "I was born in Michigan, but grew up in Seattle. But we didn't have the Seahawks yet and the Huskies were terrible. It was 1973 and I was 10 years old. While I liked the Huskies, they had a really bad season (2-9). I think as a kid you naturally gravitate toward the things your Dad likes. So I became a big Michigan fan. And they were winning, which always makes it easier to be a fan.

"At age eleven, I wrote a letter to a newspaper called the Michigan Daily describing how much I loved Michigan football. I sent them some money. And I started receiving issues of the Michigan Daily. They also sent me several player photos that were signed by the players."

When Millen was in his mid-teens, he was looking at future Husky schedules, when something jumped out at him and seized his imagination. "It was 1980," he said. "I remember seeing that the Huskies were traveling to Michigan in 1984. I wanted to be a part of that. You've got to understand that I was a HUGE Michigan fan... As an example, I had a Los Angeles Rams helmet and some fishing line. I peeled the Rams stickers off, and painted the Michigan design onto the helmet. Then I took the fishing line and used it to suspend that helmet from the ceiling in my bedroom... Are you getting the idea here?"

By 1984, after a two-year stint at a junior college, Millen had transferred to Washington and become the starting quarterback. The Huskies boarded a plane destined for Ann Arbor, Michigan. The hosting Wolverines were ranked #2 in the nation, after beating #1 Miami the week before.

"It was the first game that I ever got on a plane and traveled in my life," said Millen. "Michigan's defense had intercepted Bernie Kosar six times the week before. I'm watching film all week and seeing this. We were so cognizant about not turning the ball over. I didn't want to go into Michigan Stadium and turn the ball over six times."

Millen reflected on the twenty-four hours prior to kickoff.

"What struck me was that at the team hotel, there were all these boosters everywhere, and the Husky band was there," he said. "I was totally unprepared for the party that was going on. There were thousands of Husky fans in the hotel and there were people everywhere having a great time. For some reason, I had this idea that you just go on the road and play Michigan and then go back home."

Prior to kickoff, and with most of the players on both teams still in the locker room, Millen walked through the tunnel and emerged at midfield, entering the stadium he had idolized for the previous ten years. "I go out there to warm up my arm. I look around and think, "Its Michigan, here we are!" Then a handful of Michigan players come out onto the field. I was looking at their uniforms and their blue was much more of a vibrant, royal blue, than the navy blue I had always seen on TV. I even wondered for a moment if they had changed their uniforms. Of course, they probably hadn't. But I had such a clear idea in my mind as to what their uniforms were like, and the reality was different.

"Going into the game, I had a great mindset. I said to myself, 'You've waited so long for this day to arrive, so go out and make it as fun as possible.' I was in a great mental state to compete. If anything, the nerves helped me put a little more on my deep outs... Once the game started, I never looked up. I never wanted to look up. I didn't want to take in the size of that stadium, and see the 103,000 people, and start freaking out."

As the game started, the Husky defense established a ferocious tone. The Husky offense, playing conservatively, put together an 18-play drive that resulted in a field goal. The first half was a nearly-even slugfest.

It was in the third quarter that the Huskies held to a 10-3 lead and had the ball on their own 27- yard line. As they broke huddle, Millen brought the offense to the line of scrimmage. At that point, he had completed 10 of 12 for 69 yards. As he leaned over center and began barking out signals, one of the season's great plays was about to unfold.

"We were going to go into a 7-step drop and hit (wide receiver) Danny Greene on a deep hook route," recalled Millen. "But Michigan came with a blitz and brought their safety down. It's Pattison's job there– he's clearing out on a post route. In a situation like that, the QB has to beat the safety, and the receiver has to beat the cornerback. We were in a protection with play action, and if we can get a hat on everyone then that play will succeed. If one guy blows his block, the play probably won't work... Michigan tried to disguise the blitz, and it was there for the taking."

The pass protection was perfect. Millen dropped back, wound up and heaved a deep, arcing spiral down the center of the field that connected with Pattison. The Husky wide receiver, having beaten the defender by two yards, raced untouched into the end zone. The stadium fell silent. The Husky sideline was going nuts.

"I remember getting back to the sideline", said Millen. "Now it was 17-3. Our defense was playing so well. Michigan was utterly inept against our defense. To me it was like a baseball game, with Randy Johnson pitching and now you're sending in Mariano Rivera to wrap it up. I felt our defense was in total command."

Millen chuckled at another memory he had as the Huskies attempted to run off clock in the 4th quarter.

"Trying to milk the clock– once you have some experience as a QB, you look at the play clock, and try to break huddle at under fifteen seconds. So we break huddle and we're up to the line, and I thought, 'Oh, I broke huddle too early.' So we get into a set position, and Michigan is set, and I am looking at the scoreboard. For the first time during the game, I look around. I suddenly realize that there were 103,000 people waiting for me to take the snap. And I'm looking at the play clock slowly tick down: 14...13...12...11...10... It seemed to take forever.

"That was such a surreal moment for me."

When the game clock expired, Washington had stunned #2 ranked Michigan 20-11. The exuberant Huskies poured onto the field. Late Michigan coach Bo Schembechler met Don James at midfield to shake his hand, then began heading toward the locker room. Suddenly, Hugh Millen was standing in front of him.

"I was twenty years old at the time," said Millen. "At this point, I don't know what I was thinking. But I stuck out my hand and told him that I had been a big Michigan fan and had wanted to play for him. He shook my hand, but there's no real story to tell here. He didn't exactly want to engage me in a conversation."

Years later, Hugh Millen summed up the game. "My parents were in Germany, at a military base. But that game was actually on the Armed

Forces Network, so my Dad got to see the game. That was certainly a surreal experience for him... It was also the ideal Don James way to win a football game. It was total domination by our defense. I only threw the football 16 times. We had a great game plan and we were so completely prepared to win that football game. It all stemmed from Don James' preparation. It was a great day for the defense, and a great day for the Washington Huskies."

Chapter 22 — January 1, 1985

Purple Reigns Supreme

Washington vs. Oklahoma (Orange Bowl)

IT WAS ABOARD A cruise ship off the coast of Miami that players from Washington and Oklahoma almost got into a brawl. Until that point, these pre-game activities leading up to the 1985 Orange Bowl had been congenial enough. Trips to the Everglades and Disneyworld made for fun memories and lots of laughs. But as the cruise ship left port and skimmed eastward toward international waters, the confined quarters led to friction.

"There were three open bars and a casino on board," said former Husky strong safety Jim Rodgers years later. "When we got out beyond the U.S. border, the casino opened for business, and everybody was drinking and gambling at the tables. It was a weird thing to be at a Blackjack table and look over and see (Oklahoma Coach) Barry Switzer sitting next to you."

"Everybody was having a good time," added weak safety Tim Peoples. "And the Orange Bowl people brought in girls for the players to dance with. Everybody was drinking. Next thing you know, somebody said something to someone, and both sides were in each other's face. It almost turned into a brawl. The Sooners were pretty cocky and talking a lot, like those Miami teams of old."

"We had that deal out on a cruise ship," recalled Husky linebacker Joe Kelly. "I don't know why, but they put two teams about to go to battle on the same boat. I remember the arrogance of the Oklahoma players who were walking around. But being that we had a lot of guys from California, we weren't cocky, but we were confident. Well, the Sooners started mouthing off. We weren't going to cross the line because Don James wasn't going to accept that. But at the same time, Don James turned his head a couple of times. The guys on our defense were talking to Oklahoma like, 'Hey, we're gonna whup you in a couple days, but we'll whup you tonight, too!' So they saw that we weren't just a bunch of northwest... I don't know, whatever they thought we were."

Kelly went on to describe Oklahoma linebacker Brian Bosworth's confrontation with Washington's Reggie Rogers. The story goes that Bosworth, wearing jeans and cowboy boots, climbed up onto the table where Rogers sat, then started dancing in a mocking manner. Rogers reportedly kicked the table out from under him, and Bosworth landed on his feet, before the two converged and jawed face to face.

"Bosworth was a show-off, but Reggie was the biggest showoff on our team," said Kelly, laughing. "Bosworth probably didn't know that about Reggie. But yeah, on a couple of occasions down in the bar, a couple of guys said words I can't repeat, and Don James would turn his head and then it was nose to nose. It didn't come to a physical altercation. It got resolved without going there. Then Don James would come back, and we'd sit down like nothing happened.

"The fun part about the casino," added Kelly, "was that while Don James was upstairs, (Sooner Coach) Barry Switzer was down there with us. And he's cussing and fussing. We were in awe. I couldn't picture Don James with a gin and tonic, smoking, swearing and gambling. But that just wasn't U-Dub, that wasn't DJ."

Confrontations aside, Washington was to enter the game with a 10-1 record and the #4 ranking in the AP poll. Oklahoma sported a 9-1-1 record and the #2 national ranking. The entire nation recognized several Sooner players— like Tony Casillas, Brian Bosworth, Keith Jackson and Steve Sewell. The Huskies, on the other hand, arrived with little fanfare, aside from their defense's catchy moniker as "The Purple Reign," from the movie starring Prince. That defense was comprised of ferocious hitters and led the nation in turnover ratio. The Husky offense possessed quality players like tailback Jacque Robinson and receiver Danny Greene, but sputtered much of the season behind quarterback Hugh Millen.

"The defense played two seasons' worth, in terms of minutes," said Rodgers. "The offense couldn't stay on the field long enough for us to catch our breath." Added Peoples: "Don James finally told the defense to not say anything bad to the offense, to get off their case. But we were often quite angry at them. I don't feel Don James handled that situation very well."

"Our defense was really beat up," said Rodgers. "Tim Meamber was deaf in one ear, and I was playing with a broken arm and an injured knee. We had worked really hard and were ready. Then two days before the game, Lambright decides to go live (full goal-line scrimmaging). So what happens? Our linebacker Joe Krakowski blows out his knee and is out. The whole defense was so fucking pissed off."

Jim Lambright subsequently altered the defensive scheme, and placed responsibility on freshmen linebackers David Rill and Albert Tufono. "There they were draining 60 CCs of blood out of my knee, and what does Lambright do?" asks Rodgers. "He puts me on the motion guy! Lambright is a great guy, and he and I can laugh about this now, but god damn it!"

Both teams took to the field, and a throng of 56,000 fans buzzed amid evening air that was thick with heat and humidity.

Husky offensive tackle Al Robertson fumed with animosity toward Oklahoma linebacker Brian Bosworth. From the very start, the two engaged in multiple heated exchanges. The whole Sooner team was giving Washington an earful. The field was in awful condition, and was basically a mixture of gravel and dirt between the thirty-yard lines, and at midfield the Orange Bowl logo had simply been painted atop the dirt. As center and captain Dan Eernissee recalled, "If you look at pictures of me from that game, I'm absolutely filthy."

The Huskies came out with a great game plan, utilizing fullback and tailback trap plays that kept Oklahoma's bull-rushing defenders off-balance. Don James also utilized something else that is common now, but was a novelty back in 1985. He lined up the tight end in a 2-point stance, and then right before the snap, moved him in motion to the other side. This befuddled the Sooners.

Eernissee had a plan for the constant challenge of blocking All-American Tony Casillas. "I had no chance if I tried to overpower Casillas, as he was just too strong. So I used a scramble blocking technique, with the key being to get to the point of attack before he did, using my quickness." That blocking helped lead the way for the game's MVP Jacque Robinson, who tallied 135 rushing yards on 21 carries including a touchdown.

On offense, the Sooners achieved early success by running right up the middle. Heading back to the huddle after surrendering a 12-yard gain, Jim Rodgers went up to Husky freshman linebacker David Rill and grabbed him by the facemask. "David motherfucker!" he shouted. "These bastards are running right at you! You just gotta stick your nose in there and don't give 'em another fucking inch!"

Rill responded, and the Husky defense clamped down. By the second quarter, Washington held a 14-0 lead, which could have been 21-0, had Husky receiver Danny Greene not bobbled a sure touchdown throw from quarterback Paul Sicuro. Oklahoma utilized a couple of big plays and tied it at 14-14 going into halftime. But even then, the Huskies felt confident. "We knew we were thirty minutes away from beating Oklahoma," said Rodgers. "We felt we still had momentum."

In the third quarter Sooner kicker Tim Lasher booted a field goal to apparently provide Oklahoma with a 17-14 lead. A procedure call negated this, but a distraction prevented fans at first to realize a penalty had occurred. The famous Boomer Schooner Calistoga wagon suddenly rambled onto the field to celebrate. It proceeded to drive right through the middle of the clustered Washington defenders, parting them like the Red Sea. A male Sooner cheerleader was hanging out of the back waving the OU flag right in the Huskies' faces. Husky linebacker Joe Kelly swung his foot in the direction of the wagon in disgust, and several players reacted animatedly. It was at this point that Jim Rodgers had his only regret of the evening. "In high school my Dad had sternly warned me about throwing tantrums," he said. "He said that he would never let me play football again if I ever lost my temper on the field. That thought raced through my head. That was the only thing that kept me from reaching up and grabbing that damn flag and yanking that little bastard right out of the wagon!"

The subsequent 20 yards worth of penalties left the Sooners with a longer field goal attempt. Safety Tim Peoples roared around the left side and smothered the kick. The Washington sideline went berserk. The NBC announcers were giving the credit to Ron Holmes for getting a big mitt on the ball. "It wasn't Holmes, it was me. I got a hand on it," said Peoples. "They were always giving Holmes all the credit!"

Oklahoma did ultimately take a 17-14 lead into the fourth quarter. Hugh Millen entered the game to replace Paul Sicuro as Husky quarterback. On a key 3rd down and twelve, Millen delivered a beautiful 29-yard throw to Danny Greene on a crossing pattern up the left sideline. Toward the end of that drive, the Husky offense broke huddle and approached the line of scrimmage. It was one of those awkward moments when there is a TV timeout and both teams just stand at the scrimmage staring at each other. By now, Oklahoma sang a different tune.

"The Sooners were a bunch of good ole boys," recalled Eernissee. "They were suddenly saying 'Man, your coaches are awesome! We don't have a clue what the hell is going on! Or what you're gonna do next. And what's the deal with moving the tight end around?'"

On the next play, Millen hooked up with receiver Mark Pattison for a 12-yard timing pattern for a touchdown. This put Washington in front 21-17 late in the game. Jeff Jaeger kicked off down the left hashmark, the ball sailing high in the air. As is descended toward the orange pylon near the front of the end zone, it bounced off the facemask of Sooner return man Buster Ryhmes, rolling out of bounds at the 2-yard line. The Sooners were in desperate straits as they huddled up in their own end zone. On first down, Sooner Quarterback Danny Bradley immediately dropped back to throw. Husky tackle Ronnie Holmes roared past his blocker and knocked Bradley's pass straight into the air. It was intercepted by linebacker Joe Kelly.

"I caught it at the 10-yard line and took off toward the end zone," said Kelly. "I got so excited, I thought I was gonna run over this big 325-pound guard from Oklahoma. But after I hit him, all I remember is standing up from the ground and I was facing the other direction, so I knew I didn't make it into the end zone. I was about 208 pounds. I could have easily dodged him, but it was that toughness in me. It was mano-a-mano. I wanted to run him over. But I lost that battle."

Husky fullback Rick Fenney promptly plowed up the middle for the touchdown. Washington now led by the final margin of 28-17. As the final seconds ran off the clock, the players lifted Don James atop their shoulders and carried him around, before the NBC network sideline announcer beckoned for an interview. Washington would finish ranked #2 in the nation—behind undefeated BYU from the weaker WAC Conference.

"We had a final chance to bond and finish off that era of the Purple Reign," recalled Joe Kelly. "It was great that it ended as it did. It was a special bunch of guys. We felt confident that we had earned at least a share of the national championship. It was a great night, although disappointing later to not have won it all." Both Tim Peoples and Dan Eernissee stated that this was the biggest win in their Husky careers. Said Eernissee: "Taking on Casillas, the best lineman in the country the last two seasons, and shutting him down, was very satisfying."

Jim Rodgers is more pro-active in his remembrances of that game. He laughs as he says, "Every time I meet a new woman and we have a first date—out comes the Orange Bowl tape!"

Chapter 23

A Visit with Ron Holmes

RON HOLMES ARRIVED AT Washington in 1981 at 6'4" and 197 pounds, and a prospect of middling caliber. By the time he completed his senior season in 1984, he was 6'4" 290 lbs, and a Consensus All-American. He played on UW teams that won both the Rose Bowl and the Orange Bowl. He went on to become a first-round NFL draft pick for the Tampa Bay Buccaneers, and later played in a Super Bowl for Denver alongside the legendary John Elway.

Derek Johnson: Tell me what the recruiting process was like for you in relation to Coach James, as you were coming out of Timberline High School in Lacey, Washington.

Ron Holmes: The one thing I can say about Coach James is that he taught me everything outside of football. When Coach James came to my house during the recruiting stage, he made a promise to my parents. He promised that when I left the U of W, I would have a chance to get my degree, a chance to be a positive part of the community, and a chance to be a better man. He never even mentioned football. By the time he left my house, my parents were so wrapped up in him. Every word he said, they felt that outside of the Bible, they were the truest words. That meant a lot to them and to me. Every other coach that recruited me talked about how I could contribute to the team and what a great player I could be. They never talked about how life would be for me after football. Those were the things that Coach James was talking about.

My Dad was part of the military all his working life. So, he had read a lot of books on psychology and war time strategies. Coach James had a conversation with him on that level, and my Dad felt it was very meaningful. My Mom was very involved with religion, and Coach James spoke at length with her about his beliefs, and he had a very interesting view of religion. He wasn't afraid to express that. He made it clear that Christianity provided balance to his and Carol's life. So by the time Coach James left our house, my Mom and Dad had already made up their mind where I was going. As Coach James was walking back to his car, we were watching him. My Dad said to me, "Now *that's* a man."

If you talk to my teammates Jacque Robinson or Tim Meamber, they will tell you the same thing. Whenever Coach James called you into his office, it almost always had to do with bettering yourself in life. It was almost *never* about football. It would be about grades, or something related to your future. But it was never to tell me that I wasn't playing well enough. Only once did that happen, going into my senior year. He said to me, "I know that you play hard and you play hurt, and you do all the things we ask you to do. But in regards to how people and pros scouts are viewing you, I am asking you as both a human being and a football player, to show more of a presence in the weight room. I don't want to hear whispers about how you're not strong enough or you're not dedicated enough."

That was really about life, he was trying to help me out in life. He knew that I was in shape and dedicated, but he had answered those questions a few times, and he told me to just make it easier for them to see that I was giving everything that I had.

Johnson: One of the chapters in this book has to do with the 1982 Apple Cup, when the Cougars knocked you guys out of the Rose Bowl. In the previous two weeks, you guys had knocked off two top ten teams. Don James told me in an interview last year that during the week of the '82 Apple Cup, he got disgusted with the team's practice display, and even kicked everyone off the field one day. Tell me about that week from a player's perspective.

Holmes: That 1982 Apple Cup game felt out of place all around. In practice, we were on the defensive side of the field, but we could hear Coach James up in the tower on the bullhorn yelling at the wide receivers, "HEY! IF YOU DROP THE BALL, GO PICK IT UP AND RUN IT BACK!" Some of them were leaving the ball there. Then he started yelling at the defense, "HEY! HOW MANY TIMES ARE WE GOING TO HAVE TO RUN THIS PLAY BEFORE WE GET IT RIGHT?"

We got back to the huddle, and we were like "Ah man, we know what we need to do." But we were *really* lax. We had the assumption that all we needed to do was show up against the Cougars. Everyone knew that we had just knocked off two undefeated teams. We were 9-1. We were going to just show up, beat the Cougars, and go to our third straight Rose Bowl. Everything was going to work out because we thought we could turn it on when we wanted to.

Johnson: But typically, Coach James never yelled at players from the tower, right?

Holmes: Oh, no! Never! Whenever Coach James talked through the bullhorn, it was always instructional, and it was almost always directed toward the assistant coaches. Normally the plays would run, and the assistant coaches would look to the tower. Coach James would just shake his head, and that meant that we had to run the play over. They were all in sync with that. But during that week prior to the Apple Cup, there he was suddenly yelling down at us, "HEY! PICK UP THE BALL AND RUN IT BACK!" At one point, suddenly we saw him climbing down from the tower. We thought *"Oh-oh! God's coming down from the tower!"* We thought he was going to yell at us, then put us back to work. But he just said that he was sick of watching us slop around, and he was ending practice early. For the moment, it was shocking to see him do that. But then we got to thinking, "OK! This is just one of those psyche jobs!" Because we were always trying to stay one step up on him.

To be honest, I think many of us players were feeling so good about ourselves that we decided that Coach James felt we had been working too hard, and that this was his way of *giving us some rest!* But when we played against the Cougars, we were in for a rude awakening. Those Cougars really showed up to play. We didn't think they would, but they did.

Johnson: I had an immensely enjoyable interview with former Cougar Coach Jim Walden. Among other things, we talked about the 1984 Apple Cup when the Cougars were making fun of Jacque Robinson's weight during practice leading up to the game. The word is that the Huskies got pretty upset about it.

Holmes: (Laughing) That was bad year for Jacque and his weight thing. Everywhere he went, he was hearing it from opponents. Cookie Jackson and Sterling Hinds starting getting a lot more carries because Jacque wasn't down to his playing weight. We players didn't really get upset about it, but Jacque was upset. Jacque was heated! There were "vicious rumors" coming out of Pullman that the Cougar players were going around dressed up like the Pillsbury Dough Boy. So that was the Cougar way of letting fat boy know that he was carrying too much weight. But you know, Jacque always had that little bit of weeble to him. Anyway, he went out and had a great game and we beat those Cougars.

But I had a few situations that I was hearing it from the opponents, too. I had one game in 1984 against Houston at Husky Stadium (a 35-7 UW win). I had been in a car accident two days before, with shattered glass and all that. I had a splitting headache and I could barely fit my helmet over my head. I wasn't playing very well. And all game long, I was wondering why our fans couldn't be louder, because I was hearing it from the Houston sideline: HEY HUSKIES! WHERE'S YOUR ALL-AMERICAN? WHERE IS HE? WHERE DID HE GO? WHERE'S YOUR ALL-AMERICAN? WE DON'T SEE HIM! I'm telling you man, it was ugly! (Laughs)

Johnson: On the flip side, one of the great dominant individual games in Husky history was your performance against #2 Oklahoma in the 1985 Orange Bowl. You had that epic moment in the fourth quarter where you charged through the Sooner line and knocked QB Danny Bradley's pass into the air, where it was picked off by your teammate Joe Kelly. Tell me about that night in Miami.

Holmes: A series of events happened. Just like the Houston game, the Oklahoma guys were ragging me. They clipped my knee early in the game. Dr. Bramwell was talking to me on the sideline and telling me that my knee was blowing up on me. I told him there was no option and that I was going to play. I hadn't come all the way down there to Miami to not play and be embarrassed by these cowboys. You know, Oklahoma had this thing about them that really rubbed me the wrong away. We got down there to the Orange Bowl, and it was like we didn't even exist. Everyone was assuming that they were going to roll over us. Everyone had these predictions of how much Oklahoma was going to beat us by. They had this arrogance about them. They had a bunch of big guys and they were definitely corn-fed. They really, truly believed that they were invincible. And we were totally convinced that we were going to kick their butt.

Well, the first defensive play of the game, they set me up with a chop block. So now, I am really kind of heated. Not just that they were playing dirty, but that they were *laughing* about it. But by the end of the third quarter, the knee wasn't even an issue with me anymore. And a series of events just started to happen. We got the blocked field goal, and we got that pass that I tipped up in the air. Stuff like that happened, and we won 28 to 17. The Washington Huskies left Miami as Orange Bowl Champions and 11-1.

Johnson: I interviewed Tim Peoples awhile back, and he complained that you were given credit for blocking that field goal, when it was actually him. He said people were always giving you credit instead of him.

Holmes: (Laughing hysterically) Go tell Tim Peoples that I love him dearly, but that I have video of that Orange Bowl game, and he can go break it down *frame by frame*, and see that it was *me* that blocked it. I know I blocked it. But if he wants to say he blocked it too, that's okay with me. I don't care. As long as we came up with the victory, I don't care. We won the game.

Johnson: Tim Peoples was also one of the few guys I have spoken with who had negative things to say about Coach James. He felt that the position change from Strong Safety to Weak Safety going into his junior year cost him a lot of money in the NFL draft. He listed several things he was upset about, and then said, "I will never forgive that man for what he put me through."

Holmes: Really? Well, I don't claim to know anybody's personal relationship with Coach James. All I can tell you is this. If you wanted to be more than a football player, then Coach James was the guy for you. I love Peeps dearly and I love all those guys dearly, because that camaraderie that we had I could never replace in a million years. You say my teammates' names and something swells in my heart and I miss those guys. I wish that I could see all of them and talk about how life brought us together years ago, and how life has brought each of us to where we are now, over twenty years later.

But let me give you an example of what Coach James put Tim Peoples and all of us through. I look at Jacque Robinson as a perfect example of illustrating this to you. Jacque Robinson came out like a shooting star, like a blaze. Boom! Do you remember? He was the MVP of the Rose Bowl as a freshman! He had the world by the tail. Coach James was no different with Jacque Robinson as a freshman than when Jacque Robinson was a senior. If you called up Jacque right now on a conference call and asked him if Coach James rode his ass, Jacque would say *"Not only did Coach James ride my ass, he rode it like Zorro."* I'm serious. Coach James didn't care if you were the first pick of the first round or the never pick of the never-was round. He was going to drive you until you gave your best as a person. He would tell you that this isn't about becoming the best on the football field. This is to teach you about not quitting on yourself when it comes to life. So if you felt that you were of a certain stripe and that Coach James wasn't going to make you work as hard as others, then you were in for a big surprise.

I can only say this—Coach James treated me fairly, and everyone I saw he treated fairly. Because he treated everyone exactly the same. You can call up Steve Emtman and Napoleon Kaufman and all those guys, and they'll tell you that Coach James rode them hard yet treated them all the same.

I will also say this about Peeps. There have only been a couple or three guys who have come to the University of Washington that I have looked at and thought *"Damn! That guy has got to make it to the pros!"* Tim Peoples was one of those guys. He had so many God-given skills. He could leap like a gazelle. He could literally jump like nobody else. I love Tim, but he never maximized his talent. He played in the NFL, but he left Washington untapped. I always thought he was going to be a better version of (former Husky) Ray Horton. Tim had such strength and speed and God-given athletic ability.

Johnson: There were many great characters on your team, but tell me the story about the late linebacker Fred Small when you guys were freshmen.

Holmes: This one is for him. God rest his soul, Freddie Small. Early on in my freshman year in 1981, (Assistant Coach) Skip Hall knew I was going to be a defensive lineman but they were starting me off at linebacker. We were doing drills. Our freshman class was like hell on wheels. We wanted to cause as much destruction as possible. We were doing drops back into coverage, taking turns, one after another. We started the drill with 12-13 guys, but it soon thinned out to 3-4 guys. We were all getting quite winded and fatigued. It got to be my turn and I said to Freddie, "You go ahead and take this one." And Freddie said to me, *"No! You take it yourself."* I turned around to look at him, and he said, "Hey man, I come from *COMPTON*!"

I was so used to being THE GUY, and suddenly I realized that I wasn't anymore. Little ol' me, I didn't come from Compton. I came from Lacey, Washington!

Johnson: Your teammate and defensive back Jimmy Rodgers once told me that you guys were scrimmaging, and he turned to Freddie and yelled at him for being out of position or some such thing. Freddie got right into Jimmy's face and said, "Don't you ever tell me what to do again, you white motherfucker, or I will kill you right on this field!" And Jimmy, no slouch himself, replied "Yes sir!"

Holmes: (Laughing hysterically) That's Freddie, man! That was Freddie! I want to say that we were all for one on that defense, though. There wasn't any discrimination going on or anything... But hearing these guys' names, talking about these guys' names, I miss them. I loved my teammates. We were the Purple Reign. We let that purple rain fall on us while we worked on that field down by Lake Washington, and we were as happy as could be. We were known as the tough guys who didn't mind working in the rain.

Chapter 24

A Visit with Husky Radio Announcer Bob Rondeau

BOB RONDEAU HAS BEEN the Husky play-by-play announcer since 1979, with the exception of the years 1986-1988, when KIRO took over the radio rights from KOMO for Washington football. When the Dawgs cross the goal line, he is famous for his call, "Touchdown Washington!"

Derek Johnson: In your written introduction for the book *Husky Stadium: Great Games and Golden Moments,* you mentioned that you were nervous the first time that you did the play-by-play of a Husky football game. Can you describe that day?

Bob Rondeau: It was in 1979; that was the game at ASU that Frank Kush got fired. We actually did broadcasts in 1978 also. Bruce King did the play-by-play and I was doing to color. We were still doing that in 1979. What happened was KOMO-TV decided to broadcast that Washington-Arizona State game live and so Bruce went over to do the telecast and I went and did the radio play-by-play live for the first time. But I had done booth color the preceding year and all the games up to that point in the 1979 season. Then Bruce left to take a job in New York, and I became the play-by-play guy.

Johnson: What were your first impressions and experiences in dealing with Don James?

Rondeau: The best thing with Don James was that he was always very patient with me—answering questions and so forth. We would book time to record the pre-game show and then have time afterwards for my questions and his observations. He was very generous with that, even from the first. Of course, the more you do it, the more comfortable you get. Don was always really good that way and put up with a lot from me. Along with Jim Lambright, who also helped me a lot in the early days, in trying to get a little more sophisticated in my knowledge of the game. Don made it very easy in that regard. He was always pretty even-keeled and very open—at least off the record. If there were things he didn't want to talk about he would let me know, but for the most part he gave me what I needed to know, at least off the record. He was great that way.

Johnson: One of my favorite recollections of games you called was from the win over undefeated Arizona State in Tempe in 1982. My Dad and I sat in his den listening to your broadcast on KOMO. There are three things I recall vividly: My sweaty hands, the smell of Dad's pipe smoke, and your description of Aaron Williams' one-handed diving touchdown catch.

Rondeau: (Chuckling) That was a great night! That was the night when they did a closed-circuit telecast back to Seattle. ASU was third in the nation, we were seventh. ASU's defense was all the rage. I think Paul Moyer, our buddy from the Seahawks, was a safety on that team. They were just killing people. And my recollection is that we didn't give up a sack that night— in addition to the great play you mentioned by Aaron Williams. There were Sun Devil fans throwing roses around because Arizona State was finally supposed to be going to the Rose Bowl for the first time. But the Dawgs put together a great game and won 17-13, knocking ASU out and setting themselves up for the Rose Bowl. Which of course, was torn asunder the following week in their loss to Wazzu.

Johnson: In your years of dealing with Don James, what game stands out?

Rondeau: The game that stands out for me was the Stanford game in 1982. The Dawgs were undefeated and ranked #1 in the nation, and Stanford had John Elway and all that. This was at the end of October, and there was a lot of talk that Don James was going to be the next coach of the Seattle Seahawks. So that had been bandied about for a long time and really had gotten serious that week. Don finally just decided to put an end to it. He held a press conference right before getting on the airplane to head to Stanford, and he announced that he was staying at Washington and telling everyone to end any speculation that he might be leaving to coach the Seahawks. That was one of the few times that Don was really feeling the pressure. Certainly the football pressure never bothered him as much. But the external pressure of the media and having his name tossed around like that, especially as coach of the #1 team in America, I think it really, really bothered him.

I remember that we had already recorded his pre-game show, and he didn't want to do it again. So I wound up having to do some serious editing that Friday night before the game, but we managed to get it done. Of course, the next day, Washington was upset 43-31. John Elway had a great day, and needless to say, Don was upset with that too, losing the #1 ranking and all. That was certainly a trying week for all concerned.

Johnson: What was it like doing the weekly radio show with him?

Rondeau: It was always great. Don was always the competitor. Anyone who knows him knows how competitive he is. Whether it's a football game, or a golf game, his mindset was always the same— he wants to win. He enjoyed doing the talk show, particularly the people who would take issue with him, as opposed to those who wanted to bow down to Don. And believe me, when it was going well, the calls were always prefaced by 'Coach, I think you're the greatest thing ever!' I think he appreciated that, but got a little tired of it. He enjoyed the jousting with people who would take issue with players or play calling. Don was never one to shy away. He would engage the caller. I think it made for some of the better moments of the show.

Johnson: Given your close proximity to Coach James, what would people be surprised to learn about him that they may not have seen from a distance?

Rondeau: His wit and a very dry sense of humor. Don James is a sharp man. I don't know if that always came out, but it certainly did with me. Maybe not always on-the-air, but certainly off-the-air. He enjoyed conversation, and if the conversation got competitive, he enjoyed it that much more. I enjoyed talking with him a lot. I think he came across to many people as the guy up in the tower, very stoic and very stern. A little bit like current Washington Coach Tyrone Willingham nowadays, in a different kind of way. But you know, Tyrone has a better sense of humor than a lot of people realize, and it was the same with Don James as well.

Johnson: There are several similarities between the two men. However, I don't believe that Don James ever referred to himself in the third person.

Rondeau: No, I don't think that ever occurred.

Johnson: In post-game interviews, what was the most agitated or frustrated you ever saw Coach James?

Rondeau: There was a game here in 1980 that a lot of people don't remember, but Washington had won five of its first six games and looked like a pretty good football team. And Navy came into Husky Stadium and beat Washington 24-10. The Huskies just looked awful. The tackling and general defensive play was WAY below Don James' standards. And he was NOT happy after that game. He was pretty upset. But it's interesting, the next week the Huskies came right back and shut out a pretty good Arizona State team 25-0. And that's a reflection on Don James. As a player, you really didn't want to upset him, because he was going to make you pay for it, but he would also make you better. But that Navy game was as put-out as I ever saw him after a game.

Johnson: What was the most excited you ever saw him after a game?

Rondeau: He always prided himself on great road wins, as a mark of a great football team and a great coaching staff. I remember that game at Michigan in 1984. Going into Ann Arbor and the Big House, with over 100,000 fans. Michigan was ranked #3 and had just beaten Miami the week before. Don felt really good about that game. You didn't have to read too far in between the lines, he was confident that his team could go in there and win. I remember that Doug Looney from *Sports Illustrated* was in Seattle that week before the Huskies headed east. Looney was the writer who had listed the top three coaches in America. His list was: 1. Don James 2. Don James 3. Don James.

I remember asking Don point-blank at the end of the show, 'Can you beat these guys?' And he said, 'Yea, we can beat this guys.' Of course, they went out and played a great game and won 20-11.

Also, the road win at Nebraska in the National Championship season of 1991. That win delighted him to no end, especially the way it finished. Those two stand out for me.

Johnson: Those must have been fun interviews for you to conduct.

Rondeau: They were. And you know, win or lose Don was always up-front. Perhaps he didn't give the electrifying quotes that you wanted, but he always addressed the questions. What I liked about him was he would talk about his team, but would seldom bad-mouth his players. Rarely would he single out a player for doing something wrong.

Johnson: Going back to August 1993, where were you the moment you heard that Coach James had resigned?

Rondeau: Oh, it was unbelievable. I was also working at KOMO television at the time, anchoring the weekend sports casts. That Sunday morning I remembering watching the Pac-10 sanction stuff come down on television. They had live coverage on the hearings and announced their verdicts. So I started calling around for some sort of reaction. I talked to one prominent Husky booster at the time, someone I am not going to identify, and he said, "You know that Don is resigning?" And I said, "No... I didn't know that." Obviously it was a jolt, and a huge news story. I was working television that day. We called around to several sources to confirm it, and then we ended up going on the air and breaking that story in Seattle, on KOMO-TV.

I don't take any pride necessarily in breaking that story— I was just doing my job as a reporter. But let's just say that it was a very difficult story to break. And Don wasn't doing any interviews and sequestered himself away. They immediately named Jim Lambright as the interim coach.

That following Monday, Don agreed to do two interviews. It was myself for radio and Keith Shipman for the coach's show on Channel 13. Those are the only two Don wanted to do. We did a radio interview into a tape recorder at Don's house. I begged him, "Don, can we put this on TV?" And he said, "No, we've done radio with you all the time and on TV with Keith. We will do it the way we have always done it." So we recorded it and excerpted it and put it on TV, with a picture of Don while the recording was played. It was reflective of Don James' great loyalty. He said "You and Keith have been loyal and I've enjoyed working with you, so I will give you guys interviews. But that's it."

The newspaper guys, whom Don wouldn't speak with because he was angry with them, they came down and got quotes off our story to run for their stories. That was a very, very difficult time.

Johnson: What was the national impact of that story from your perspective as a reporter?

Rondeau: Well, Washington's place in the national landscape at that time was as good as it got. It was enormous news, both locally and nationally. ESPN's Mike Torrico was on the phone to me not twenty minutes after the story broke wanting to talk to the one who broke the story. There must have been thirty phone calls of that ilk that came over the next couple of days.

And the thing that was most unfortunate was that some people were quick to call Don James a quitter and a coward and all that kind of thing. That was very, very unfortunate. It showed no understanding of who he was and what he was about.

Johnson: And then there was the situation with former UW President William Gerberding, who wrote a guest feature article in 1990 for the *Washington Post* back in the nation's capital. In the opening paragraph, Gerberding wrote: "If I could rewrite American history, I would not attach to our colleges and universities the task of providing mass entertainment for the American public."

Rondeau: I will say that personally I got along great with Bill Gerberding. I thought he was a smart guy and I enjoyed my relationship with him. It was a shame that loggerheads came as they did between him and Don and Mike Lude. That was always a difficult process and a tough place to be.

Johnson: Before the sanctions and resignation stuff hit the fan, did you sense tensions building between those two sides in the preceding years?

Rondeau: Yes, though it was probably more between Dr. Gerberding and Mike Lude, rather than with Bill Gerberding and Don James. Certainly Don was involved by extension of his relationship with Mike. But I think that Bill was always wary of the power that Mike wielded in the athletic department, and he wanted to make sure that at the end of the day, that this is an academic institution. He felt that was the priority, and all else should be secondary. And yet, he felt that sometimes Husky football didn't seem secondary at all. So by nature, I think that bred tension into the situation.

Johnson: In looking back at the Don James era in its entirety, what do those days mean to you?

Rondeau: Well, I was fortunate enough to be part of a golden era of Husky football. I think people in my age bracket and younger, perceive that time as the absolute best that Husky football has ever been. I was fortunate enough to get on that train and ride it.

Chapter 25 — October 19, 1985

Pride Goes Before a Fall

Husky Stadium — Washington vs. Oregon State

OREGON STATE SERVED AS comedic fodder to the Seattle media that entire week. After all, the Beavers were an awful football team. They hadn't scored a touchdown in a month. They hadn't won a road game in seven years. They hadn't beaten Washington since 1974. They had a walk-on freshman starting at quarterback. And they were having their faces rubbed in it. It started with Don James, during his weekly radio show, when he said: "You always want to win big, but I would particularly like to get the opportunity to play (backup quarterback) Chris Chandler." On Tuesday, the rhetoric was ratcheted up several notches, when *Seattle P-I* columnist Steve Rudman scathed: "Oregon State has ceased being a joke. The Beavers are not only an embarrassment to themselves and their fans, they are an embarrassment to the Pac-10 Conference." *Seattle Times* columnist Blaine Newnham wrote a feature at mid-week, on how the top recruits in the state of Oregon wouldn't even pay a visit to the OSU campus. Rudman also added in additional column: "Oregon State is the Barney Fife of College Football."

The capper was what happened Friday night before the game. It was witnessed at the Bellevue Red Lion, as dozens of Oregon State players watched the local sports news on KING-5. Television personality Tony Ventrella, with characteristic mischievousness in his eyes, told viewers that a spy had managed to smuggle secret video from a recent Oregon State football practice. The camera cut away, and suddenly upon the screen was old black-and-white footage of *The Three Stooges*, bungling their way through a football drill. Throughout the Puget Sound region, thousands of Husky fans chuckled. At the Bellevue Red Lion, however, disbelief rapidly gave way to anger. The Oregon State Beavers fumed deep into the night.

During his pre-game radio interview, Don James indicated to announcer Bob Rondeau that he wished the Huskies had the same ammunition that the Seattle media gave the Beavers all week. Washington was a 37 ½ -point favorite to win this game. *Sports Illustrated* had ranked them as the #1 team in the nation at the start of the year. The Huskies were the defending Orange Bowl champions. Though they had lost a lot of talent off that 11-1 team, they were still far bigger, stronger and superior to the Oregon State Beavers.

An eerie feeling permeated the stadium early on, as the Beavers' freshman QB Rich Gonzales rolled to his right and heaved the ball far down the right sideline to fullback Darvin Malone. Washington's All-American linebacker Joe Kelly was stride-for-stride in perfect coverage. But as Kelly later recalled: "I had it read one-hundred percent! The QB threw the ball, and being the linebacker I was - and showing the reason why I wasn't a running back - I jumped up and the ball went right through my hands and the fullback caught it for a touchdown. Oh, man! That was a tough one. It really hurt."

In the second quarter, facing second down from the Beaver ten-yard line, Husky QB Hugh Millen dropped back to pass and threw toward Lonzell (Mo) Hill in the end zone— but Oregon State's Reggie Hawkins stepped in front to pick it off. In the third quarter, Washington's Jeff

Jaeger lined up to attempt a chip-shot field goal; but the snap was bobbled and the holder rolled out and heaved a desperate pass, and was intercepted. Still in the third quarter, with first and goal at the Beaver 1-yard line, Husky tailback Vince Weathersby got decked and coughed up the football. Beaver Lavance Northington pounced upon it to secure possession, thwarting the Huskies yet again.

Still, by the fourth quarter it appeared that Washington would gut out an ugly victory. Husky punter Thane Cleland stood back at his own 20-yard line with 1:46 left, and his team leading 20-14. At that point, the Husky defense was playing well and the consensus in the crowd was that the Beavers couldn't score with that little time remaining. The snap rifled back to Cleland at chest-high and Cleland caught it cleanly and proceeded to step forward to boot it downfield. An UW blocker, however, blew his assignment. Oregon State's Andre Todd shot through the line and converged on Cleland, as the punter's foot made impact with the ball. There was a sickening double THUD-THUD! Cleland went sprawling, the kick's trajectory was obliterated, and the ball went skittering twenty yards backwards into the end zone. For a moment, it appeared the ball would roll out of bounds, until the ball suddenly shifted course and stayed in the end zone. A mad scramble ensued. An official's arms suddenly shot up skyward. Oregon State's gleeful Lavance Northington emerged with the football. His teammate Paul Sanders began jumping for joy with him— like kids at Christmas. The Beaver sideline went berserk. A prolonged anguished groan emanated from the Husky Stadium crowd. On the radio broadcast back to Oregon, Beaver play-by-play announcer Darrel Aune was almost unintelligible; screaming into the microphone, at the point of tears, pleading for fans to go hug their family and friends and remember where they were on this glorious day. Moments later, kicker Jim Nielson booted the extra point, and the Beavers had the game 21-20.

"Nothing is better than this," said Beaver Coach Dave Kragthorpe afterward in the raucous the locker room, revealing to reporters that he had read Steve Rudman's article aloud to his players before kickoff. "Nobody gave us a chance. A lot of nasty things had been said about us, and I told our kids that they could earn respect they weren't getting... I asked them to play hard and come off the field with their heads up."

Beaver Fullback Darvin Malone talked about seeing the Three Stooges video clip. "They said it was the Beavers. It was humiliating. We took that to bed with us." Oregon State offensive tackle Tom Emmons was speaking with *Seattle Times* columnist Blaine Newnham. "I don't know what paper you're from," said Emmons, "But it would be like you having a problem in your family and then somebody from the outside trying to capitalize on that problem for their own benefits. Trying to be cute at our expense isn't very cute."

Meanwhile, a terse Don James addressed the media. "We've got to give a lot of credit to Oregon State," he said. 'They played hard. They did a better job. Better than we did. You've got to give them all the credit in the world."

Several years later, Jim Lambright looked back upon that game. "It still sends a chill up my spine every time I remember it."

Chapter 26 — September 20, 1986

Payback

Husky Stadium — Washington vs. BYU

BYU CORNERBACK JEFF SPROWLS shouted into a Seattle TV camera: "Welcome to the WAC, Washington! This was our national championship game, and we just crushed the Huskies!" In the locker room, Sprowls's teammates were spouting off. All-American defensive tackle Jason Buck said: "All that press hype about Washington made you expect more," he said. "I liked killing them." Added Quarterback Robbie Bosco: "That is the biggest win in school history. I've never seen us so happy after a game."

Washington had just traveled to Provo, Utah early in the 1985 season with the intent of settling the snub from the 1984 national championship debate. But in the blistering heat near the Wasatch Mountains, the BYU Cougars, of the supposedly weaker Western Athletic Conference, blasted the Huskies 31-3 on national TV.

Washington's final drive ended in failure at the goal line. UW tailback Aaron Jenkins went air-born and fumbled the ball away. It was the last of many brutal Husky blunders. The capacity crowd was delirious. On the sidelines, Don James stood motionless, staring out toward the field in fury. A *Seattle Times* photographer captured a picture of Aaron Jenkins as he returned to the bench— slumped and with his head buried in his hands. Meanwhile, the clock's remaining seconds were expiring, and Mormons throughout the nation began to celebrate.

In the Husky locker room, Don James scolded his team behind closed doors. Washington football was 0-2 for the first time since 1975—James's first season. He looked at the players and expressed his embarrassment, before ordering them to provide only compliments for BYU while speaking with reporters. He said he didn't want to open up the paper the next day and read anything derogatory. Then James opened up the locker room and addressed the media.

"I was embarrassed by the way we played," James said. "It is probably the worst game we've played with quality players. In the early years when we started out, we weren't very good, but I think we've got more talented players now. At least I thought we did."

A reporter asked James why he had replaced running back David Toy. "I was looking for somebody who wanted to run hard," he said. Another reporter asked if this meant that the tailback job was open.

"All jobs are open," James snapped. "We're going to look at everything."

A year later in September 1986, back in the damp and cool Pacific Northwest, BYU was making it's first-ever trip to Seattle. During his Monday press conference, Don James described what it had been like to lose in Provo the year before. "We were on national TV and we had the flap over who was number one the year before, and just like they wanted to show us, we wanted to show them," said James. "Then we go out and flop in front of all those people. That was not a lot of fun."

James also let it be known that for the first time in his twelve-year career at Washington, he scheduled an extra practice during a game week. The primary reason, he said, was to prepare for BYU's exotic passing attack.

As Washington's Jeff Jaeger booted the opening kickoff high into the air on September 20, 1986, Husky Stadium was packed with fired-up fans. In his white jersey with blue pants and trim, BYU's Robert Parker waited at the six-yard line for the ball to descend to him. As he caught it and advanced up the field, he couldn't believe his eyes; a colossal wedge to the right side had cleared a hole large enough for a dump truck to rumble through. Parker scampered through that hole untouched for 94 yards until he reached the end zone. Twelve seconds into the game, and BYU already led 7-0. A mega groan rolled heavy through Husky Stadium, as the Cougars caroused on their sideline. "It's going to be just like last year," BYU's Jason Buck yelled to his teammates: "We're going to walk all over these guys!"

Late in the first quarter, with the Huskies leading 13-7, BYU was backed up against their own end zone, facing a third and long. Quarterback Steve Lindsley came up to the line of scrimmage and froze with confusion. He felt compelled to call time out. The Husky defense had lined up showing two down linemen and nine pass defenders. Following the time out, when both teams lined up again, Lindsley tried to size up the Husky formation, but now was thinking too much and felt intimidated. He took the snap and dropped back but was immediately blasted to the turf for a safety by Husky lineman Reggie Rogers. The Huskies now led 15-7.

The TV cameras panned in on Lindsey as he held both hands to his helmet and hobbled off the field. The irrepressible broadcaster Sam Adkins exclaimed, "Ouch! They don't hit this hard in the WAC!" Lindsley said later: "I was worrying too much about the rush. I knew sooner or later they were going to get me."

Following that safety, and led by quarterback Chris Chandler, the Huskies began steamrolling up and down the field and scoring at will. Chandler threw four touchdowns in the second quarter. One of them was magnificence in artistry. Chandler took a snap and saw

BYU safety Jeff Wilcox approaching up the middle like a heat-seeking missile. Chandler made his seven-step drop, waited until the moment before Wilcox's impact, then threw the ball downfield—right to the spot Wilcox had vacated— and receiver Mo Hill hauled it in for the easy touchdown.

This extended Washington's lead to 28-7. Chandler got up from the turf and began dancing about with his hands extended high to signal touchdown. He glanced over at the BYU bench and saw an assistant coach with *his* hands in the air, mocking Chandler's dance. "I went over and told him to keep coming after us with the blitz," said Chandler. "I probably shouldn't have, but I was fired up."

By halftime, the game was a grotesque massacre, with Washington out front 42-7. By the 6:00 mark in the fourth quarter, and the Huskies leading 52-7, Don James took out his last remaining starters. BYU had 70 yards of total offense. Washington had registered 10 quarterback sacks for (-87) yards. In those closing minutes, BYU was able to take advantage of sloppy defensive play and score two touchdowns against Washington's back-ups. Amazingly, Don James would require his team to engage in extra conditioning the following week, because they had lost the fourth quarter. Nevertheless, as time ran out, the scoreboard at Husky Stadium read: HUSKIES 52, COUGARS 21.

Washington receiver Darryl Franklin was all smiles with multiple microphones hovering before his face. "Two years ago, they took our national championship away from us and last year they took away the respect the nation had for us by beating us so bad on television," he said. "Then they said they didn't respect us. I think they do now."

Don James was smiling and in a better mood compared to the previous year's game. "I didn't like the start and I didn't like the finish," he said. "But in between it was pretty good."

Chapter 27

A Visit with Chris Chandler

WHEN SOPHOMORE QUARTERBACK CHRIS Chandler took over for the struggling Hugh Millen late in the 1985 season, it was immediately clear that the position would be in good hands for the next two seasons. Heading into his senior campaign of 1987, Don James surprised some people by singling out Chandler with this comment: "I don't know who the best player in the country is heading into this season, but I've got to believe that Chris Chandler is somewhere in the top ten. To win the Heisman Trophy, the team has to have a great year and Chris has to have a great year individually. All of us — his teammates and coaches—believe he deserves the consideration and opportunity."

Derek Johnson: When I think of the name Chris Chandler, the first thought coming to mind is the 98-yard drive late in the fourth quarter to beat USC in 1985. Talk about dramatics, Don James benched the struggling Hugh Millen and gave you your first start as a sophomore. This was at Husky Stadium on a cloudy, overcast day. With 4:00 left in the game, USC was leading 17-13 and had the ball on the Husky 1-yard line. The handoff went to Trojan tailback Ryan Knight. Can you describe your perspective of everything that occurred from that point forward?

Chris Chandler: It wasn't looking good. The ball went to Knight and he dove in there. From where I was standing on the sideline, I didn't see the fumble. It looked like a big scrum at the goal line, and I was just waiting for the touchdown sign. The next thing I knew, my teammate Ron Hadley is holding the ball up and jumping up and down.

Now, that was exciting. However, getting the fumble was one thing, but driving 98 yards to score a touchdown was another. But you know, everybody was pretty calm in the huddle. It was really strange. There were a couple of fourth downs that we converted. Everybody up front did a great job blocking. David Trimble made a big catch. There were some big passes along the way. When we got down to the USC 13-yard line, we caught them in a goal line defense. I got us up to the ball pretty quick and signaled for Mo (Hill) to run a corner route. Mo had single coverage and had his guy beat pretty well, and it really wasn't that hard of a throw. Everything just fell into place on that drive. It was as exciting a football moment for me that I have ever had.

Johnson: I also recall from that drive that there was a fourth-down throw where the ball barely whizzed past the outstretched hands of two USC players and into Mo's hands. Just an inch or two off, and the pass would have been knocked away or picked off, and USC would have won.

Chandler: Yea, well, when I threw that one, I remember that Mo looked a lot more open than what he turned out to be. Fortunately, the ball had just enough tamale sauce on it to get to Mo.

Johnson: There's a picture I have going into this book of you and Mo Hill smiling and grabbing each other just moments after the touchdown to beat USC. You two guys always seemed to have a special rapport and connected on many big plays.

Chandler: Oh, yea. That's always going to be a big connection right there. And he was a huge reason why that game came out as exciting as it did for myself and the rest of the team.

Johnson: Do you remember any interactions with Coach James on that last drive?

Chandler: You know, I really don't. The reason for that is probably because of all the coaches I have ever played for, including the ones in the NFL, he is the one guy who never got ruffled. He never got too excited. He just stayed totally level and consistent. And that was a good thing. Especially being around a bunch of young college kids who are getting excited because they have a chance to beat USC, he was such a calming influence, just from his personality. I don't ever recall one time where he did anything different in a game than what he would do in practice or any other time. He was just amazingly consistent that way.

Johnson: I interviewed Dana Hall a few weeks ago. He told of the time in 1990 when the Huskies were really putting it to USC. Hall said he looked over at the sidelines and saw Coach James waving a towel—and Hall said it stunned him to witness that.

Chandler: Yea, well, if I had looked over and saw that too, I would have felt the same way! Perhaps as Coach James got a little older, he got a little more excitable. But I certainly never saw anything like that during my time at Washington. He was unusually consistent in everything he did.

Johnson: Another big game from your Husky career would have been the opener in 1986 at Husky Stadium. Washington crushed tenth-ranked Ohio State 40-7.

Chandler: I remember that Ohio State just blitzed a lot. It afforded us big plays. We did a great job picking up the blitzes and were able to score some points. I suppose that perhaps Ohio State thought I was a young guy and that they needed to bring the house, so to speak. But they exposed themselves, and we got the best of them.

Johnson: I remember that late in the second quarter, Washington was ahead 17-0 and the defense recovered a fumble on your own forty yard line. The story I heard was that Don James told you to run the clock out, but you pleaded with him to throw deep. Then you went out there and hit Mo Hill deep down the left sideline. What do you recall of that?

Chandler: Well, I don't ever recall trying to tell Coach James what to do. But I do remember thinking that a big play was possible right there.

Johnson: When I interviewed Napoleon Kaufman, he spoke of the privilege he felt during the recruiting process when Don James came to his house. Do you recall what that experience was like for you?

Chandler: Oh, definitely. Growing up in Everett, I remember seeing how he turned the Washington program around. I watched the 1978 Rose Bowl, and I watched Jacque Robinson going nuts against Iowa in the 1982 Rose Bowl. I saw all of that. I mean, in the Seattle area, who wasn't a Husky fan? By the time I was being recruited, the legend of Don James was huge. When he came to my house and walked through the front door, I definitely felt it to be a privilege—as much for my parents to meet him, because they thought so much of him. I was just proud that Don James was in my house.

Johnson: By the way, you were heavily recruited; before committing to Washington, were any other schools on your radar?

Chandler: Pretty much Washington and Stanford. You know, Stanford has a beautiful campus. And there was a lot of romanticism about going down there, because John Elway had just left for the NFL. But it really wasn't my place. It was easy to get sucked into what they were telling me, "Oh you're going to be the next John Elway." But in the end, I'm a Washington guy, you know? This was the place for me.

Johnson: Once when I interviewed Don James, we talked about you. He said that of all the quarterbacks he ever had, you were the best overall athlete. He also indicated that if he had a regret it was that he didn't surround you with some better talent. We talked about the 1986 Sun Bowl against Alabama and the 1987 loss to Texas A&M, when their superior team speed overwhelmed you guys. Don James realized that UW's team speed wasn't where it needed to be.

Chandler: (Sounding surprised) Well that's a heck of a comment for him to make. I appreciate the compliment. But I mean, I didn't notice a difference. Especially guys like Darryl Franklin and Mo, they were as good as I've ever seen. Especially coming from Everett, as I did. The guys I had around me at Washington I thought were the best in the world.

Johnson: Then there was that 29-22 loss to Oregon down in Eugene in 1987. You and the whole team struggled terribly. Husky fans were taunted by the Duck fans as they filed out of Autzen Stadium.

Chandler: It was a frustrating day. I think that Oregon is a better team now, maybe. But I remember when I was at Washington, no matter what the rivalry was, Oregon was just never very good. We always won. But on that day, nothing seemed to go right. We played poorly and the Ducks played exceptionally well. I had a lot to do with us not playing well. But I mean, they are Oregon, and they like to feel that they're better than they really are.

They played exceptionally well that day. It was very frustrating, especially to lose at their place. Oregon, Oregon State and Washington State, you always want to beat those teams. And to lose to them, is really unacceptable.

Johnson: By the end of the 1987 season, which was your senior season, Don James was privately feeling disillusioned and burned out. Mike Lude said that the week before the Apple Cup, he had a long talk with Coach James in front of the tunnel after practice. James was thinking about retiring after that next game, and calling it a career. From your perspective, especially as quarterback and a captain, were you privy to the fact that he was feeling that way?

Chandler: You know, in all honesty, I really wasn't. With his personality, I don't think he would ever let that kind of thing bleed over into the football aspect of things. Also, he always kept our plate pretty full in terms of things we needed to be ready for. Preparation for each game always took so much concentration and took so much out of us, that we really had no time to notice that he was feeling that way. He didn't seem any different at all. At least I didn't notice anything. But I am glad that he stuck around, because it got a lot better in the years after I left.

Johnson: Dave Hoffmann was telling me that Husky football practices were so structured and that there was always non-stop running, that when the defense made a big play in a scrimmage, they would all pig pile on each other, just to get a breather.

Chandler: Yes, there was a lot of running. At least for us during my time there, it was like an NFL- structured practice. All offense on one end of the field, all defense on the other end, and you wouldn't see those defensive guys until after practice… It was very organized and physically difficult to get through.

Johnson: I can't end this interview without asking you about the Super Bowl. While with the Atlanta Falcons in 1998, you were the first Husky quarterback to start a Super Bowl. What was that like?

Chandler: We had a great fourth-quarter drive to go into overtime and beat Minnesota to win the NFC Championship and get to the Super Bowl. For my wife and I, our third daughter was born ten days before the Super Bowl. So around that time, everything was surreal. I was on top of the world. There was a two-week wait for the game to start. The media buildup was monumental. You know, very few people ever get to experience something like that, and I am just grateful that I got that opportunity.

Chapter 28

A visit with Former UW Athletic Director Mike Lude

WHEN MIKE LUDE WAS the athletic director at Kent State University in 1971, he hired a defensive coordinator by the name of Don James to be KSU's head coach. James resigned four years later to take the Washington job. By 1976, with James entering his second season in Seattle, UW athletic Director Joe Kearney announced his retirement. James immediately began lobbying to bring Lude to Washington.

At the time Mike Lude assumed control of the UW athletic department in April 1976, it was running a $400,000 deficit. By the time Lude was forced into retirement in 1990, he had overseen the development of the Hec Ed Pavilion and Addition, the Lloyd Nordstrom Tennis Center, the band headquarters, the north upper deck of Husky Stadium, and the Assembly Room, located halfway up the Husky tunnel. The department was also $20 million in the black.

Derek Johnson: In the week prior to the 1987 Apple Cup vs. Washington State, you and Don James had an interesting conversation. Can you describe it?

Mike Lude: I believe it was during practice that week, and Don and I were standing over by the tunnel. He was quite concerned and stressed, and he told me that he was thinking about retiring after that next game against Washington State. We just weren't winning like we used to, we were 5-4-1 heading into that game. And Don felt like he had done everything he could to get the program back to an elite level. He said maybe it was time to just hang it up.

I told him, "Look, I'm not planning on leaving here until June of 1992, when my contract expires. I don't want to have to spend time at the end of my career having to interview candidates and hire a new coach. If you're thinking about retiring, let's first get this thing back up to where it needs to be, and then let's go out of here together. It can't end for you like this."

Then we played WSU that Saturday, and beat them soundly. Afterward I talked to Don and I asked, (with a joyous voice) "So did that take care of the problem?" He said, "Yes Mike, it did."

Johnson: The 1987 season opened against Stanford, featuring the beautiful new north upper deck of Husky Stadium. Please describe the story behind that.

Lude: After I arrived at the University of Washington on April 1, 1976, every day I would leave our new home in Bellevue and drive across the 520 Bridge. I would look at Husky Stadium and think to myself that it looked like a one-winged seagull. Not only would it esthetically look better with another upper deck, but it would increase our attendance and help out the overall athletic program. Well, in that 1976 season, which was my first year and Don's second, we didn't have a very good season. I didn't say anything to anyone about the stadium idea. I didn't during the 1977 season either. But as luck would have it, we were able to go to the Rose Bowl and defeat Michigan. After that, I was sure that we could do an upgrade. Our season ticket sales became more pronounced. There was a lot of enthusiasm for Husky football. I started to proceed on the project.

In 1979, Dr. William Gerberding arrived as the new President at the University of Washington. He said that I should do a feasibility study, which I did, and showed that it was feasible. We immediately went to work on it. All along, I was consulting with John Skilling (of Skilling Construction) and we put it together.

Construction began early in 1987. We had a little problem halfway through when it collapsed. We got one section up and the workers disengaged the cables that were anchoring it. They had big heavy steel spikes grounded into the old practice field. The structure began to twist and then collapsed. It was a big deal in the media. But the General Contractor told me, "Mike, I can bring this in on time if you keep everyone (bureaucratic red tape) away from me." Well, I did keep them away from him, and he brought it in on time.

We were working right up to the morning of the game getting it ready. All of our staff and construction people were putting the decals on thousands of seats so that the fans could find where to sit. We had the dedication ceremony before the game, which went great. We released about a billion purple and gold balloons into the air. We beat Stanford 31-21. It was a happy affair!

Johnson: It should be noted that you had hoped for luxury suites, too.

Lude: I had wanted to put in luxury suites at Husky Stadium, but President Gerberding thought it seemed elitist. Our feasibility study also showed that there wasn't a lot of interest in those. After some negotiation, I got him to concede for a large meeting room that would overlook the field. That became the Tyee Center, which later was appropriately renamed the Don James Center. We set a price of $50,000 for the rights for someone to buy two tickets for ten years. Within two weeks, we sold it out, over five hundred seats.

Johnson: Did you watch the games from the Tyee Center?

Lude: No, my wife Rena and I would go up there before the game. But I always stood at the very top above the press row, in the press box. First I would greet the reporters, visiting dignitaries and the opposing athletic director. Right before kickoff, I would go into the radio booth and give Bob Rondeau a high five and a hug. Then there was a stairway that led to where the statistics group sat, and right in front of that door was a platform. I would stand there and watch the game by myself. At the start of the fourth quarter, I would go down to the field. I would usually stand in the east end zone in front of the temporary bleachers. Then with about five minutes left in the game, I would go over to the sideline and stand next to Don James.

Johnson: In your book *Walking the Line*, you described multiple situations where you and Gerberding locked horns. You wrote that Gerberding fought hard to terminate popular basketball coach Marv Harshman and attempted to keep Washington from accepting an invitation to the 1986 Sun Bowl against Alabama. You said that you were consistently embarrassed and confused by the treatment you received from Gerberding. Was part of the impetus to write your book stemming from the public not knowing the truth behind what occurred between you and Gerberding?

Lude: No, that never bothered me. I want to emphasize that for the first twelve years of my time at the University of Washington, President Gerberding and I had a good and effective working relationship. It wasn't until about the last two and a half years that things changed. I didn't know what was happening at first. But things were suddenly much more difficult than they had been before. I suddenly had to justify everything. I'd have to prepare an agenda of everything that was going on, and it became more and more difficult to get things done. One day I finally said to myself, "Judas Priest it's hard to get things done around here!"

Johnson: In your book, you wrote: *"The Bill Gerberding I got to know was far different from the picture of composure and control he projected in public. I remember too vividly the Gerberding who fumed and criticized and who could be hostile to the point of insulting in the presence of someone with whom he disagreed."*

Ultimately Gerberding forced you into retirement a year earlier than had been previously agreed to. He also took stances that seemed intent on harming the football program. Why was he antagonistic and what went wrong with your agreement?

Lude: I don't know. Some people at the university suggested to me, "We don't know what happened. It seems that Gerberding and upper campus are jealous of the success that you and Don James have had." Now, I don't know that for sure, but that was what was told to me.

Johnson: You received a terse memo stating that your time was through, and it was the culmination of two years of frustration. Former Husky tailback Beno Bryant told me of seeing you enter the locker room to say farewell to the players. He said, "Guys were crying, coming up to Mr. Lude and saying good-bye and giving him a hug. It was tough to see him pushed out like that."

Lude: Well, the feeling was mutual. I cared a great deal for Beno and for all of our players.

Johnson: Being pushed out early cost you a chance to be part of the 1991 Washington football team that went 12-0 and won the National Championship. But as bittersweet as that must have been to watch from afar, you ended being a part of it after all.

Lude: Don and I had worked fifteen years to get to that point of winning the national championship, and to not have my name on the trophy, along with all the other fine people who contributed to that success, was a sad thing for me. I had moved on to become the Executive Vice President of the Blockbuster Bowl. It was January 2, 1992, and it was the day after the Huskies had just won the Rose Bowl. I arrived at my office in Florida at six o'clock in the morning.

At about nine o'clock, suddenly the phone rings. I pick up the receiver and it was Don James. He doesn't say hello, he doesn't identify himself. He just says "Mike, what size ring do you wear? Carol and I just got the message— we're number one!"

I was really appreciative of Don for including me in that.

Linebacker Chico Fraley signs autographs for youngsters.

Linebacker Andy Mason fires his six-shooters to the sky,
in celebration of a sack against Nebraska in 1992.

Quarterback Cary Conklin lets a pass fly in 1989.

All Pac-10 defensive lineman Dennis Brown

Soft-spoken cornerback William Doctor in action in 1991.

Beno Bryant breaks a punt return during 48-0 win over Toledo in 1991.

Center Ed Cunningham protects quarterback Mark Brunell during Washington's 31-0 win over USC in 1990.

All- Pac-10 tailback, Greg Lewis.

Linebacker Donald Jones became a force that some compared to Junior Seau.

Fearless safety Shane Pahukoa in action during Washington's 56-21 win against WSU in 1991 Apple Cup.

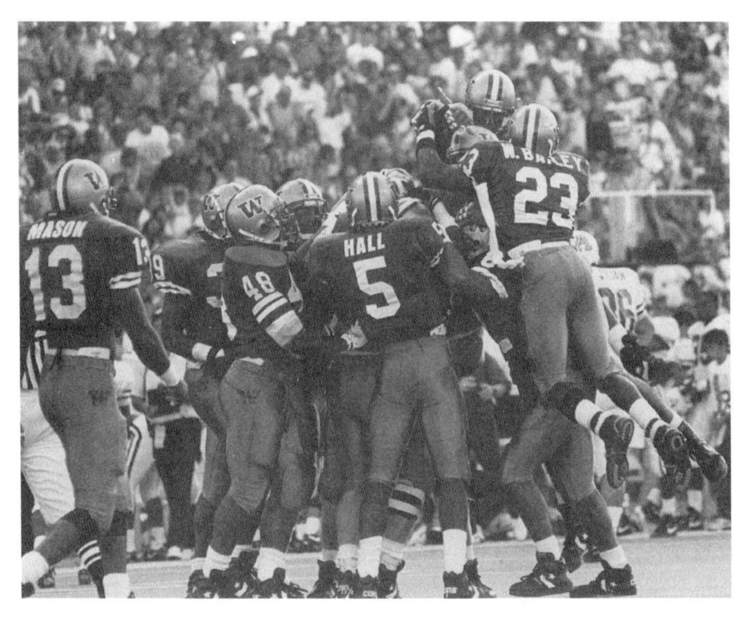

The Husky defense celebrates a big play during 1991 season.

Linebackers Dave Hoffmann and the late Jaime Fields

Steve Emtman poses in front of the Rose Bowl

Don James and his captains celebrate their 46-34 win over Iowa in 1991 Rose Bowl.

Safety Tommie Smith was considered by teammates
as the best athlete on the team.

Record-breaking wide receiver Mario Bailey hauls
in one of his seventeen touchdown catches in 1991.

All Pac-10 tight end Aaron Pierce looks for running room in 1991.

Don James poses with the National Championship Trophy

Don James and wide receiver Mario Bailey

James Clifford, Jim Lambright and Dave Hoffmann

Don James exits the field following Washington's 56-3
win over Kansas State in 1991.

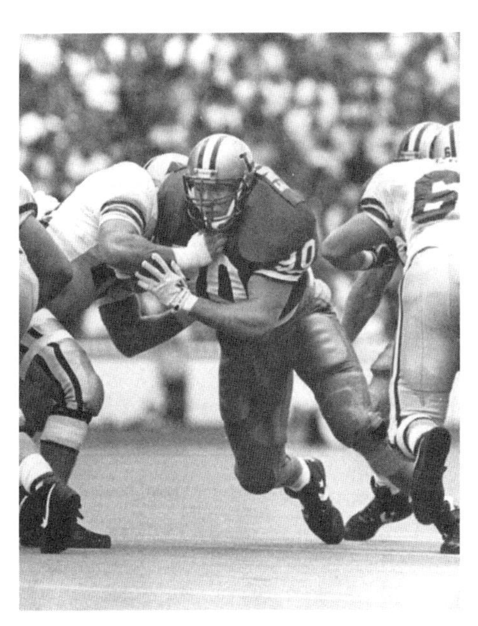

Outland Trophy and Lombardi Award winner Steve Emtman

Outland Trophy and Lombardi Award winner
Steve Emtman signs autographs for fans.

Quarterback Billy Joe Hobert breaks free for a gain during UW's 41-7 win over Stanford in 1992. It proved to be Hobert's last game as a Husky.

All-American tackle Lincoln Kennedy and All Pac-10 quarterback Mark Brunell talk during the 1993 Rose Bowl.

All-American tight end Mark Bruener goes out for a pass route.

Former University of Washington President, Dr. William Gerberding, "If I could rewrite American history, I would not attach to our colleges and universities the task of providing mass entertainment for the American Public." (Photo: University of Washington)

With Don James watching from the coach's box above, Jim Lambright looks on as the final seconds tick off the clock in UW's 31-14 win over Stanford in 1993.

Keith Gilbertson was the architect behind Washington's high-powered offense in 1991 when they won the national championship. Thirteen years later as UW's head coach, he oversaw the worst season in Husky football history.

Tyee Open Golf Tourney, late 1990s. Dave Torrell, Chuck Ainslie, Don James and Ron Johnson.

Warren Moon and Don James - 20 years after the '78 Rose Bowl.

Derek Johnson and his Dad, Ron Johnson.

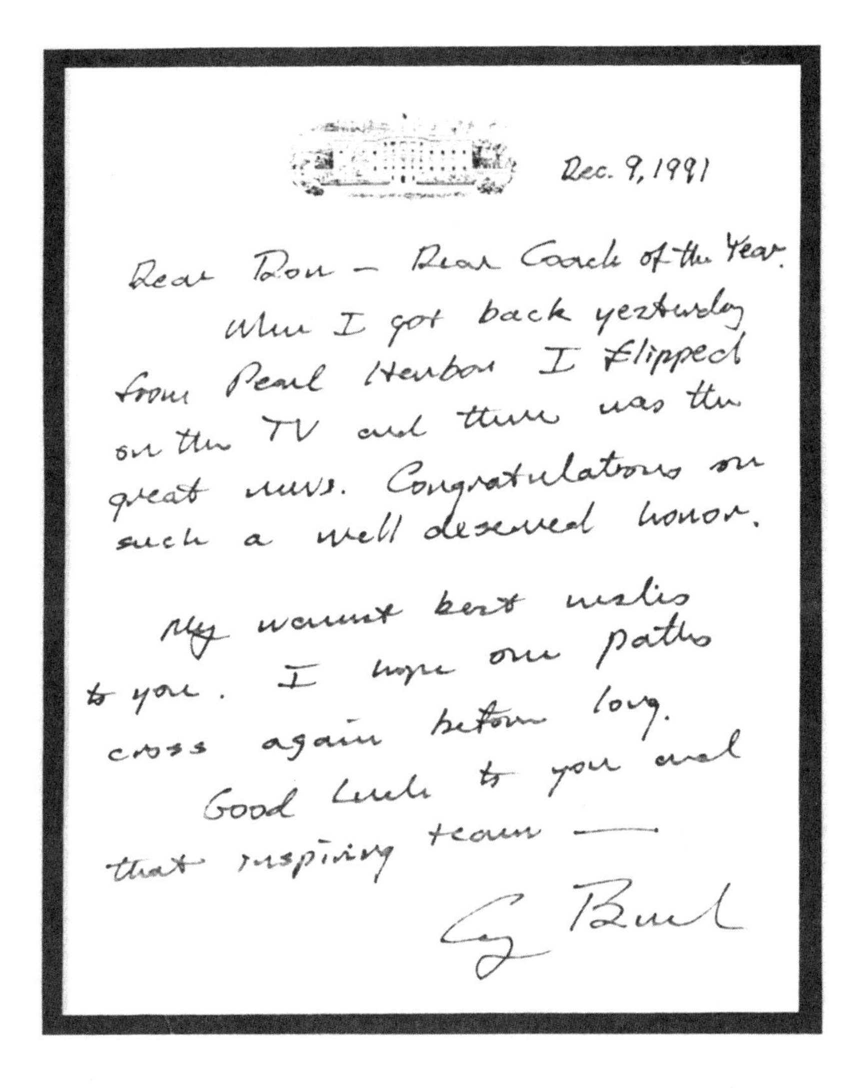

Dec. 9, 1991

Dear Don — Dear Coach of the Year.

When I got back yesterday from Pearl Harbor I flipped on the TV and there was the great news. Congratulations on such a well deserved honor.

My warmest best wishes to you. I hope our paths cross again before long.

Good luck to you and that inspiring team —

G Bush

A hand-written note from President George H. W. Bush to Don James, as the undefeated Huskies prepared to face Michigan in the 1992 Rose Bowl. President Bush had just returned from Hawaii commemorating the 50th anniversary of the Japanese bombing of Pearl Harbor.

Chapter 29 — November 19, 1988

The Darkness Before the Dawn

Washington at Washington State

IT WAS IN THE final minutes of the fourth quarter, and Don James stood on the sidelines as his punt team ran onto the field. The Huskies were clinging to a 28-25 lead. It was snowing in the Palouse darkness. James's fingertips, face and feet were bitterly cold. His counterpart — WSU Coach Dennis Erickson— was across the way, extolling his Cougars to make a big play. Husky Punter Eric Canton took a good snap and stepped forward with what he thought would be a great kick. Cougar defender Shawn Landrum had other plans. Landrum shot in from the left side and took the football right off of Canton's foot. It ricocheted backwards along the frozen turf and randomly undulated, before Cougar Jay Languein recovered it at the Husky 13-yard line. Four plays later, it was fourth down and two from the five. The snow continued to fall. The home crowd screamed for blood. Quarterback Tim Rosenbach took the snap and dropped straight back, before tucking the football and running a draw straight into the end zone. The subsequent extra point gave Washington State the 32-31 victory.

The Cougar players immediately scooped up Dennis Erickson and carried him off the field. He wriggled free in order to find Don James and shake his hand, before embracing Rosenbach with a wild hug as photographers and fans clustered around both of them. This win gave Washington State an 8-3 record and a berth in the Aloha Bowl against Houston. Almost as delightful to Cougar fans, the Huskies slipped to 6-5 and would be staying home for the holidays for the first time in ten years.

Back in Seattle, watching on their dormitory TVs, were redshirt freshmen Dave Hoffmann, Lincoln Kennedy, Mark Brunell, Darius Turner, Steve Emtman and others. They grew indignant and vowed revenge, as TV cameras captured scenes of Cougar players frolicking about and taunting the Huskies.

The celebration at Martin Stadium quickly turned violent, as drunken fans ignored pleas from the stadium announcer and stormed the field, overwhelming the security forces. The field became a mass of swarming humanity. Ambulances attempted to wedge their way through the crowd, to reach a handful of injured spectators near one of the goal posts.

The Washington Huskies got to their locker room, showered quickly then left town. The flight back to Seattle was one of the most despondent and quiet trips that assistant coaches could recall. Within the next few days, a couple of newspaper columns came out claiming that Don James' best days were behind him. Opposing schools throughout the Pac-10 were suddenly telling recruits that Don James was on his way out. Some UW underclassmen, like offensive lineman Ed Cunningham, felt disillusioned and strongly considered transferring. It was a month later on Christmas Day, however, that the final ignominious insult took place.

In the glorious Hawaiian sunshine, Dennis Erickson and his Washington State Cougars were on their way to a convincing Aloha Bowl victory over the Houston Cougars. It was late in the fourth quarter, after a final big play had just sealed the triumph, that a TV camera panned the ecstatic Cougar bench. It zoomed in on one player in particular. As millions of Americans looked on, he turned toward the camera, and with a bright smile and a wave, shouted, "MERRY CHRISTMAS HUSKIES!" before motioning his hand dismissively in the air and cockily reclining in satisfaction.

"I think we all remember the meeting on December 28, 1988," recalled Don James years later. "That's where we committed to doing whatever it took to get better. We were all tired of mediocrity. I know coaching a 6-5 team wasn't much fun for me."

Chapter 30 — September 9, 1989

"I Sense a Chemistry Developing"

Husky Stadium — Washington vs. Texas A&M

IT WAS ON DECEMBER 29, 1988, that Idaho Head Coach Keith Gilbertson was in his office when the phone rang. It was Don James, and the Husky coach didn't even say hello. "All he said was, 'I want you to take the chalk'" reflected Gilbertson years later.

Gilbertson arrived at Washington soon after as the offensive line coach—but also to help revamp the offense. He had been a disciple of Dennis Erickson's revolutionary one-back spread offense. Together, they refined it to where Wyoming, Idaho and finally Washington State achieved startling success in moving the football against superior opponents. It was designed to spread defenses by using as much of the field as possible—both horizontally and vertically. Said Gilbertson, "To make it work, you better have a guy pulling the trigger who can throw," he said. "Receivers have to have the ability to run after they catch the ball. They don't have to be 6-foot-5 with 4.5 speed, there's not a lot of those guys around. What there are a lot more of are compact, shorter kids who can really catch and run. This is for them."

"We just weren't going to make it with the old offense," recalled 5'8" wide receiver Mario Bailey. "No way was it going to work. But once Coach Gilbertson arrived, everything changed."

Gilbertson's personality also helped to mold the Husky offensive line into a cohesive unit. "Gilby really made you feel comfortable playing your game," recalled All-American Lincoln Kennedy. "He could be a hard-ass like any good coach, but he also builds you up. Personality-wise, our offensive line was all across the shelf. But one chubby little Italian comes up and firmly shakes your hand and says 'Hey, how ya doin'?' And you felt that love. We were ready to be accountable to one another."

"Gilbertson's probably the best coach I've ever played for," offensive lineman Adam Cooney said at the time. "It's a whole new feeling with him. There are a lot more emotional ties. We're more of a group within the team. We're not a bunch of individuals- there are not guards and tackles. We're one entity."

A rematch at home against Texas A&M served as the season opener for 1989. The Aggies, led by first-year Coach R.C. Slocum, didn't feel sufficiently at ease in merely scouting Washington's games from the year before. Slocum and his assistants also conducted a background check on Gilbertson. "We've scouted around a little on Coach Gilbertson to see what he's done in the past," said Slocum. "I think he's one of the top coaches around. I've got tremendous respect for him."

In Washington's third offensive series of the game, a nine-play drive in the first quarter, there was mischievousness in Gilbertson's play-calling. The Huskies lined up seven times in the supposedly antiquated I-formation, once in the wishbone, and just once in the new one-back set. On the drive's final play, sophomore Husky wide receiver Mario Bailey was going one-on-one with Aggie cornerback Mickey Washington; Bailey made a cut to separate from the defender before leaping high to haul in Cary Conklin's spiral, before dragging one foot in the end zone. 69,434 fans were ecstatic in the September sunshine, as Washington took a 7-0 lead.

In the second quarter, Texas A&M's Kevin Ellis thundered a 50-yard punt downfield that was downed at the Husky 16-yard line. But a penalty on Texas A&M nullified the kick, so the play had to be run again. This time, the snap back to Ellis was errant. In desperation, he scrambled and tried to throw downfield. The ball fell incomplete, and Washington took over at the Aggie 30-yard line. The end result was a John McCallum field goal, extending UW's lead to 13-3 heading into halftime.

In the second half, the main story was the domination of defensive lineman Dennis Brown and the rest of the Husky defense upon Texas A&M running back Darren Lewis. The Heisman candidate was limited to a mere 52 yards on 15 carries. Meanwhile, Washington's Greg Lewis racked up 133 yards on the ground. Husky QB Cary Conklin was solid, completing 23 of 37 passes for 224 yards and 1 touchdown. Senior receiver Andre Riley made a sensational third quarter catch going down the sideline, reaching behind the defender to make the one-handed snare. In the words of *The Seattle Times'* Blaine Newnham, "The Huskies blocked, ran, caught, threw and tackled better than they have in a long while... By almost any evaluation, it was the most impressive and important win by the University of Washington since the Huskies thrashed Ohio State 40-7 to open the 1986 season."

"Last year I know I felt a step behind," said offensive lineman Ed Cunningham in the game's aftermath. "Today I felt a step ahead. Only once did I find myself thinking about what I was supposed to be doing. As Coach James said, 'if somebody gets in your way, nail them.'"

"We knew that they'd throw the ball more than they have in the past," said A&M's Slocum. "But we didn't think it would be like this. They kept us off balance with short passes and did a good job of running the ball."

Oddly enough, Husky Defensive Coordinator Jim Lambright was gushing about the new offense. "I love it," he said. "We had time to get our guys together on the sidelines, to get them rested, to make adjustments. We haven't always had that kind of time." Then Lambright paused, before adding: "I sense a chemistry developing, an intermixing of offense and defense."

Chapter 31 — September 30, 1989

Death of a Quarterback

Husky Stadium — Washington vs. Colorado

IN MARCH 1989, IT was widely-publicized that Colorado quarterback Sal Aunese was suffering from inoperable stomach cancer. For the next six months, he would receive thousands of cards and letters of support from across the nation. Come September, he even received a get-well card from President George H.W. Bush and an encouraging phone call from former United States President Ronald Reagan. Aunese was a charismatic and cheerful personality, and deeply loved by many teammates and friends. He attracted people with his friendly smile. Despite his deteriorating condition, Aunese had attended fifth-ranked Colorado's first three games of the '89 season. He sat up in the booth, watching the Buffalos destroy each opponent. However, his internal organs seared increasingly with pain, and he began struggling to breathe. Finally, knowing his body was capable of only a few more hours of life, Aunese dictated to his sister a letter for his teammates.

Meanwhile, as Colorado prepared to play against Washington, Coach Bill McCartney gathered his team into a group before practice. Ashen-faced, he told his players that Aunese would probably be dead within twenty-four hours. The Buffalo players fell silent until several started sobbing.

Hours later, a hush descended upon the Colorado campus. Sal Aunese was dead. The next day, news of the tragedy was splashed across the front pages of newspapers nation-wide. A moment of silence was held in his honor at the Denver Bronco-Oakland Raider game. And as 2,000 mourners filled an auditorium on the Boulder campus, a choked-up McCartney addressed the crowd. He spoke to the courage and humility that Aunese had demonstrated. And he publicly acknowledged for the first time that Aunese's six-month old child had been by his own daughter. Then McCartney pulled from his pocket the letter Aunese had dictated on his deathbed. It read:

> *Dear Brothers and the family whom I hold so close,*
>
> *I come with love and encouragement for you to continue what you've been doing when the season first started, to excel and better yourself mentally, physically and spiritually.*
>
> *Unity is strength and love is our guide from here on in. Don't be saddened that you no longer have me in the flesh because I assure you I'll always be with you in spirit.*
>
> *Hold me close to your hearts as you know I do you.*
>
> *Strive only for victory each time you play and trust in the Lord for He truly is the way. I love you all. Go get 'em and bring home the Orange Bowl.*
>
> *Love, Sal.*

Later in the week, as Colorado boarded a plane destined for Seattle, McCartney noticed a fierce determination in the eyes of his players. That Saturday, as they headed down the tunnel in Husky Stadium, each Colorado player carried a copy of Aunese's letter. Wearing black pants, white jerseys and gold helmets, the Buffalos poured out of the tunnel, assembled at mid-field to take a knee, and pointed to the gloomy skies above. A gasp rippled through the Husky Stadium crowd, as fans took stock of Colorado's take-no-prisoners demeanor.

Then stunned cheers emanated from the crowd as Washington emerged to take the field. The Huskies were dressed entirely in purple, both jerseys and *pants*. The seniors had made this decision. Don James signed off on it, but wasn't overly enthusiastic, having just told them in the locker room: "It's not the color of the pants that will make the difference- it's the guys wearing them."

If this game was likened to a heavyweight boxing match, Colorado came out swinging at Washington with a merciless and mechanized fury of combinations from their rushing attack. Despite the recent influx of talent, Washington's inexperienced defensive players were on their heels throughout the onslaught. Colorado averaged nearly eight yards per play. Buffalo QB Darian Hagan (Aunese's replacement) orchestrated the option attack to perfection. Be it handing off to burly fullback George Hemmingway, or keeping around end and using his own deceptive moves, or pitching to the trailing Eric Bieniemy and J.J. Flannigan for big chunks of real estate, Colorado ran all over Washington.

Colorado offensive tackle Mark Vander Poel entered the game afraid that Washington's defensive tackle Dennis Brown would tear his head off. Early in the first quarter, however, Vander Poel was telling his teammates in the huddle, "Brown is very quick, but just an average player. I've got him under control."

By the end of the third quarter, Colorado led 38-6. Husky fans were streaming to the exits by the thousands. By the end of the game, Colorado won 45-28—and it wasn't that close. The Buffalos rushed for 420 yards on the ground and scored 45 points. It was the most rushing yards ever against a Don James team. It was the most points ever scored against a Don James team in Husky Stadium.

"This exceeded anything I'd hoped for," said Colorado Coach Bill McCartney after the game. "This speaks a lot about the intensity and resolve of our players." Said Colorado QB Darian Hagan: "The polls and Sal are keeping this team together. We dedicated this season to Sal and this victory gives us a chance to move up in the polls."

In the next day's *Seattle Times,* columnist Blaine Newnham fretted: "Don James still believes his defenders have improved their speed and strength through a rigorous off-season program and better recruiting. He couldn't explain what is missing, other than execution and discipline. What is missing is leadership. A player to rally around. A chemistry that made the 1984 group a noxious mixture... The collapse of the defense leaves the Huskies vulnerable and hapless for the rest of the season."

Newnham also quoted Washington defensive coordinator Jim Lambright. "You can't play on your heels," said Lambright. "We don't seem to be mature enough to handle pressure. We're worried more about what just happened to us, than what is happening. We ended up setting and catching, instead of attacking."

(Note: Colorado would go on to finish the regular season 11-0 before losing in the Orange Bowl to national champion Notre Dame).

Chapter 32

A visit with Dave "Hammer" Hoffmann

DAVE HOFFMANN PLAYED LINEBACKER for the Huskies from 1988-1992. In his senior season, he was an All-American, a finalist for the Butkus Award (Presented to the nation's top linebacker), and named the Pac-10 Defensive Player of the Year. His Husky teammates bestowed him with the nicknames of "Hitman" and "The Hammer," due to his ferocious hitting and intensity on the field.

Derek Johnson: It was in November of 1989, and you guys had just lost at home to Arizona State 34-32 to fall to a record of 5-4. The defense was terrible in giving up about 500 yards. The following week, prior to playing Oregon State in Corvallis, Don James and Jim Lambright decided to scrap the read-and-react defense and begin attacking.

With the first quarter underway, you guys were still playing the old defense. But as the Beavers drove a second time inside the Husky 20-yard line, Lambright finally put Donald Jones into the game at outside linebacker. As Oregon State quarterback Matt Booher approached the line of scrimmage, there were suddenly eight Huskies crowding the line of scrimmage. Booher took the snap and dropped back to pass. Jones flew around the corner at astonishing speed and engulfed Booher for a sack. On second down, Beaver left tackle Brad D'Ancona lurched offsides for a five-yard penalty. On third down, Donald Jones came around the corner so fast that Booher stepped up into the pocket to avoid him, but only to be demolished by Dennis Brown infiltrating the middle. Booher fumbled the football as he collapsed in a heap and you guys recovered. Washington led 37-6 at halftime and 51-14 when the game was over.

Husky football suddenly transitioned into a new era, and you guys went on to win 33 of the next 35 games, into November of 1992. Can you describe the changes that took place heading into that 1989 Oregon State game?

Dave Hoffmann: It was initially a slight scheme and personnel change. Personally, it allowed me to play downhill the way I like to. From that point forward, my first step was never lateral on a run play, but rather toward the line of scrimmage— straight ahead or at a hard angle. On any zone coverage I read the linemen and got a fast and true read. Lambo taught us how to read three linemen at once, and to see the whole offensive line as an animal and how it would have to move to try to run the ball to certain places. With his teaching we could make these reads in a fraction of a second and then it was time for high-speed destruction.

Although we changed our scheme before this game, the success we had was due to having players that loved to dominate with a great leader at Defensive Coordinator—Jim Lambright. It was as though we had been blessed to play more reckless and up-field. Coach James and Coach Lambright realized we had the people to do it and the defensive backs to cover us. We started attacking.

Johnson: Lincoln Kennedy told me about a team meeting that you and Steve Emtman led amongst the underclassmen down at the Connibear Shellhouse the week of the 1990 USC game. It was the Centennial game celebrating 100 years of Husky football. All sorts of legends like Hugh McElhenny and Don Heinrich and Sonny Sixkiller and many others were coming to town. You guys went on to crush the Trojans 31-0. It was the most excited I have ever seen a Husky Stadium crowd. What do you recall of that informal players-only meeting?

Dave Hoffmann: It was a momentous time for the program. I don't want to say it was do or die, but USC had long been King of the castle, and if we were as good as we thought we were, it was time to do it. The intensity and focus for that game was coming to a head, and I said some things, not in a rah-rah sense, but very matter-of-fact. To let guys know, that this is serious.

We typically had the forty-eight hour rule, which was installed by Don James. Forty-eight hours before game time, there was to be no laughing or joking around. Discussions should only be about the game, aside from schoolwork, of course. No messing around with TV and that sort of stuff. That was something we were used to. We were all on the same page and we knew the importance of doing that. If you remember, there were no headphones on our road trips. Guys weren't listening to music, and in their own world doing their thing. It was all business. It was for getting ready for violent activity and executing our game plan.

But what was unique about that week against USC, was that Don James said, "Guys, I know that I normally ask you to do the 48-hour rule before each game. But for this week, we're going to do it for the whole freakin' week." That's a lot of time and a lot of focus and intensity, but we all felt it was worth it. So for that week, guys weren't sitting around in the crew house watching the Late Show and joking around. It was all focus. Not that guys didn't play an occasional game of cards, but it was real minimal. The attitude that week was all business. So when it came down to Friday night, there wasn't a whole lot left to be said. Lincoln could probably tell you closer to verbatim what I said. I just remember that all of us were ready to go.

You know, the first time I met Lincoln and Mark Brunell too, was at the California High School North-South Shrine Game. We were in a classroom, and they announced the names of everybody playing in the game. I was sitting on one side of the room for the North, and Lincoln and Mark were on the other side for the South. They announced, "Lincoln Kennedy and Mark Brunell—Washington." I looked over and we all gave each other a wink and a nod. We knew we would be hooking up soon enough.

Johnson: Well, at 6'7" and 350 pounds, Lincoln's not hard to spot. You've also told me stories in the past of the conditioning that you would go through.

Hoffmann: Oh, yea. The dark days and nights of winter, and summer afternoons by yourself, trying to get stronger, faster, better. I can remember going out onto a dirt road in my hometown of San Jose, and pushing my little Chevy Blazer around until I threw up. My brother Steve used to come do that with me. You know, what that does for your body is one thing, but what it does for your mind is even greater.

Johnson: Go into that a little more.

Hoffmann: We used to put the truck in neutral. You want to talk about full-body intensity and effort, I just felt if I pushed it along a 60-yard dirt track next to my school, it would be just perfect. Getting it started and pushing, digging and digging, it took everything you had. It was tough to do each rep. But once you got it going, you would just keep down with your body on a nice angle, and I found that it was the exact angle that I was at when striking somebody on the football field. From the tips of my toes, to my shoulders, I was going full tilt. When I would get down toward the end, my brother would count out, "Five, Four, Three..." And it was always good to hear that, because it meant you were near the end. Then we would switch, and my brother would do the same thing. At the end of it, we would throw up our guts all over the place, and then slap each other on the back and get out of there.

It's kind of like something you said to me in a previous conversation, about whether fans really appreciate all that goes into being a great football team. They saw the glory of it on Saturdays when we were jumping up and down all over each other after a big play, but do they know all the hard work and sacrifice of it? Are they aware of just how much blood and sweat that we left on the turf of Husky Stadium during the week? We loved the fans— they were a part of everything we did. But I also wondered sometimes, do they have a clue?

Johnson: I once interviewed your former teammate Dennis Brown. We were talking about the riot that took place at Husky Stadium following the 1989 Apple Cup win over Washington State. Cops used mace canisters and some of the fans were acting like animals. Dennis said that the rest of the team was having a post-game meeting but he left it and wandered back to the mouth of the tunnel by himself. He was a senior having just played his last home game. He had become an All Pac-10 defensive tackle but felt turmoil and resentment about his time at Washington. He felt ambivalence toward Don James and assistant coach Randy Hart over some issues, including their continual harping on his weight.

Dennis was standing there at the mouth of the tunnel, looking at several dozen fans rioting on the field and swinging from the goal posts like animals and getting maced. Dennis thought to himself, "Do those kids have any idea of the blood, sweat and tears that I shed on that field for the past four years? And they're running around like that!"

Hoffmann: Right, yea. Man, that's a good story. Dennis hit it on the head. Run around on the field in a drunken state just as an excuse to raid the field.

Johnson: Not to be melodramatic and draw a direct comparison, but it is kind of like church out there.

Hoffmann: Exactly. In fact, I don't want to say it was hallowed ground, but it was close to it. We had poured so much of ourselves into that place. Whenever we crossed those lines and stepped onto the field, we were always running. It was standard preparation, but it was also a type of reverence. It's that respect thing. Nobody was ever walking. In practice, after each play, you ran back to the huddle. Then you broke and ran to the ball, then after the play you ran back to the huddle. When we were done with a series of plays and it was time for the twos to take the field, we would run all the way off the field. We would run all the way across the line. That was the type of mentality that we had.

Johnson: Lincoln Kennedy told me that during the 1992 victory over Nebraska at Husky Stadium, it was the only time in his entire career that he was laughing on the field because he was having so much fun.

Hoffmann: I've been there before, when I've been laughing on the field. When you have already poured your heart out, and poured so much physical and mental energy into the game, and the whole environment of Husky Stadium. I can see how on that day he would have laughed. We always felt like we had that game. I can remember at the beginning of the game, just unloading on their center—just to let Nebraska know, "Here we are again. Just as hard as ever."

Lambo was sending quite a few blitzes off the strong side, sending the safety—either Paxton Telele or Tommie Smith. Nebraska had a hard time with that. The rest of us knew we could stop the option. Instead of sitting back and playing it soft to defend it like other teams would, we would attack it. We would make the call in the huddle, and either the outside weakside backer or the strong safety would automatically go after either the quarterback or the pitch guy and take them out of the equation. Whether he had the ball or not he was going to pay.

We had so much trust in each other, we knew that whoever had that assignment, the job would be taken care of, and the rest of us could worry about the dive, or whatever other responsibilities we had. I don't know if Nebraska had seen that before, but we had a fun time doing it. That was our style, we attacked. That is what made us good.

Johnson: What was your favorite part of Husky Stadium?

Hoffmann: One place I loved was in our old locker room. It was our row that they called "Blue Collar Row." There were a lot of guys there, and I'll spit out some names but I don't want to leave anybody out. It was myself, Emtman, Clifford, my brother Steve in later years, Mark Bruener, Ernie Conwell, Steve Springstead, Aaron Pierce, Pete Kaligis, Jim Nevelle, Danianke Smith, and just a bunch of blue collar guys, a whole cast of characters. They were all my brothers. One day after practice we were all getting undressed and joking around, and the Running Backs Coach came walking past. He just stood looking at us for a moment and then he said, "This here is Blue Collar Row!" And that's how the name stuck. Of course, it no longer exists, because they later gutted that whole place when they renovated.

Another place in Husky Stadium I loved was the corner of the end zone where you come out by the tunnel. That's where we linebackers during the week and before the games would smack each other with our butt drills. We would be down there with Lambright, and I loved that corner. It was our own little corner of the world. Later when they replaced the Astroturf, I wondered about all the great Husky linebackers through the years that had done countless drills in that corner, and how much linebacker blood and sweat was stuck into that turf.

Johnson: Your close friend Jaime Fields was a great linebacker playing alongside you. He died in 1999 as a victim in a hit-and-run car accident. In honor of Jaime Fields, describe one of your favorite moments playing with him.

Hoffmann: My pleasure. We were playing down in Los Angeles against USC in 1991. Jaime and I had been unloading on their fullbacks, linemen and tight ends, and I remember just looking over at him. When you play that long together with someone, you almost don't have to speak at times, you could just look at each other and know what the other guy was thinking.

Late in the game, USC tried a running play on third down and short. Jaime and I just engulfed it, hammered the fullback and blasted the ball carrier. We were high-fiving and jumping up and down like we always did, and running off the field. We sat down on the bench together, talking about that play we had just made. It was just like what Lincoln said to you about laughing on the field. Well, Jaime and I couldn't stop laughing. It was just the joy and excitement. The score was only 14-3, so it wasn't like we were blowing them out of the water.

But we knew that USC couldn't move the ball on us. We were just having fun and enjoying life together. I mean, that was living! There was nothing more enjoyable than to be out there together playing the game of football and doing well. Jaime was from LA, so it was extra special for him to have his family and friends in attendance. We were just in the moment together.

So Jaime and I are over there laughing like a couple of kids, and Coach Randy Hart, whom I have a good relationship with, comes over to us with his headset on. He screams, "Hoffmann! Fields! Get those smiles off your faces! Can you see that scoreboard? There's still two minutes left! This thing isn't over!" Well, Jaime and I started laughing even harder with everything we had. Coach Hart gave me a look, and then slapped me in the face. Jaime and I stopped and looked at each other for a quick second— then we started laughing even harder! And I reached up and slapped Coach Hart, and knocked his headset off!

I can remember Coach Hart just shaking his head and walking away. He knew that we had our heads in the game, and that the defense had control of things. But he was just doing what a good coach does, and playing the part. He sees a couple of his guys acting crazy on the sideline and he came over just to keep them in line.

Johnson: Knowing you have conspired with your opponent to engage in a battle, giving it everything you've got, and to savor the emotional high of a job well done.

Hoffmann: Exactly! Physically you're drained, but there was something special about that feeling. I always liked being tired, hot, sweaty, with blood usually coming off the forehead and spilling into the eyes. There was a good feeling about being half out of breath, like I had been in a fight. I can remember toward the end of that 1992 Arizona game down in Tucson. What a freaking war. I hit my ass off that day. I always loved playing in the heat and the grass. I also loved putting on the black hat and going into the other guy's backyard.

But we had won 22 games in a row, and we were about to have that winning streak snapped at Arizona. We were ranked #1 in the nation, and we were going to lose that too. I knew that it was going to feel devastating. There was only a minute or so left, and I remember getting into my stance and waiting for the snap, feeling dehydrated and hot, and I took a moment there and thought… "I love this! I love this feeling that I have right now. It's being out here engaged in the fight and it's what I love. I'm out here pouring everything I've got into a great fight, and I'm going to keep coming." I'm sure all my teammates on the field felt the same way.

Johnson: The older I get, the more I recognize that God is to be found in those little moments and in those little details of life

Hoffmann: That's exactly right, man. That's exactly right. Talking personally, I've got a faith in God, and a lot of us on the team did. There were those special little moments. Like before games, one of my favorite sounds was hearing the cleats on the hard tile floor of the showers. Almost the whole team would walk in there and hold hands and pray together. We knew it was something we had to do, whether we were in Husky Stadium, or playing at Stanford or Nebraska, or wherever. Especially in the visitors' locker room, the shower was the biggest place where we could all stand together. It was something that the players started, but our Chaplain Mike Rohrbach would come around, and nothing would have to be said. The intensity level before the games was sky-high, but we would see Mike and we knew it was time to pray. I always loved hearing the click-clack of the cleats on the tile floor of the shower, because that meant that all of the warriors were coming together. I knew that the warriors had that warrior mentality, and at the same time I knew that they had the humble appreciation that God had given them the ability to come together and do this special thing on Saturday afternoons.

Johnson: Well, one thing about Christianity that I think is overlooked is that a lot of people think pure Christianity is about turning the other cheek and being 100% peaceful and emphasizing the lack of conflict. And yet, the main part of life is the struggle itself. Tensions are the source of energy. In the case of football, you're engaged in conflict yet you're also in accord with your enemy or opponent.

Hoffmann: That's exactly right. I used to love that aspect and I still love it today. I love the verse Psalm 144:1 "Praise be to the lord God my rock. Who trains my hands for war and my fingers for battle." Because that's such a big part of life that a lot people don't want to think and talk about. But it was something that me and a lot my teammates enjoyed. We were warriors and we enjoyed the battle.

Chapter 33

A Visit with Steve Emtman

DEFENSIVE TACKLE STEVE EMTMAN played at Washington from 1988-1991, and was the most decorated player in Husky football history. He won the Outland Trophy and Lombardi Award, and was twice a consensus All-American. He was the two-time Pac-10 Defensive Player of the Year, despite leaving for the NFL prior to his senior season. He was the first player selected in the 1992 NFL draft.

After being crushed by Washington 54-0 in 1991, Arizona Coach Dick Tomey had this to say: "All I can think about is that defense. Washington is a fantastic team. They have it all, but that defense is the best I've seen since I've been at Arizona. The only player I can compare Emtman to is Junior Seau at USC, both dominant players you can't block. But this Washington defense is more suffocating than those USC defenses. It doesn't give you a chance to breathe."

Derek Johnson: Let's start with talking about the recruiting process. By no means were you a blue-chipper. Dave Hoffmann told me the story of when you guys were being recruited. He said that a handful of recruits were out on a boat on Lake Washington. You personally were wearing blue jeans and boots, and had a scowl on your face looking like a kid who just had his lunch money stolen. He was thinking, "Who's this guy?" Of course, over time you guys became great friends. Tell me about the overall recruiting process.

Steve Emtman: (Laughing heartily) Well, I don't know about having a scowl on my face like I just had my money stolen, like Hoffmann says. If anything, I was probably getting ready to kick Hoffmann and James Clifford's ass for being so damn cocky. I don't recall hating the world. But there was a funny story from that time. I had it in my mind that I was going to Washington State. Dennis Erickson was the coach there, and I had tremendous respect for him. About a week before I took my trip, a WSU alum sent me a letter, saying that Washington was only recruiting me because WSU wanted me, but that Washington had no intention of playing me. The alum said that I would just get lost in the shuffle, and that there would be no playing time for me on the defensive line behind Mike Lustyk and Lincoln Kennedy.

I had an OK trip at U-Dub. I got to know Hoff and some of those guys on the boat. By the end of the trip I was talking to Coach Gary Pinkel. It was the very last thing I did before I left for home. I told him about the letter I received the from WSU alum, saying that Washington was just recruiting me to keep me from going to WSU, and that I would never see the field if I went to Washington. Coach Pinkel looked right at me and said, "If you're scared to compete for a job, we don't want you. Go to WSU."

On the plane ride home, it was a late-night flight. I was looking out the window thinking, and it really sunk in. I felt like, "Yea, that's what I'm about. I will compete for a job, and I'm better than any of those other guys." Pinkel made you think that way, and I thought it was kind of cool. It was the attitude that most of us Huskies had at that time. I know that me and Hoff, when we became friends as freshmen, well I felt like I was better than Mike Lustyk, and Hoff felt like he was better than James Clifford. It's hard to say that you're better than James Clifford when he just led the Pac-10 in tackles as a freshman. But that's the kind of competitors we were. We were pissed off and working out and trying to get better. I know that I had to earn my spot and earn respect.

I bitched a bit about not traveling with the team. But we would work out our aggression in the weight room, and it kind of became addicting. I just grinded and slowly but surely got better and better.

The big selling point for us was that weight room, we had the best weight room in the country, it was quite the deal. That's how you get those competitors in there. Guys that want to work hard and compete. Our team was built on that. We had some highly recruited guys, like Napoleon Kaufman. But for the most part, we had guys like me and Hoff. Neither one of us was a blue-chipper. In fact, I don't think I got a single blue chip vote.

Johnson: Back in 1988 I remember reading about your recruiting class, and feeling mildly disappointed that there were no big names. Including your name; I just was like, "Steve Who?" I wondered if Don James was slipping.

Emtman: Right. Well, I always use that foxhole analogy. Any of those guys I played with on defense, I would take into a fox hole with me, and know that we would come out on top. Because I could count on them. Especially playing a gap defense, where you only had to worry about your responsibility, because you could count on everybody else to do their job. We had a letdown every once in awhile, but very few.

Johnson: Speaking of letdowns, I talked with Hoffmann about the most prominent one, which was the 88-yard touchdown run by UCLA's Brian Ball, in the Bruins' 25-22 stunning upset at Husky Stadium in 1990. Hoffmann decries that he can still see that play like it was yesterday.

Emtman: Ah! That's the game I remember most, which is probably a bad thing. I probably need a few psychologists to help me out there. But that loss cost us the national championship. It's kind of funny, but I heard some years later, there was a player on our team, and I won't mention his name, who was out after the game with some UCLA cheerleaders and a couple of players or some such thing. When I heard about that, I wanted to go kill him. And this was ten years later! I was like, "How can you be out like that when we just lost a game in which we were 24-point favorites?"

Johnson: Following the 1991 Rose Bowl win over Iowa, I have heard that Ed Cunningham gave a speech to the team on the plane ride back to Seattle.

Emtman: Ed stood up in the plane and said "Seniors, good job. Way to go out a winner. But to the rest of us, I'll say this: We're going to win them all next year, and we're coming back home with a national championship. That's our focus, and we're going back to work on Monday."

The following Monday, we all went back to work. It wasn't mandatory, but we didn't take any break after the grind of the season we had just been through. But we enjoyed it. I actually enjoyed practice. It's easy to say in retrospect, but I can truly say, we got a lot done and had fun doing it.

Johnson: Where was the point for you along the way when it occurred to you that you could be something special?

Emtman: There were times in my freshman year that I felt like that things were screwed up and that the coaches were screwing me over. It's kind of funny how you remember the little things, but I remember once calling my Dad to do a little whining and get a little sympathy. He was like, "Well, work harder." In retrospect, it wasn't like he was going to say to me, "Oh, it's too bad they're screwing ya, please come home."

My Dad said, "Work harder and make it obvious." So I just kept grinding. I really had nowhere to run and nowhere to hide. I really attribute my success to Eric Cohen and Rick Heugli in the weight room. That's where I found my drive. You start by putting your numbers out there and I started to make sure that I had better numbers than anyone else at my position. I don't know if any of my teammates knew it, but that was a big thing for me. One time, Rick Huegli showed me my chart of everything I had done from day one and it was pretty cool to see the progress. To see me go from being a mid-300 bencher to a 475 or 485 bencher was great.

Johnson: Lincoln Kennedy told me about meeting that a bunch of underclassmen had in 1990 at the Conibear Shellhouse. It was prior to the USC game, following less-than-inspiring wins over San Jose State and Purdue. Lincoln said that you and Hoffmann were the ones doing most of the talking. What do you recall of it?

Emtman: I don't really remember details about that. The thing about our team was that so much leadership came from the players. The coaches didn't have to motivate and lead as much as you see on other teams. As a player, you respected your position coach and you respected all the coaches and you *certainly* never questioned Don James. I've never seen a coach that got so much respect from his players. And I played for Jimmy Johnson, Don Shula and Ted

Marchibroda. It was amazing to see Don James compared to them in how the athletes would respect him. He kept everyone in line, because you were terrified to screw up. You didn't want to have to go face DJ. I'm sure that a lot of the former players have told you that. But we had those informal meetings—the players on our team really cared about winning and each other. And if there was something that needed to be addressed, it got addressed.

Johnson: Greg Lewis was telling me about that 1990 USC game, when you guys won 31-0. He said that he could have played that game at 5 AM, he was so fired up. That was when USC quarterback Todd Marinovich told reporters afterward that "All I saw was purple."

Emtman: Gosh, that game was intense. That game was when we felt we arrived defensively. Right before halftime, one of my teammates got a sack, and my finger got up under (Marinovich's) gums. He was bleeding. It was funny to see Marinovich looking all dazed and confused. Then we're heading up the tunnel and their running back Ricky Ervins was talking crap. We were kicking their ass, and he's coming up our tunnel talking crap. He just didn't get it. After hearing that, there was no way we weren't going to come back out in the second half and finish the job. We shouted at him, "You're a fool! You've just motivated our whole team!"

The confidence amongst ourselves really started right there. We experienced the realization that if we could dominate a team like USC, we could dominate anybody. Added to that was the thing we learned from that UCLA game the year before, we learned that we were never again going into a game and not be 100% prepared.

Johnson: What memories have you from the epic 36-21 win at Nebraska in 1991?

Emtman: The thing I remember most about that game was how cool it was to walk off the field. We had just beaten Nebraska in Lincoln, which back in the day, was THE team to beat. And their fans, a sea of red, were going crazy and applauding us for a great performance. They were true fans, as opposed to fans down in Oregon, who are just rude assholes. I never played in Oregon, but went down there as strength coach. They're just incredibly rude. But Nebraska's fans demonstrated true sportsmanship. I had never experienced anything like that. I probably have more respect for Nebraska fans than just about any other. They were pure class, you know? They were disappointed that their team lost, but appreciative of the great battle. When another team's fans pay respect like that to you, it makes you feel even better about what you accomplished.

Johnson: It raises sport to a higher level.

Emtman: Yes, it really does. It's an example you can point to and say ideally that *this* is what you would love your fans to be like. And that was such a great battle. When we won that game in Lincoln, we knew we could win the rest of our games.

Johnson: What was the most poignant memory you have of Coach James?

Emtman: Seeing Coach James win the national championship that he deserved. Seeing him get excited and emotional about it was great, considering that he always grinded and never got emotional. If anybody deserved winning the national championship, it was him. Of course, what followed after the national championship was a bunch of crap. But what he did for the university and for us as players— no other coach could have made us into what we were. We had guys who were best friends on that field, and yet so different off the field, despite coming from different backgrounds and different worlds. When we crossed that white line we transformed into a group of warriors who were dedicated to each other absolutely. It didn't matter where you came from, you respected Coach James.

And Coach James didn't ever have to say much. But he had that look he would give you, and you *did not* mess with him. And it's still the most amazing thing and I'm sure that every guy has talked about it with you; but you've got a bunch of 18-20 year old guys in the meeting room, talking loudly and carrying on. When that man walked into the room, it was instant silence. You didn't even think about finishing your thought.

It was funny for me because later on I played with the Miami Dolphins and Don Shula would walk into our meeting room, and guys would be talking and nobody was paying attention. And I was like, "Wow." That's why we didn't win while I was at Miami, because we weren't on the same page.

Johnson: What memories come to mind from the win over Michigan in the 1992 Rose Bowl?

Emtman: Leading up to that I was sick as a dog. I had done a tour for awards and whatnot, and I was worn out, and finally became sick during practice. But I remember our team's preparation for that game. We had our fun, but when it was time to work, we worked. We never let the outside world effect our preparation.

My favorite moment was probably Mario Bailey's little Heisman pose with the ball in the end zone. That was the best moment, I think. He was saying that he was the best receiver on that field, and not Desmond (Howard). All of us on the team knew it all along, but Mario had his chance to shine for the national TV audience.

We won 34-14, and we could have scored more. It makes you wonder what it would have been like had we left the offense in there a little longer to score. We never would do that of course, because that's not the kind of man Don James was. So we did the right thing by not running it up. But it still makes you wonder (If the Huskies might have won the polls outright from Miami had they poured it on). There's no question we could have scored at least another seven points in most of our games, had we wanted to.

Johnson: Just like from the 1977 game down in Eugene. I don't know if you have ever heard this story. The Huskies led the Ducks 54-0 and were at Oregon's 2-yard line. Don James had his quarterback take a knee and run out the final two minutes.

Emtman: Wow. That's says something for the man, doesn't it?

Johnson: A final question for you. Dave Hoffmann told me of the time when you guys were freshmen and it snowed. Apparently you, Mark Brunell and Dave snuck into Jackson Golf Course in the middle of the night for some furtive sledding. Care to tell your recollection of that evening?

Emtman: (Laughing and defiant) I'll let Hoffmann tell that story! I'm just glad he told that story because there were other stories that were worse, that I thought he might have told you. It's a good thing he didn't tell you about the snowball fight.

Johnson: Well you've got center stage, so take it away.

Emtman: I'll just leave it that there were some snowball fights up on Greek Row that were more than snowball fights. We had some fun. Especially when you're freshmen who aren't playing and you're angry. I'm sure that if they had camera phones around back then, me and Hoffmann would have ended up on the front page of *The Seattle Times*.

Chapter 34

A Visit with Dana Hall

DANA HALL BEGAN HIS Husky career as a safety, before moving to cornerback late in his sophomore season. He was a graceful athlete who only surrendered three touchdown passes in his entire collegiate career. He was a first team All Pac-10 selection in 1991, and was a first round draft pick to the San Francisco 49ers, in the 1992 NFL Draft.

Derek Johnson: When you arrived at the University of Washington in the fall of 1987, you symbolized the new emphasis that Don James was putting on getting players with speed. You won the 110-Meter Hurdles championship for the state of California. You had also been a class president and honor student at Ganesha High. But you told me before that within three weeks on campus, you were summoned into Coach James's office. Can you share that story again?

Dana Hall: Sure. I came from the type of (lower-class) neighborhood where not everybody likes to see someone receive a way out. I had been a model student, but I gotten into a scuffle earlier that year. Well, what kid doesn't get into a scuffle at some point, you know? Well, somebody called up to Washington and let them know about it. Coach James called me into his office. For whatever reason, he felt that maybe I was a guy who wanted to run with the crowd. He talked to me about not being part of the crowd. Maybe he saw in me a guy who had potential if he could just straighten me out. I remember that he wanted to know why I was wearing an earring. Well, everybody was just starting to wear earrings. Coach James looked right at me and said, "You know what Dana? If you act like everybody else, you're going to be just like everybody else. You're going to just be an average player. But if you want to be different, you need to create your own identity. Don't be a follower. Learn how to lead."

That meeting changed my perspective of who I was as a person. As I left Coach James's office, I took out the earring and I haven't worn one since.

Johnson: It was in November of 1989 that defensive coordinator Jim Lambright and Don James switched to the high-pressure attack defense against Oregon State in Corvallis. You guys went in there and crushed the Beavers 51-14. In that game, you were a sophomore, and made your first start as a Husky. You earned two "Big Hit" Awards from the coaches.

Hall: Yes, I did. It was just a really exciting time. We were a tight-knit group, and we trusted each other absolutely. Playing that type of defense, trust is one of the biggest things. Especially being a corner. If trust that I won't need to cover for that long, I can be aggressive and trust that the guys up front will get to the quarterback.

Johnson: I was talking with Dave Hoffmann recently, and he says that he can remember the Husky defense surrendering that game-breaking 88-yard TD run to UCLA's Brian Brown like it was yesterday. That loss late in the 1990 season cost you guys dearly. You had been ranked #2 nationally going into that game, and #1 Notre Dame lost that same day.

Hall: Like Dave, I remember that play. It swung the ballgame to UCLA and in losing that game we lost the shot at winning back-to-back national championships. All the players and coaches were stunned. But it gave us a renewed focus. We immediately put it to use. We decided to not let that happen again. We decided that every opponent from then on was going to get our 100% focus.

Johnson: You guys went on to win the Rose Bowl over Iowa and finish 10-2, and during the following spring practice everything seemed in place for a run at the national championship. Suddenly during a scrimmage, a defensive player accidentally crashed into quarterback Mark Brunell and tore up Brunell's knee. How did that affect the team from your perspective?

Hall: We were devastated because Mark was our guy, and we didn't know what Billy Joe Hobert could do as an unproven sophomore. But the record shows that he responded to the challenge just fine.

Johnson: Do you remember the point when the team felt confident that Billy Joe could lead them all the way?

Hall: It was that Nebraska game, winning in Lincoln. We saw right there that Billy Joe had what it took to lead us. Defensively we were already in the mindset of stepping it up to help compensate for losing Mark. Our thing was, if the other team doesn't score, they won't beat us. But at Nebraska, we saw that Billy was fully capable.

Johnson: I'm going to rattle off some names from your defensive unit and tell me what thoughts or memories come to mind. We'll start with the late linebacker, Jaime Fields.

Hall: You know, Jaime Fields was a different kind of individual. I don't even think the coaches could figure out Jaime. He was quirky, he was different. Sometimes he would have this look in his eyes, and you'd wonder "Does Jaime know what planet he's on?" He often appeared to not know what was going on, and yet he was one of the more heady players on our defense. He was a ballplayer. He brought it every day in practice and in games.

Johnson: Dave Hoffmann and Ed Cunningham both say that Jaime was an immensely humble guy.

Hall: He was, he was.

Johnson: Defensive Tackle Steve Emtman.

Hall: Unstoppable. But the story about Steve Emtman is this: When he came in as a freshman, here's this country boy from the farm, coming to the big city. For him to take over the way he did was unbelievable. I had to answer so many questions from my peers and guys I played against, saying "Ain't no way that guy got that good without some kind of enhancements." But I told them, "I watched this guy work day in and day out. If you watched this guy work out you wouldn't say that." He worked so hard in the weight room and on the field, and it translated into being the #1 pick in the NFL draft.

Johnson: Linebacker Dave Hoffmann.

Hall: Dave was another one of those guys who overachieved far more than anyone thought he would. He was a fierce competitor. He hung out more with Emtman and Clifford and Mark Brunell and those guys, so I didn't get to know him well enough to have any stories or anything like that. But he was just a fierce competitor, and wanted to be the best at whatever he did.

Johnson: Safety Tommie Smith.

Hall: Tommie Smith! (Prolonged chuckling)

Johnson: I don't know what you want to put on this, but Greg Lewis told me that teammates referred to Tommie endearingly as "Dummy Smith."

Hall: (Still chuckling) Yea, Tommie wasn't the sharpest tool in the shed. But we love him. We loved the guy. But here's a guy, in regards to Xs and Os, who was not one of the better guys. But as far as athletically, he was always one of the best athletes on the field at any time, regardless of our opponent. He always had a knack for being around the football. But in terms of academics, school wasn't Tommie's thing.

Johnson: Amongst the defensive players, was there ever talk that Tommie should have been a running back?

Hall: Yea, naturally when a player is arguably the best athlete on the team, there's always a rumor that he will get switched to running back.

Johnson: Linebacker Chico Fraley.

Hall: Yes, Chico was my roommate my freshman year. We were both from California. I remember the first day of classes, it was raining. I looked at him and said, "Are you going to class?" He said, "No." He said to me, "Are you going to class?" I said "No." By the third day, it was still raining. I turned to Chico and said, "You know, it's probably not going to stop raining. We should probably go to class." I loved that guy. Chico was my roommate for three of the five years that I was in college. We would drive home to California together during breaks and stay together during summers.

Johnson: Andy Mason.

Hall: Here was guy who hailed from Portland, I think.

Johnson: No, Mason actually came from my Dad's hometown of Longview, Washington.

Hall: Oh, OK. Well, Andy hailed from down near the Oregon border. This guy was all upper body and no legs. He was a heck of a sprinter and baseball player in high school. Andy was another one of those guys that Jim Lambright saw something in and he got plugged into a position and excelled. Andy had extreme upper body strength.

Johnson: And he loved yappin' out on the field.

Hall: Yes, Andy was a talker. He was out there trash talkin' to the other team. But that was what he did to motivate his game, and so that's what he did.

Johnson: Safety Shane Pahukoa

Hall: Big Shane! Another guy who was very deceptive, speed-wise. I remember when he came in, we didn't know what he could do physically. We thought he might be OK. But he had this self-confidence about him, even from the days way back when he had his accident (Pahukoa has severe burn marks along one side of his face and neck). I don't know how old he was when the accident occurred, but he probably grew up getting all the stares and comments and whatnot. But he developed a real self confidence about himself that he could do anything, and he carried that with him at Washington.

Johnson: It's interesting in life. One person can go through something like that and it can destroy them emotionally, while for someone else they can use that to make themselves stronger.

Hall: Exactly. It depends on how you look at yourself. If you take it as 'Woe is me," then you probably won't make it. But if you take it as 'Why not me?' then you can persevere and be successful, and that's what he did. He even played a couple of years in the league (NFL). I'm very proud of Shane.

Johnson: Defensive Tackle Tyrone Rodgers.

Hall: T-Rodge! When that guy talked, we couldn't understand what the heck he was saying.

Johnson: You mean because of a southwestern accent?

Hall: Yea, well, I don't know what it was. We would be like, "What did you just say?" We used to call T-Rodge "Scooby." Just like the TV show *Scooby-Do*. And in that show, only Shaggy knew what he was saying. So when Terrance Powe was on the team, we would call him "Shaggy." We used to tease T-Rodge. He would say something, and we would turn to Shaggy and say "What did he just say?" We just couldn't understand the guy. But Tyrone was just another great defensive lineman. Maybe that helped Steve Emtman be so good, because teams couldn't afford to always double team him because Tyrone was so good too.

Johnson: Cornerback Walter Bailey

Hall: Walter B! Walter was the resident team barber. He used to cut everybody's hair on the team. He was an incredible athlete, and always around the ball. I think that one year, he had 10 picks. Quarterbacks seemed to throw his way more than my way, and I'm not sure why. But they would keep throwing at Walt, and he would keep burning them.

Johnson: Well it was probably because— as Don James once said— that when teams threw at Walter, it was usually six points, either for the Huskies or the other team.

Hall: Yep! That was Walter Bailey! He took some chances. The defensive linemen were always thinking they better get to the QB quickly, because they didn't know what the heck Walter was doing back there.

Johnson: Defensive back William Doctor.

Hall: When you have name like William Doctor, you obviously are going to get the nickname of "Doc." He was my roommate for two years. He was a military child, from El Paso, Texas at that. He was very musical, always singing. He was very bright, very intelligent. Probably the brightest guy in the bunch (amongst the secondary). But he was very quiet and unassuming, until he got around us, and then he became a different person.

Johnson: An hour from now I am going to be talking with Napoleon Kaufman. I know that you only spent one year with him as a teammate, as you were a senior when he was a freshman. And I know he was on offense, but can you tell me any stories you recall about him at Washington?

Hall: I don't remember much about Nip. Besides the fact that he was super fast. *That* I remember. But I didn't really spend a whole lot of time with him when we were at Washington.

Johnson: And here's a guy who I love, and who was a defensive lineman early in his career at Washington, Lincoln Kennedy. One teammate once described Lincoln's face as looking like "an overstuffed Gary Coleman."

Hall: Yea, ol' Big Link! You know, I was one of Lincoln's hosts when he came up to Washington on a recruiting trip. He was a big, slow defensive lineman from San Diego. He was a Baby Huey kind of guy. It's true what they say sometimes: It's the big guys who are the most gentle. And he was truly a gentle giant. But he was just too slow to play defense. He had to do more than just sit there and clog up the middle. We'd tell him, "Hey, we've got to figure something out here!" But the best thing that ever happened to him was the move to the offensive line. He became an All-American and it translated into a long NFL career. You know, Washington has been notorious for that, defensive players moving to offense and becoming good enough for the NFL.

Johnson: Linebacker James Clifford.

Hall: Cliff was another guy who was crazy and the typical frat guy. He was out there. He had an "I don't care" attitude.

Johnson: I read a quote that a teammate anonymously stated that Clifford was so demented, if he had the chance, he would hit his own grandmother. Also, he was described as "Charles Manson in shoulder pads."

Hall: Yes, that's about right! That sounds like Cliff! He was always looking for something to run into.

Johnson: Brett Collins.

Hall: From our true freshmen year, he and I went down to Oregon for a trip. My parents were living in Vancouver, Washington at the time. I went to Brett and Bo Yates' old high school in Oregon to see a game. They would put three or four running backs in the backfield, and just keep running the same play, and push right on down the field. I was like, "This is high school football?"

But Brett was another guy who probably overachieved a bit, but became a great player.

Johnson: It's a curious thing about Brett, considering that he was a captain of the National Championship team, that he never became very well known.

Hall: For whatever reason that was, who knows? Another guy like that was Paxton Tailele.

Johnson: I remember one year he knocked somebody's QB out of the game.

Hall: That guy was built like a Greek God. A hard hitter.

Johnson: Linebacker Donald Jones.

Hall: He was another guy who was built like a rock. When Don was a fullback, nobody wanted to hit him in practice. We were like: "I don't want to hit that dude!" But Jim Lambright, being the genius that he is, saw that Jones would be perfect in the new scheme he was trying to create in 1989, which started during that Oregon State game. He was so quick off the ball, he was unstoppable.

Johnson: In some of those line-of-scrimmage TV camera angles of the 1992 Rose Bowl, his movement when the ball was snapped was absolutely simultaneous.

Hall: Oh yea. When that ball moved, Don was gone. It was like he was shot out of a rocket.

Johnson: I was always surprised that he didn't have a long and glorious NFL career.

Hall: Yea, me too. I don't know what happened either. He had the skill set to succeed there. But you know— the NFL is a strange nut to crack.

Johnson: Finally, what was the best and toughest thing about playing for Coach James?

Hall: Coach James was fair but consistent. He was tough. You had to be on time for meetings. On time for Coach James meant 5-10 minutes early. He was notorious for closing the door early. It was all based on his clock. He was domineering. He would go up into the tower and let his coaches coach. He wouldn't say much to us players, unless he needed to correct something blatantly outrageous.

But the best part was how he evolved. He was always consistent, but he also evolved right along with the rest of us. By my senior year in 1991, he wasn't the same type of unapproachable coach as when I came in. He developed respect for the guys in my recruiting class. I remember one game against USC in 1990. USC had kicked our butts three years in a row, and then we beat them 31-0. We saw Don James waving a towel on the sideline. It gave us players a whole other perspective of Don James. It's a lot easier to play for a guy that you think is for you rather than against you. Coach James was definitely adversarial. He wanted us players to unite against him in order to unite together.

Johnson: That's interesting. You didn't feel he was on your side?

Hall: No, we didn't feel he was on our side. He did that on purpose because after that first whistle (of a game) you're out there on your own and Don James can no longer help you. It made us mentally stronger. In that environment, over time, I matured into a man. The two most influential people for me on that campus were Don James and Jim Lambright. It would take me hours and hours to express my admiration and respect for those two guys.

Chapter 35 — September 22, 1990

"All I Saw was Purple"

Husky Stadium — Washington vs. USC

DURING THE WEEK LEADING up to the monumental game against #5 USC, assistant coach Keith Gilbertson decided to have his usual moment of fun in practice. Pass-rushing terror Donald Jones always got an amazing jump off of the snap of the ball from his linebacker position. He would shoot forward at the first sign of movement by the other team's Center. The joke among Husky players was that all opposing teams ever had to do to catch Jones off-sides, was to alter the cadence and snap the ball on two. As the Huskies commenced to do their 11-on-11 drills, Gilbertson gathered up the first team offense into a huddle and called the play. "OK! Let's make Donald Jones offside, on two... Ready, BREAK!"

As usual, it worked to perfection.

Ironically in light of Gilbertson's joke, there was a tremendously stern attitude pervading the Huskies during the entire week leading up to the game. The focus was all USC. The Huskies were 2-0 but were lackluster in their wins over San Jose State (20-17) and Purdue (20-14). Now would be the time to step it up, if they were to achieve the lofty goals they set during the previous spring and summer.

"We had a goal in the off-season, *N.B.R.*, which was Nothin' but Roses," recalled Husky All-American running back Greg Lewis. "We had been really dedicated that off-season. A lot of guys were staying in Seattle to work out. We knew we were set at every position, but that the only question was at QB."

Lewis stated that everyone on the team knew that Mark Brunell was a great young talent, but the question was whether he could lead the Dawgs while being so raw and inexperienced. Meanwhile, USC was coming off of impressive wins over Syracuse and Penn State. They had the highly-proclaimed "Robo-QB" Todd Marinovich and Ricky Ervins at tailback. Unlike miserable weather-related experiences in the past, the Trojans were pleased with this day's weather report for Seattle. Temperatures were to be in the 90s with blue sky.

Amongst Husky players, there was much talk of how much disrespect they were getting from the Trojans. "Those guys from USC were real cocky," said Lewis. "They were talking trash in the tunnel, on the field, even in the newspapers. USC is just that type of team."

As the Huskies strapped on their helmets and exited the locker room, Lewis was bursting inside. "I could have played that game at 5:30 AM!" he said with a laugh. "I didn't sleep much the night before. Coming down the tunnel I felt like a horse being corralled. All I was thinking was 'Let me get out there!' I was thinking that this was THE GAME. We were in a position to prove something. It was my senior season, and I knew that if we lost that game against USC then all the things I had worked for over the past four years probably wouldn't come to fruition. And the number one reason that I came to Washington was to play in the Rose Bowl."

As the game began, Lewis watched the dominating Husky defense from the sidelines and in a sense felt bad for USC quarterback Todd Marinovich. "It was pretty much pick your poison out there with our defense," said Lewis. "If you're an opposing QB, you've got Donald

Jones on one side and Jaime Fields on the other. Then you've got Steve Emtman and Tyrone Rogers collapsing the middle. There's really nothing you can do."

Marinovich entered the game as a Heisman Trophy, but quickly began to wilt in the face of the blast furnace pressure applied by the Husky defense. On most of his attempts to drop back and pass, the Husky defense engulfed Marinovich in waves of defenders. With every attempt to run the ball, running back Ricky Ervins was smothered.

The capacity Husky crowd reached a zenith of intensity in the second quarter. The fans smelled blood. The Huskies began scoring. First they drove 66 yards in 10 plays, culminating in a 1-yard plunge by Lewis. This would be followed by a field goal by Mike Dodd, then a 1-yard run by Darius Turner and finally a 12-yard passing strike from Mark Brunell to Mario Bailey. Suddenly it was halftime, and an anticipated tight battle was surprisingly Washington 24, USC 0.

When asked what was going through his mind at halftime about the circumstances and USC, Lewis said: "That for all their talk, these guys couldn't play with us. Our defense was constantly three and out, and their defense had to stay on the field a long time. It made it easier for our offense. We were getting push with our offensive line. There was one play that I remember well. The O-line was blocking well and I cut it back inside and I didn't see a single maroon jersey until I was forty yards downfield. That just showed how much our offensive linemen were dominating them."

Washington scored again in the second half, and posted a 31-0 triumph. This outcome startled the rest of the Pac-10 and secured notice throughout the country. As Husky fans left the stadium, random cheering continued to erupt—all the way out to the parking lot.

The Pac-10 named Greg Lewis as its Player of the Week, after he rushed for 126 yards and a touchdown. Husky quarterback Mark

Brunell came of age, showing leadership, and completing 12-of-23 passes for 197 yards and a touchdown. Linebacker Travis Richardson led the defense, recording seven tackles and two quarterback sacks. The Husky defense held USC to 28 yards rushing. Todd Marinovich had the nightmare game of his career, completing a paltry 7-of-16 passes for 80 yards. The Husky defense intercepted him three times. Following the game, he was wearing dark sunglasses, still dazed and battered, as he conversed quietly with reporters. He uttered words that ultimately defined that era of Husky defensive football.

"I just saw purple, that's all," said Marinovich. "No numbers. Just purple."

Chapter 36 — November 3, 1990

Nothin' But Roses

Washington vs. Arizona

IN THE POST-GAME MEETING room, Rose Bowl representative Roy Cohts began to address the entire Washington team. When he uttered the words "formally inviting" the rest of his speech was drowned out by cheers and shouting from the Husky players and coaches. Back-up senior lineman Shell Mays grabbed and bear-hugged Don James. Offensive line coach Keith Gilbertson raised his arms in triumph and was quickly engulfed by several players. Running backs Coach Matt Simon started sobbing upon the shoulder of secondary coach Larry Slade.

The #3-ranked Washington Huskies had just buried the #23-ranked Arizona Wildcats 54-10, on a gloriously overcast day at Husky Stadium. They had improved their record to 6-0 in the conference and 8-1 overall. They had beaten their Pac-10 opponents by an alarming average score of 44-11. Even though there were still two games left in the regular season, Washington was officially the Pac-10 champion for the first time since 1981.

"This is what we've worked so hard for, for so long," said senior defensive back Eric Briscoe with a gigantic smile across his face and roses in-hand.

"The guys really went out and played again, didn't they?" said UW defensive line Coach Randy Hart. "They're a special group. This team is unparalleled in its ability to prepare. They refuse to *not* be prepared. In every phase, they want to know what the other team is going to do—and they're ready."

For Don James, this was to be his fourth Rose Bowl. He admitted that it felt good to prove the naysayers wrong that he could still coach. A reporter asked him what type of experience this was for him at fifty-eight years of age. "It's a thrill to see the kids enjoy it," said James, with a big smile and the game ball tucked under his arm. "They're going to have a lifetime experience. I'm getting a lot out of it—that's what I'm getting out of it—enjoying it with these kids." Another reporter asked James how difficult it was to see his friend Mike Lude recently forced out as Athletic Director. "It hurts to see it happen that way," said James. "I'm in a position where I have bosses too, the same ones that he has, and we all have jobs to do. We all have those situations where decisions are made and we don't always agree with them, but you still have your job to do."

Standing a few feet away from James was a teary-eyed Mike Lude. "This is the best team I've ever been around," he said, raspy-voiced to a nearby reporter.

The display by the Husky defense that day had been astounding. In Arizona's 57 plays from scrimmage against UW's first-team defense, 31 plays went for no gain or lost yardage. On offense, Washington's onslaught was sparked by big plays, including backup running back Beno Bryant, who returned a punt 70 yards for a touchdown and busted a 73-yard touchdown run in the fourth quarter. And with three minutes left in the game and Washington running out the clock with a 54-10 lead, freshman backup quarterback Billy Joe Hobert startled his teammates and angered Don James, when he dropped back in the pocket and threw a bomb.

"I was sitting on the bench, and all I could see were helmets on the field when we would run a play," said starting quarterback Mark Brunell. "All of a sudden, I see the ball in the air. I said, 'Oh, no!' But that's Hoby. He loves to go for it."

"That was a mistake," said Don James afterward.

Afterward in the visitor's locker room, Arizona Coach Dick Tomey was effusive in praise for the Huskies. "If they're not the best team in the country they're right there with whoever is. If they're not the top choice, I don't know who is." "That's the best team I've ever seen," said senior Wildcat offensive guard Rob Flory. "They've got to be number one. We came in thinking we could play with them, but after awhile—after halftime—you could see some of our guys giving up. Washington was too good."

A reporter asked Husky offensive lineman Dean Kirkland about the possibility of a national championship. "We've got the roses," said Kirkland, as he smiled and pumped his fist repeatedly. "And we're up there in the rankings! We've got a shot. We've got a big shot."

Chapter 37– January 1, 1991

Pasadena Onslaught

Washington vs. Iowa (Rose Bowl)

AS FAST AS IT took UCLA running back Brian Brown to scamper 88 yards for a touchdown, Washington's dream of a national championship disintegrated on November 10, 1990. Despite having been 21 ½ point favorites, the Huskies had just lost at home to UCLA 25-22. This defeat devastated and disgusted the whole team, and dropped UW from #2 to #10 in the Associated Press poll. They also lost All-American running back Greg Lewis to a knee injury. A week later, the Huskies (without Lewis) took to the field in Pullman with revenge in their minds and carnage in their hearts. In the frigid and bleak elements, they ran roughshod over Drew Bledsoe and the Washington State Cougars 55-10. In the locker room after this game, the 9-2 Huskies still felt hurt from the UCLA loss, but also relief and happiness at returning to the Rose Bowl for the first time in nine years.

The team doctors conveyed doubt that Greg Lewis would heal in time to play in the Rose Bowl, which was forty days away. Lewis decided privately that he would do whatever it took to play in Pasadena. Prior to its renovation, Hec Edmundson Pavilion used to have a running track encircling the interior. Just two weeks after his surgery, a member of the UW training staff spotted Greg Lewis running sprints around that track—something that was not a part of his prescribed rehab program. Soon after, Lewis worried he wouldn't make it. "There was one point in practice when I planted on the knee and something popped," recalled Lewis years later. "But I came back from that quickly and by January 1st I was ready to go."

The 8-3 Iowa Hawkeyes stood between the Huskies and a 10-win season. Washington privately felt immense confidence in how they matched up with the Big 10's representative. "The Iowa defense looked extremely slow on film," said Lewis. We didn't respect their speed, and we were disappointed to be playing them, instead of Michigan or Ohio State. With the exception of one player, their entire defense looked slow."

In practice, Lewis routinely had to block one of the best pass-rushing specialists in Husky history. Coming off the corner from his down-linebacker position, Donald Jones amply prepared Lewis for anything that any college team in America could throw at him. "Having to block Donald, I wasn't worried about Iowa's rush defense," said Lewis. "He even broke my face mask a couple of times leading up to the game."

Greg Lewis went on to describe stepping onto the Rose Bowl turf, in an experience that was borderline mystical. "I still haven't experienced anything like that, before or since," he said. "The sense of euphoria of running out onto the field, the pageantry, the rose painted on the field, and our team's name painted in the end zone. And knowing that Keith Jackson was up in the booth broadcasting our game to millions of people around the world, and wondering what he was saying about *me*. I had played in that stadium a couple of times before, but it's a different place when it's for the Rose Bowl. Seeing the stands completely full, and everyone wearing one color on one side of the stadium and a different color on the other side, it's very different."

As for the game itself, the Huskies came out with the mentality of an 800-pound gorilla, and sat wherever they damn well pleased. From the opening kickoff, they overtook and engulfed the Hawkeyes. Early on and on fourth down, Iowa lined up in a bizarre formation, out of which they attempted to punt the football. Washington's Andy Mason came up the middle and smothered the kick. Teammate Dana Hall scooped it up and raced in for a touchdown.

Following two Husky field goals, Husky cornerback Charles Mincy picked off a pass from Iowa quarterback Matt Rogers and raced 37 yards for a touchdown. Minutes later, Husky QB Mark Brunell displayed his speed by racing five yards for a touchdown via a broad, winding arc around left end, outracing all defenders and scooting into the end zone. The first half was capped off by a Brunell pass to Mario Bailey. Washington took a 33-7 lead into the locker room. "Going into the game, we wanted to prove that the UCLA game was a fluke," said Lewis. "We wanted to show that we were clearly better than the best team that the Big 10 had to offer."

Lewis and other starters were pulled from the game with several minutes still remaining in the third quarter. In just over two quarters of play, Lewis tallied 128 yard rushing on 19 carries. Unbeknownst to the doctors and training staff, Lewis had removed the prescribed knee brace to increase his mobility. "It was too bulky and cumbersome," said Lewis. "And let me tell you, we starters wanted to stay in the game. The only reason that we didn't win by an even greater margin is that Don James is a gentleman." But even in light of the mild disappointment of being pulled from the game early, Lewis and his teammates were having a great time on the sideline. "We were celebrating, enjoying the fact that we were going to be Rose Bowl Champions. We knew that we were about to accomplish our goal that we set from the start of the season."

With Washington's second unit in the game, the 77th Rose Bowl grew a tad more interesting. With admirable pluck, Iowa came roaring back with a flurry of points. With 5:07 left in the game, the image of giant Hawkeye running back Nick Bell rumbling 20 yards up the middle for a touchdown sent tremors of mild panic through Husky fans. The lead had been trimmed to 39-26. But the Huskies recovered the subsequent onside kick attempt. With some starters re-inserted into the game, Washington promptly marched down the field for another touchdown. Iowa added one more tally, to create the final score of Washington 46, Iowa 34. The 80 points racked up between the two teams were the highest combined total in Rose Bowl history. The Huskies finished the season at 10-2 and ranked #5 in the nation.

On the flight back to Seattle, junior Center Ed Cunningham stood up to address the team. He lauded Greg Lewis and the other seniors for finishing their careers on such a high note. "But for the rest of us," said Cunningham, "We are coming back to Pasadena next year, and we are going to settle for nothing less than 12-0. See you all in the weight room on Monday."

Chapter 38 — September 21, 1991

Slaying Big Red

Washington at Nebraska

AS THEY EMERGED FROM the locker room, it was the calm before the gridiron storm. Amid the relative quiet of pre-game warm-ups, the defending Pac-10 champion Washington Huskies took to the field at Lincoln, Nebraska. There was a mixture of excited anticipation and introspection. It was to be a prime time night game, on national TV. Looking around Memorial Stadium, Don James knew to expect the obvious. "I knew it was going to be red, and it was going to be full," he said years later with a chuckle.

Former Husky tailback Beno Bryant was a bit more prescient from the players' point of view. "We knew it was going to be amazing to beat them in Lincoln, the whole team felt that. Billy (Hobert) didn't like to lose, nobody on the team did."

The Huskies were ranked #4 in the nation, after thrashing Stanford 42-7 on the road in the opener. Nebraska entered the game with a #9 ranking and a 2-0 record. The first half was a slugfest. Then halfway through the third quarter, with the Huskies trailing 14-9, UW's Beno Bryant set up near the 10-yard line to return a punt. The pivotal point of the entire season was about to unfold.

"I got caught up in the moment," recalled Bryant with a laugh. "I saw all the red in the stands. Here I'm a little kid from South Central L.A., playing on national TV… My eyes were too big for my stomach." To the Huskies' horror, Bryant went against convention and attempted to field the punt from the two-yard line, but he bobbled the ball and Nebraska recovered. "We had a 10-yard (line) rule, unless it was kicked flat," stated James. "Beno actually thought he had recovered the ball, but apparently it was taken away at the bottom of the pile."

In due time, Bryant would have his redemption. In the meantime, that didn't stop Nebraska's Derek Brown from plunging into the end zone, to provide his Cornhuskers with a commanding 21-9 lead. The harrowing din of 76,304 raucous fans rattled Memorial Stadium to its foundation. The Huskies trudged back to the sideline. The clock showed 5:32 remaining in the third quarter. The sway of emotion was all Nebraska's. Several Huskies started shouting at each other along the sideline. They were recalling the bitter pain of the UCLA loss the year before that had cost them the national championship. They had spent so much time training and preparing for this opportunity, and they didn't want to suffer the regret of another lost opportunity for the rest of their lives. Extraordinary examples of leadership suddenly emerged from the 1991 Washington Huskies. It was most manifest when a distraught Beno Bryant slumped upon the bench following his gaffe at the goal line.

"On the TV they showed a picture on the sidelines," said Bryant. "Everyone on the sideline kept coming up and shaking me, saying "C'mon… It'll be OK. It'll be OK". Not one person said anything negative. Everybody was encouraging me... Then suddenly Billy Joe Hobert comes up and grabs my neck. He just looked at me and said matter-of-factly, "We're not gonna lose," and then just walked off… That changed everything for me."

On the ensuing drive, the Huskies faced 3rd down with a daunting 27 yards to go, from the Cornhusker 49. Hobert dropped back and felt tremendous outside pressure. He stepped into the pocket then scrambled straight ahead into the open to pick up 19 yards. Still, it left 4th -down with 8 yards to go. Don James explained that normally for any given situation of down and distance, there would be three play options planned ahead of time. It would usually be up to the coordinator to select which would be called. This 4th down situation called for action from the special teams. But James had the spontaneous urge to strike while the opportunity presented itself.

"I made one change to the plan," said James. "We had moved the ball a bit, and while talking into the headphones, I used that four-letter word and said let's go for it. Gilby (Offensive Coordinator Keith Gilbertson) had already gotten up to go to the bathroom or grab a Coke, and they had to call him back… I was just thinking, 'How many more times are we going to get down there?'"

Beno Bryant recalled that fourth down play with relish. "Gilby called a slot receiver, straight up field. Orlando McKay underneath, and Billy threw a bullet." McKay hauled in the pass for a first down. Soon after that, Beno Brant broke free and scored on a 15-yard touchdown scamper. "It was a roll play", said Bryant. "I took a belly step to the right, and a little crack opened up, and I shot through it for the touchdown."

The deficit was now trimmed to 21-16. The Husky defense stuffed Nebraska in three plays and forced a punt. Washington took over on its own 31-yard line with 13:39 left in the game. The Dawgs proceeded to march 69 yards in 6 plays. Hobert found Orlando McKay with an 8-yard strike. The startled Nebraska crowd suddenly saw the Huskies take a 22-21 lead.

The Cornhuskers started the next drive on their own 40-yard line. But on 2nd down, late Husky linebacker Jaime Fields leveled Nebraska

QB Keith McCant, forcing a fumble and giving the Huskies the ball right back.

Washington marched unabated down the field. Six plays later, Hobert bulled over from the 3-yard line. Washington's lead extended now to 29-21. Nebraska was now thrashing to stay above water. An exuberant Washington team kicked off. Once again it was three downs and out for the Cornhuskers, as all attempts to move the ball against Steve Emtman and the swarming Husky defense proved futile. Nebraska punted, and Washington took over at its own 21-yard line. Nebraska was physically wearing down and time was running short. The Cornhuskers began pulling their linebackers up in an effort to stave off the UW rushing attack. On 3rd and 12, Husky tailback Jay Berry took a handoff and bounced it around right end. A Nebraska linebacker took a poor angle born of fatigue.

Barry bounced off the attempted tackle, and motored through the drawn in Cornhusker secondary, passing jubilant teammates along the sideline for a backbreaking 81-yard touchdown. Said Bryant, "I started running down the sideline alongside Jay, shouting encouragement... I knew he was gone when he took the handoff." As the Huskies celebrated in the end zone and on the sideline, ABC-TV's commentator Keith Jackson depicted the reality. "That was the sound of the door slamming shut."

Jay Barry's run and subsequent extra point by Travis Hanson gave the Huskies the final 36-21 margin. In the final tally, in front of the entire nation, Washington amassed an ungodly 618 yards of offense against the mighty Cornhuskers. Beno Bryant had 139 yards rushing on 17 carries. Jay Berry had 110 yards on 11 carries. Sophomore Billy Joe Hobert, starting just his second collegiate game, completed 23 of 40 passes for 283 yards. Several thousand Nebraska fans rose to their feet and provided Washington with a standing ovation as the Huskies came off the field. Said Nebraska's legendary coach Tom Osborne afterward: "Washington's offense is good. Their defense is superlative. They compare with some of the very best, including Miami in the Orange Bowl three years ago. There will probably be a lot of good teams that won't come as close as we did tonight."

Years later, Don James called this victory in Lincoln the biggest road win of his head-coaching career. "The end of the game was probably the best twenty minutes of football we have ever played," he said. "Especially back then, teams just didn't go into Lincoln and win. It was certainly one of the supreme highlights of my career."

Chapter 39 — October 19, 1991

"Wow... Now This is College Football!"

Washington at California

THE SUFFOCATING HEAT RADIATED off the artificial surface of Berkeley's Memorial Stadium. It compounded Beno Bryant's miseries during pre-game warm-ups. The Husky tailback had been suffering all week from intense head cold pressure and plugged ears. Now, his nose started bleeding, and while standing along the sideline, he fainted and collapsed. Bryant came to a few minutes later, looking into the face of a trainer who suggested that Bryant sit this one out.

"All I remember was getting dizzy and walking over to someone and grabbing on," recalled Bryant years later. "The next thing I know they're sitting me up and telling me to move my legs."

Much depended, however, on this showdown against the 8th-ranked Bears. Washington and Cal were both 5-0, and the Huskies possessed one of a possible 59 first place votes in the USA Today/CNN coaches' poll. The winner would secure the inside track to the Pac-10 Championship and the Rose Bowl berth. Bryant told the trainer he was going to play.

"It was tough," said Bryant. "It was real hot. Cal was ridin' high and the team was hitting. But I was sick, and I felt heavy."

With 2:30 left in the first quarter, Bear quarterback Mike Pawlawski connected with Sean Dawkins on a 59-yard TD strike to put their team up 7-0. It was the first touchdown surrendered by the Husky defense in ten quarters of football, and this one came against Washington's best cornerback — Dana Hall. The Huskies didn't blink, however, and countered immediately with a 35-yard touchdown completion from Billy Joe Hobert to Mario Bailey to tie things up. The game was extremely physical with both teams bringing sky-high intensity. The raucous Berkeley crowd of 74,500 helped to fuel the Bears on. Both teams traded field goals, before a 9-yard touchdown run by Jay Barry enabled the Dawgs to take a 17-10 lead into the locker room.

Despite his ailments and the stifling heat, Bryant had a moment of appreciation during the first half for the scene before him. "The crowd was really into it and very loud," he said. "There was a hill overlooking the stadium that had people sitting up there. And I couldn't understand all of it, but the students were jumping in rhythm and chanting something like this:

"You know the story!

Something something something,

You're in BEAR TERRITORY!"

"And I was like, 'Wow, now *this* is college football!'" recalled Bryant.

The battle resumed in the second half. As Cal's offense approached the line of scrimmage for the final play of the third quarter. Like a bolt of lightening, Bear running back Lindsey Chapman took a handoff and flashed up the middle, racing 68 yards untouched to tie the score 17-17. Entering the fourth quarter the Bears and their fans were sky high. Beno Bryant's Godbrother, Sean, who was seated near the Husky bench, caught Bryant's attention. "He was shouting 'it's your turn, it's your turn.'" Said Bryant. "And I shouted back, 'You just watch!'. Suddenly, a gigantic teammate loomed in front of Bryant.

"Ed Cunningham grabbed me off the bench and threw me back onto the field!" said Bryant.

Three plays later it was 3rd and 11. Bryant took a handoff on a draw play and zipped up the middle through a gaping hole in the Cal line, created partially by Cunningham. Ten yards downfield, Bryant encountered a Cal defender but veered off to the right and was past him and suddenly flying at warp speed down the sideline and into the end zone. The home crowd reacted like it had been walloped in the collective midsection by a Steve Emtman right hook. Placekicker Travis Hanson converted the PAT and the Huskies now led 24-17. But there was still a quarter to play. Beno Bryant peered into the facemask of some of the Bear players. "We saw it in their eyes, in their faces," he said. "They were at the top of the mountain, but could they climb over?"

Two gigantic plays by the Husky defense staved off California's potent offensive attack. First, linebacker Jaime Fields picked off a Mike Pawlawski pass and returned it 29 yards to the Bear 27-yard line. "It was a perfect call by Coach Lambright," said Fields after the game. "I was sitting right there and Pawlawski threw the ball right to me." The second play occurred in the fourth quarter as the Bears drove downfield. Husky linebacker Dave Hoffmann shot through the line on a blitz and smashed into Pawlawski, who fumbled the football then watched helplessly as the Huskies recovered. "It was a call from Coach Lambright," said Hoffmann. "I got a pretty nice hole to run through and when I saw Pawlawski start to raise the ball I just tried to club it. I was fortunate to knock it loose."

The game came down to the nerve-racking final moments late in the fourth quarter. Mike Pawlawski had driven his team to the Husky 23 yard line with eight seconds showing on the clock. After two long passes fell incomplete, there would be one final heave into the end zone. Washington's undefeated season lay in the balance. Pawlawski dropped back to pass and lofted a well-placed ball into the left corner of the end zone. Bryant watched from the sidelines.

"It may not have looked like much on TV," said Bryant. "But from the sideline, Walter Bailey's vertical leap had to be about twenty feet! He really got up there, and knocked the ball away." Washington prevailed 24-17, to run its record to 6-0. The march toward Pasadena continued.

Chapter 40 — November 23, 1991

Perfection

Husky Stadium — Washington vs. Washington State

WSU QUARTERBACK DREW BLEDSOE dropped back in the pocket and scanned the field for his receivers. It was early in the 2nd quarter and Washington was leading by a mere 12-7 count. With the pocket collapsing around him and the roar of the Husky crowd reaching a crescendo, Bledsoe stepped forward and rifled a throw to his left— only to see the ball tipped into the air, and Husky cornerback Walter Bailey snare it and sprint unfettered down the sideline—37 yards for a touchdown. The President of Pasadena's Tournament of Roses was on hand at Husky Stadium, and he exalted at the Washington TD. He was giving high-fives to everyone around him up in the VIP box. The Huskies went for a 2-point conversion and got it, and this upped the lead to 20-7.

For the day, Washington's defense sacked Bledsoe seven times. Husky sophomore quarterback Billy Joe Hobert threw for 236 yards and three touchdowns, including two to acrobatic receiver Mario Bailey. UW linebacker Jaime Fields recorded a safety-producing sack of Drew Bledsoe in the third quarter. His "Compton Quake" dance sent Husky Stadium into deliriums of joy. Quarterback Mark Brunell subbed for Hobert and tallied a rushing touchdown with 3:50 to play in the 4th quarter. Washington led 56-21, as the regular season reached toward closure.

At game's end, Husky fans may have been ecstatic, but the Washington players were fairly matter-of-fact. Roses were passed out along the sideline to the entire team. Around mid-field, a timeless photograph was taken by a *Seattle P-I* cameraman. There were three Husky players posing for the photo, all possessing smiles. Cornerback Dana Hall was holding up two index fingers to signify 11 wins; Defensive lineman Tyrone Rodgers had his fingers contorted to illustrate zero losses; and All-American Steve Emtman has his hand stationed above theirs, with a single index finger extended skyward, to indicate Washington's place in college football's pantheon. The Dawgs had plowed through their season with unmatched ferocity. Aside from the wins over Nebraska and Cal, they had destroyed Stanford 42-7, Kansas State 56-3, Arizona 54-0, Toledo 48-0, Oregon 29-7, Arizona State 44-16 and Oregon State 58-6. This perfect regular season was UW's first since the Gil Dobie days from 1908-1916, when Washington won 39 games in a row and boasted a 63-game unbeaten streak (still a NCAA record).

"I wasn't very pleased with the way we played," said James with stern sincerity, in the aftermath of the Apple Cup. "I don't think we could play like that and expect to win a lot of games." This statement solicited some private chuckles amongst reporters. Particularly galling to James was that Washington was flagged for 11 penalties totaling 109 yards. But the Cougars were flagged for 16 penalties of their own, and turned the ball over six times as well. Washington State did manage to gain more yards than any other team had against UW's defense all season. They racked up 430, stemming mostly from Bledsoe's 334 through the air. But Washington had gained 460 yards themselves, and featured an enviable balance in the process, with 194 rushing and 266 passing.

The double collision course was now set for New Year's Day. Second-ranked Washington (11-0) would be squaring off with third-ranked Michigan (9-1-1) in the Rose Bowl. Top-ranked Miami (11-0) would be confronting fifth-ranked Nebraska (9-2) in the Orange Bowl. Speculation ran rampant across the country as to whether the Huskies or Hurricanes would be crowned national champion.

Chapter 41 — January 1, 1992

"A Great Day in the Life of a Football Coach"

Washington vs. Michigan (Rose Bowl)

AS THE UNDEFEATED HUSKIES practiced for their Rose Bowl showdown with third-ranked Michigan, place-kicker Travis Hanson became unnerved in practices and was having trouble even converting extra-points. This worried Don James to an extent that he brought in former Washington All-American kicker Mike Lansford to try to help Hanson through it. Boosters fretted amongst themselves-what would happen if the Rose Bowl came down to a field goal?

"The kicker wasn't going to decide that game," recalled former Husky and current ESPN broadcaster Ed Cunningham. "Our attitude was, so what? He will miss extra points and field goals—it doesn't matter. As long as he can kick it off, it doesn't matter. Never in my life have I been around anything that focused yet that relaxed the entire time. We just fully trusted what was being taught to us, we fully trusted the game plan. The coaches fully trusted us in executing it. There was just this amazing calm."

At 2:10 PM Pacific Time, the Rose Bowl was packed with 103,566 fans. The rest of the nation gathered around television sets to witness the drama. This game would be followed by the Orange Bowl, featuring

#1 Miami and Nebraska. The National Championship was on the line, as the Rose Bowl's opening kickoff sailed through the air and thousands of flashbulbs popped throughout the crowd. UW Freshman sensation Napoleon Kaufman took it at the five and returned it all the way to midfield. Michigan would force the Washington to punt, but in the trenches, Center Ed Cunningham felt an advantage.

"We were beating the crap out of them," said Cunningham. "I don't think our own coaches realized just how physical we were. On that first drive, their poor nose guard — me and Kris Rongen literally pummeled him into submission. He was done right there."

Michigan took possession. On their third pay from scrimmage, quarterback Elvis Grbac dropped back looking for a receiver. Husky tackle Steve Emtman shoved his blocker backwards and smashed him into Grbac, causing a fumble which was recovered by the Wolverines for a 7-yard loss. Michigan's offensive line had given up only six sacks all season, but would soon surrender six more. Washington regularly sent eight or nine defenders at Grbac, repeatedly knocking him down, causing errant throws, and throttling the running game. "I can't remember being sacked that many times," said Grbac. "Not even in high school. They're ten times better than Notre Dame or Florida State."

Washington led 13-7 in the third quarter, when they mounted a drive inside Michigan's ten yard line. Cunningham came into contact with Michigan's Butkus-award winning linebacker Erick Anderson. "I rolled up on him on the goal line and I grabbed a hold of him and pushed him all the way through the end zone," said Cunningham. "Halfway through the play he said 'Dude, stop, you got me.' The white flag was out."

Soon after, Washington's Billy Joe Hobert dropped back, before rolling to his right looking for a play. Throwing across his body, Hobert connected with tight end Mark Bruener in the back of the end zone for the touchdown. Bruener exhibited incredible coordination—hauling in the catch while maintaining his feet in bounds.

"I actually saw the whole thing," said Cunningham. "As a center, sometimes it's your job to check for blitzing linebackers; if they don't come, you go help out, and you can look downfield. You have to remember that Mark was a true freshman playing in an era when not many true freshmen played. It puts another footnote into why that team did what it did. This is a true freshman— he should not be on the field helping a team win a national championship. But he was good enough to. He was a devastating blocker, an incredibly physical player on the line of scrimmage for a true freshman. Yet he was athletic enough to go make what was an amazing catch. He reaches almost behind his head, and tip-toes on the back of the end line — a beautiful catch."

It was in the fourth quarter, with Washington leading 27-7 that Michigan's Elvis Grbac took the snap and dropped back. He threw a pass to Jesse Johnson on a crossing route. The late Jaime Fields, coming from his linebacker position, viciously walloped Johnson, causing a fumble. Johnson crumpled backwards to the turf and lay motionless for a moment. Fields was immediately beset by exuberant teammates, including close friend and fellow linebacker Dave Hoffmann- who grabbed him and bellowed, "Nice hit, brother!"

"I was eagerly standing on the sidelines and saw that hit," said Cunningham. "That was one of the little mini-stories that went through the team. Jaime wasn't even supposed to play that much that year. That was Brett Collins' position. Brett broke his ankle before two-a-days. Jaime stepped in and played better than anyone thought he would. Jaime was such a great guy, as a teammate, as a competitor, as a guy who worked hard in the classroom. It was one of those exclamation points, like Mark Bruener. That's the way it was supposed to happen."

Soon after, the Huskies stuffed Michigan on fourth down and took possession at the Wolverine 38-yard line. On the next play, Husky backup quarterback Mark Brunell lobbed a beautiful long toss to receiver Mario Bailey at the goal. Bailey dove and rolled in the end zone. The official signaled touchdown, which would extend the lead to 34-7. Bailey immediately jumped to his feet, turned toward the Michigan sideline, and invoked a Heisman pose, taunting Heisman-Trophy winner Desmond Howard. From several vantage points however, it appeared that Bailey may have bobbled the football as he hit the ground.

"We got to the sideline," said Cunningham, "I kind of guessed he didn't catch it. Because of the way he rolled and the ball was kind of loose. I was like— 'Dude you didn't catch that ball did you?' He was like, 'I caught it clean! I caught it clean!' I looked at him, and said (condescendingly), '*Mario?*' He laughed and said, 'I *think* I might have caught it clean.'"

When time ran out, the Huskies had beaten Michigan 34-14. It was a 12-0 campaign—the first perfect season for a Pac-10 team since the 1972 USC Trojans (back in the days of the old Pac-8). The Washington team swarmed the grass turf. Media microphones besieged Coach Don James. The Rose Bowl Trophy presentation took place at midfield. Thousands of Washington fans chanted WE'RE NUMBER ONE! And it echoed throughout the stadium. Later that night, three thousand miles away in the Orange Bowl, Miami whipped Nebraska 22-0. Now, it would be up to the AP and Coaches' polls to determine who was the national champion—Miami or Washington.

The AP votes came in early the next morning, giving the nod to Miami. At 6:30 AM, in the 19th floor suite of the Anaheim Marriot, Don and Carol James waited nervously for the results of the USA

Today/CNN Coaches Poll. Outside their door, a media throng waited along with them. The phone remained silent. Don James turned to his wife, and said: "Its 9:30 on the east coast. Nobody's got the nerve to call us and give us the news."

"We just felt every kind of bitter disappointment," recalled Carol James. "It was unbelievable—the feeling—everything went through our hearts and minds. It was almost like somebody in our family had died. I know that's not fair to compare—we've been through that. But that's the feeling we had—more for the team than for ourselves."

Suddenly, at 9:41 AM, the phone rang. Carol James answered. A representative told her that the Washington Huskies were the number one team in the USA Today/CNN Coaches Poll. She dropped the phone, exclaiming, "Don, you've won it!" Carol immediately began calling family and friends. Don called Mike Lude, as well as Don Heinrich—the legendary Husky quarterback from the early 1950s who was now dying from cancer. "You're a part of this," said an emotional James, to the appreciative Heinrich. Meanwhile, the news rolled through the hotel. Players, friends and family members shouted and cavorted from room to room, and up and down hallways. Back in Seattle, special news reports interrupted radio and television programs to trumpet the news. It was Washington's first national championship in football.

Later that morning, Don James stood on the dais in the ballroom of the Marriot Hotel. His wife Carol sat amongst the dozens of reporters who had congregated. James began to speak, and stunned everyone by starting to cry. "Tears..." he said, pausing to collect himself. "It's so difficult to express the feelings I have for these kids... I don't know what more our kids could have done... It's a great day in the life of a football coach."

"We had been up until 5 AM partying," recalled Cunningham. "It was pure happenstance that I walked into the back of the room of the press conference. I was the only player there. It couldn't have been a more important moment. To see Coach James get emotional was incredibly special. It felt like we were in a room full of strangers. Don James was saying that in all his years of coaching he never looked at individual players during the game, he always looked at the clock, and managed the game. But this time, in the Rose Bowl, he said that halfway through the 3rd quarter he caught himself watching individual players. He looked at Donald Jones run right past their offensive tackle. He looked at Jaime Fields and Dave Hoffmann crushing Michigan's ball carriers. He watched Dana Hall shut down Desmond Howard. He watched Steve Emtman and Tyrone Rodgers dominate Michigan's offensive line. He looked at Mario Bailey and Mark Bruener catching passes and our offense executing so well. And he thought to himself—*'Our guys are better than their guys.'*

"Then at the end of the press conference," said Cunningham, "Coach James and I looked at each other. He pointed and said, 'It's guys like Ed Cunningham that have made this team so special.' We were both tearing up. So for me, that's *the* moment. That is my fondest memory of my entire experience at Washington. That moment is what will make me a Husky forever."

Chapter 42

What the Nation was saying about the Huskies

- "America, say hello to the Washington Huskies. Tucked away all this time in the nation's upper left-hand corner, seemingly three time zones from college football civilization, the No. 2 Huskies finally took center stage at the time that mattered most."

  Bob Glauber, Newsday

- "I don't think Miami could ever beat Washington."

  Michigan QB Elvis Grbac

- "When Florida State lost to Miami, I put Washington #1. I think they're just a hell of a lot better football team than people give them credit for."

  Tony Barnhart, Atlanta Journal-Constitution

- "I saw Washington beat Nebraska and saw them beat California, and to dominate in Lincoln and hold on as they did at Berkeley, just impressed me more than any of the three Miami victories I saw during the season."

  Ivan Maisel, Dallas Morning News

- "No matter how the votes come out, Washington is the best college football team in the land for the 1991 season."

  Patrick Reusse, Minneapolis-St. Paul Star Tribune

- "Forget the AP and USA Today polls. If they took a Defense Poll, Washington would win by a more convincing margin than its 34-14 blowout of poor, overwhelmed Michigan. If this isn't the best defensive unit in Pac-10 history, then it's as close as... well, as the hair on Steve Emtman's close-cropped head."

  Steve Bisheff, Orange County Register

- "I can't envision a better team than Washington's."

  Michigan Head Coach Gary Moeller

- "Push me to the wall, wash my mouth out with soap and then force me to say something or else I'll just waffle. OK. Washington is No. 1."

  Michael Madden, *Boston Globe*

- "When you're growing up, your momma always says 'share.' This is the one time that we don't want to share. But Washington deserves it too."

  Jessie Armstead, Miami Hurricanes linebacker

Chapter 43

A Visit with Napoleon Kaufman

ASK ANY HUSKY FAN born after 1970 who they think is the most exciting player in Washington football history, and Napoleon Kaufman (1991-1994) is the name you will likely hear. Older fans would hasten to add the name of Hugh McElhenny (1949-1951) as being on par with Kaufman, for the sheer level of excitement generated by their electrifying runs.

Napoleon Kaufman was the Reggie Bush of his era. Had Kaufman played at USC or Notre Dame, his national aura probably would have been within shouting distance of Bush's. Kaufman's legs churned with such astonishing rapidity, that one writer likened each leg to a needle in a sewing machine. Kaufman finished his career as Washington's all-time leading rusher—with 4,041 career yards— exceeding runners-up Joe Steele (3,091 yards) and Greg Lewis (2,698 yards). Kaufman was heralded for staying at Washington through his senior season despite the probation. He was a first round pick of the Oakland Raiders in the 1995 NFL Draft.

Stanford strong safety Tommy Knecht once said, "Kaufman is the best running back I've ever played against. He freezes you, so you can't get a good lick on him. Then he blows right by you with his quickness. And he's exceptionally strong for his size. I just don't see any flaws in his game." Added The Seattle Times' *Hugo Kugiya: "Kaufman carrying the football is a musician playing jazz. While others tailbacks run, he creates. Like notes in a solo, his moves just come to him."*

Derek Johnson: In 1991 you came out of Lompoc High School in California considered by many as the top prep running back in the nation. Can you describe the recruiting process and your first encounter with Don James?

Napoleon Kaufman: The first contact I had was from Coach Tormey, and he was the one who recruited me. He did a great job. It was in my senior year that I first had contact with him. Soon after that, Coach James came by my house and that was the first time I got the privilege of meeting him.

Johnson: When Coach James made the in-home visit to your house, were you leaning toward Washington by then? Or was it still up in the air?

Kaufman: It was still up in the air. I was considering going to Nebraska or possibly USC. I was really looking at USC.

Johnson: When was the moment when you informed Coach Tormey and Coach James of your decision to attend the University of Washington?

Kaufman: I made that decision when I was up there on my recruiting trip. It got into my mind that that was where I wanted to go.

Johnson: What was it specifically that enticed you?

Kaufman: I liked the idea of getting away from California. And I just loved the University of Washington and the guys on the football team. I was up there and, it's hard to explain, but I just felt so comfortable. It felt like home.

Johnson: Lincoln Kennedy told me that when he made his recruiting trip to Seattle in December 1987, it was blue sky and about 65 degrees. After he moved up here, he learned that normally it just isn't like that in Seattle in the winter. He said, "I was duped!"

Kaufman: (Laughing) That's exactly what happened to me! Exactly the same thing.

Johnson: Speaking of Lincoln Kennedy, his comment about Don James was: "What can be said about the little man except one word: 'Intimidating.'" When you got to Washington as a freshman and began practicing, with Coach James surveying from up in the tower and all that that entailed, would you say that he was intimidating for you as well?

Kaufman: Well, yes and no. I would say he was intimidating, but for me he was a father figure. For me, I wouldn't say he was intimidating as much as I would say he was fatherly. When I would talk with him, I got the feeling like he really cared for us as players. He reminded me of a father, and I enjoyed that aspect when I spoke with him.

Johnson: What were the best and toughest aspects in playing for Don James?

Kaufman: His standard and expectations. There were things that you could probably get away with when playing for other coaches, but with Coach James you got the feeling like you couldn't get away with stuff.

Johnson: So you're saying that would be the both the best and worst aspect?

Kaufman: Yes, exactly.

Johnson: What was your most poignant moment in relation to Coach James?

Kaufman: I was out at practice one day in my freshman year. Somebody punted a ball. I went back to catch the ball, and it bounced off my helmet, so I obviously muffed the punt. But then, I just laid there on the ground and didn't go try to get the ball. Well, Coach James was standing behind me, and he got so upset. He really let me know that I was at Washington and that type of thing wasn't tolerated there. He said if I dropped a ball like that, I needed to go get it.

Johnson: I want to ask you about a couple of plays from your career. First off, from the 1992 Rose Bowl win over Michigan—you took the opening kickoff and busted it all the way to midfield. You almost broke it all the way. Describe your perspective.

Kaufman: I was kind of disappointed, because I felt like it should have been a touchdown. I was excited that I got as far as I did, but in looking back, I should have taken it to the house. It was the last guy who had a shot, and he dove and grabbed my leg, and that tripped me up just enough. It should have been a touchdown.

Johnson: Imagine that—returning the opening kickoff of the Rose Bowl for a touchdown.

Kaufman: Oh, man! That would have been something.

Johnson: The opening game of the next season against Arizona State in the desert. You guys won 31-7, and you personally racked up 159 yards rushing on six carries, as a sophomore. The first time you touched the football, you went 59 yards for a touchdown. The next day's headline in the Seattle Times read: NAPOLEON MARCHES ON TEMPE. Arizona State Coach Bruce Snyder later recalled: "It was the first option play they ran and it was right in front of me. It was one of those plays where your mouth drops and you watch the guy run by you for a touchdown. Fast. Really fast. My memories of Kaufman center around how hard and tough he plays, how energetic he is and how tough he is."

What do you remember from that night in Tempe?

Kaufman: That game was just amazing. You know, the two tailbacks ahead of me were hurt. Jay Berry had a hurt toe and Beno Bryant had a hurt hamstring. So for me it was an opportunity. On that first long run, the adrenaline was running so high. It was off a pitch from Billy Joe Hobert, and the guys up front blocked everything so well. I just ran as fast as I could to the end zone.

Johnson: In light of the fact that you are now a Pastor, you have so many people looking to you for guidance, so in a sense you're in a similar role as Coach James was.

Kaufman: Yes.

Johnson: Is there anything that you took from his example that you utilize now?

Kaufman: Yes, there are a lot of things that he taught that I carry with me. Even when you're a Pastor in a church, there has to be a standard and level of excellence that you want to convey because we're representing the Lord Jesus Christ. Because His desire to see excellence displayed and presented before people is something that I do use. You know, this is the standard, this is what God has said in his word, and this is way it should be done, and we want to make sure that we honor that and live up to His expectations. For me, in that sense, I do model how Coach James conducted himself. This is the play, this is the way it is supposed to be run, this is who you're supposed to block. Let's get the job done so that we can celebrate when it's all done. That's how I operate.

Johnson: Who were the two or three players that were closest to you on the team?

Kaufman: Beno Bryant, Matt Jones and probably Reggie Reser. And Leon Neal. I enjoyed the times with Beno, joking around and acting silly. And I enjoyed the competition with Leon Neal. That really helped push me to get better. And with Reggie Reser, he was just a nice guy and a good friend. And with Matt Jones, same thing. Plus, I loved the way Matt blocked for me and he was such an encouraging player.

Johnson: When you were a freshman, didn't you use to follow Beno around like a puppy dog?

Kaufman: Oh yes, and he helped me tremendously. In fact, he was inspirational. I loved his toughness and zeal for the game. He was a tough soldier.

Johnson: What about Lincoln Kennedy?

Kaufman: You know, I didn't hang out with Lincoln much.

Johnson: Oh, really? For some reason I thought you did. My Dad said that the thing he always loved was that when you would break a long run and get tackled by a defender, Lincoln Kennedy would always hustle downfield and get the tacklers off of you and pull you to your feet. My Dad loved that.

Kaufman: Yes, both Lincoln and Mark Bruener did that for me a lot.

Johnson: What were your memories with Billy Joe Hobert and Ed Cunningham?

Kaufman: You know, I never really got that close to Billy Joe or Ed. They were older than me, especially Ed. He was a senior when I was a freshman, so I never really got to know him. But I see him on TV as a commentator, he's doing great.

Johnson: That's if you can recognize him!

Kaufman: (Laughs) Yes, Ed's gotten pretty thin. That's right.

Johnson: A couple more names. Mark Bruener.

Kaufman: Oh yea! He was my guy. He was a guy that was such an encourager. He was so consistent and tough. He was a soldier out there. You always knew what you were going to get with Mark.

Johnson: And what about Sipiuli Malamala?

Kaufman: Oh yea, Soupey! He was so good. He was older than me so I didn't get to know him very well. But I enjoyed his tenacity and toughness. He was just a warrior out there.

Johnson: Lastly, can you describe the play where you broke Joe Steele's career rushing record against Ohio State?

Kaufman: You know, believe it or not, as much as breaking that record meant to me, I don't remember the actual specifics of the play. I just can't remember. Do you recall?

Johnson: I believe it was a carry around left end.

Kaufman: For some reason, I don't remember the specifics.

Johnson: As a fiction writer, I could just make it up and say that you broke six tackles en route to a magnificent 98-yard touchdown run.

Kaufman: (Breaks into laughter) Yea!

Johnson: Lastly, what did that record mean to you?

Kaufman: For me, that record is something that I will always cherish. And it's not just my record, it's the offensive line's record too. They were with me on every carry. But to work so hard as a young man, to be aware of all the great athletes that have been through there and to have rushed for more yards than anyone that ever went to that university… Well, it's really humbling. I cherish that and I cherish my time at the University of Washington.

Chapter 44 — September 19, 1992

"One of those Nights to Remember"

Husky Stadium
Washington vs. Nebraska

WASHINGTON FOOTBALL WAS IN the midst of a sixteen game winning streak and also the two-time defending Rose Bowl Champion. Gone was offensive coordinator Keith Gilbertson, who had taken the head coaching job with the Cal Bears. He had been replaced by Jeff Woodruff, who was Don James' son-in-law. The Huskies were 2-0 and ranked #2 in the nation, following wins over Arizona State and Wisconsin. The Nebraska Cornhuskers entered the game highly ranked and unabashedly stating that they were coming to Seattle to avenge their 36-21 loss the previous year back home. They were averaging 559 yards of offense per game, and possessed what their legendary Coach Tom Osborne described as the greatest offensive line he had ever had.

"Nobody on our team had played a game at Husky Stadium that ran into the evening before," former Husky Lincoln Kennedy recalled years later. "Come the day of that game, the weather was so beautiful. It was the anticipation of Nebraska coming to our place, and it being the true point of proving as to whether we could repeat as champions.

"It was one of those nights to remember," said Kennedy. "Because when you came into the stadium, the air was so thick with anticipation, it was almost jubilation. You really had trouble containing yourself. The late afternoon sky had pigments of orange and pink to it, and as it grew dark, the night was so clear. You actually felt like you could do no wrong. Those kinds of moments in life don't come along very often."

73,333 fans filled Husky Stadium, along with the ESPN crew and a horde of national media. In the Husky locker room, safety Tommie Smith was dressed early, well before his teammates. He paced back and forth like a bull as he hyperventilated. Defensive linemen D'Marco Farr and Mike Lustyk continued their superstition of helping each other with their jerseys and eye black. They were 16-0 when carrying this superstition out... Kickoff was drawing near, and Farr and his teammates barked and chanted as they made their way down the tunnel toward the thunderous din of the field.

Washington received the opening kickoff and things got off to an uneasy start. The two defenses battled through the first quarter. Following back-to-back procedure penalties, Nebraska faced 2nd and 12 from their own six-inch line. In effect Washington had nine men on the line of scrimmage, and Nebraska QB Mike Brandt dropped back to pass. Husky safety Tommie Smith flashed in unabated from the right side and blasted Brandt to the end zone turf. The crowd exploded and the Huskies grabbed an unorthodox 2-0 lead.

Key plays were made throughout the first half. Eric Bjornson emerged with 3 catches for 72 yards. Both Napoleon Kaufman and Beno Bryant had touchdown plunges from 1 yard out. And receiver Joe Kralik made a dubious diving reception in the back of the end zone for a 23-7 halftime lead.

Lincoln Kennedy had been all set to do battle with one of Nebraska's star defensive lineman, John Parrella. The Nebraska defensive end had stated publicly that he was eager to battle with Kennedy. But Parrella was injured in the first quarter, and his wet-behind-the-ears replacements were shuttled into the game thereafter. Kennedy was asked which players he went against for the rest of the way.

"I had a montage of gentlemen that I can't remember now," said Kennedy with a chuckle. "It was the one time in my career that I was actually laughing during the game. I had these different guys lining up across from me, and they were literally shaking. I don't know if it was from my reputation or what. They didn't know what to do. You can smell fear on the football field. And they had no clue. And I felt so great out there! I had enough energy to literally play four football games in a row."

The second half was a toe-to-toe defensive slugfest. When the game concluded, the scoreboard read Washington 29, Nebraska 14. The Huskies improved to 3-0 and solidified their position at the top of national picture. In leaving the field and coming back up the tunnel, the jubilant parade of Huskies barked out in unison, "WHOSE HOUSE?... DAWGS' HOUSE!... WHOSE HOUSE?... DAWGS' HOUSE!"

Seattle P-I writer Dan Raley was also heading toward the tunnel when Husky QB Billy Joe Hobert jogged up to him. Raley probably knew what was coming, as he had predicted in a column that Nebraska would win— and should UW win, he wrote, that he would jog one mile for every point the Huskies won by. "What size shoes should I buy ya?" blurted Hobert with a smile. Raley patted his own stomach. "Hey, I do need to work this gut off anyways." Both men then laughed.

A smiling D'Marco Farr was talking to some media: "We laid the '91 defense to rest tonight... Nobody can play like Steve Emtman, but we did a pretty good imitation, didn't we?"

Two other players who had ambled off the field were Washington's Lincoln Kennedy and Nebraska's John Parrella. They were carefree, joking and laughing. Then Kennedy took his helmet in hand and peeled off the **W** decal, giving the adhesive to his counterpart. Parrella took it back home to Nebraska, where he would plaster it upon his locker for the rest of the 1992 season.

Washington had improved to 3-0, and the following Monday they ascended to #1 in the national polls. It seemed like the good times were going to last forever. But life never works like that. On the distant horizon, ominous storm clouds were gathering. Within the next few weeks and months, the monolith of Husky football would prove true the saying: *The bigger they are, the harder they fall.*

Chapter 45, October 31, 1992

Dissolution

I REMEMBER THAT FINAL DAY of glory from the Don James era, an overcast Halloween afternoon at Husky Stadium, October 31, 1992. I was with my Dad, in our seats upon the steep tier of the north upper deck. Washington was trailing #15 Stanford 7-0. But the Husky defense had just stopped the Cardinal offense cold and forced a punt. Back deep to receive was sophomore sensation Napoleon Kaufman. As the ball sailed through the air and began its descent toward Kaufman's waiting arms, the stadium pulsated in anticipation. Kaufman caught the ball, accelerated forward and broke through a seam. He darted and zipped 65 yards to the Stanford 4-yard line. It was an electrifying return. This play brought my Dad and I to our feet, and the whole stadium crowd to a delirious frenzy. Two plays later, fullback Leif Johnson plunged across the goal line. Those were the first of what would be forty-one consecutive points scored by the Dawgs.

Washington would go on to thrash Stanford 41-7. The football program unwittingly stood at its apex. The Huskies were 8-0 and ranked #1 in the nation. They were the defending national champions. They had won twenty-two straight games and two consecutive Rose Bowls. The program was loaded with talented players who possessed an obsessive work ethic. And they were led by one of the top coaches in America. But it was all about the change.

The hometown newspaper, *The Seattle Times,* had been clandestinely at work on a blockbuster story. For the past month, *The Times* had been following an anonymous tip and allocated resources for two prize-winning investigative reporters to dig into the background of star quarterback Billy Joe Hobert. It was during an interview with Hobert that the reporters duped him into divulging details of his financial struggles, among other personal troubles. What Hobert's statements seemed to confirm was the largest improper loan to a student-athlete in college football history.

Five days after the Stanford game, on November 5, 1992, *The Times* headline blared "HUSKIES' HOBERT GOT $50,000 LOAN." Hobert had actually received three loans totaling $50,000 from a wealthy Idaho scientist named Charles Rice, who it was later determined had no connection with the University of Washington. The article revealed that Hobert had gone on a wild spending spree, purchasing a Camaro, golf clubs and bankrolling wild weekends with his friends. He spent it all in just a few months. But NCAA rules stipulate that its amateur athletes cannot receive loans based on potential future earnings. It seemed self-evident to most that Rice loaned the $50,000 based on the likelihood of Hobert's future in the NFL.

Suddenly, the bloom was coming off the Husky rose. Speculation raged on the potential penalties facing Washington. UW Athletic Director Barbara Hedges promptly suspended Hobert, pending an internal investigation. This decision ended Hobert's collegiate career. Don James was preparing his team for #23-ranked Arizona, and was clearly irritated at being besieged by reporters about the Hobert case. Especially galling to him were the assumptions he should have known his QB had received a personal loan of that magnitude.

"If he's violated rules, then there would be discipline," said James at the time. "But I don't have any rules that say what the hell players do with their lives. That's not my job. We have academic rules, we have NCAA rules for eligibility, but I'm not a judge. There's a lot of things that players do. I let them walk around with cellular phones, wear earrings, which I don't particularly enjoy. But I don't run their lives."

Two days later in the Tucson desert, an exhausted and dehydrated Dave Hoffmann looked around Arizona Stadium as the final minute of the game ticked off the clock. The Wildcat fans were surging forward and about to rush the field. Arizona needed only snap the football once more—then celebrate their 16-3 win over #1 ranked Washington. Not only was Arizona avenging losses of 54-10 and 54-0 to the Huskies the past two years, they were also snapping Washington's record 22-game winning streak. "We played a great defensive game and we knew we had to because our offense really struggled that day," recalled Hoffmann. "We, on defense, felt like we needed to score somehow, and we just couldn't get it done. I remember my teammates Jamal Fountaine and D'Marco Farr coming up to me after we broke the huddle for the last time, there were only a few seconds left, and they told me that they loved me, and gave me a big hug. They came to me because it was the end of a long string of dominating victories and they knew how I felt. I really appreciated them. It was a momentous occasion."

The Huskies returned to Seattle with an 8-1 record. As daily speculation raged in the media of a pending Hobert investigation, Washington had two more games left to their regular season. The following Saturday, they throttled Oregon State 45-16, before traveling the next week to Pullman for the Apple Cup. As the Huskies slipped and slid across the icy turf of Martin Stadium, Cougar quarterback Drew Bledsoe lit up the snowy skies with a brilliant passing performance—leading Mike Price's Cougars to a 42-23 upset.

On the bright side, Washington boasted a 9-2 record and had captured its third consecutive Pac-10 title and Rose Bowl berth.

However, the next ten months would be an extended period of ugly headlines and anxiety. On November 19th, linebacker Danianke Smith was arrested for four counts of drug possession. On December 6th, the *Seattle Times* ran another exposé, this time detailing alleged jobs benefits given to players during the summer by two Los Angeles-based Husky boosters. On December 9th, *The Los Angeles Times* featured a headline on their front page, posing the condemning question: "WASHINGTON FOOTBALL—A PROGRAM GONE AWRY?" The article, written by Danny Robbins and Elliott Almond, was the first of a series alleging booster violations at Washington. These violations involved boosters making payments to players for jobs requiring little or no work; defensive tackle Dennis Brown's undisputable use of a truck registered to a booster; free lodging for players during the summer and a summer's job arranged by a booster while a prospective recruit was still in high school; and Jim Heckman, then-publisher of *Sports Washington,* was allegedly involved in attempting to coerce a WSU player to transfer to Washington. What wasn't emphasized in the article was that the majority of allegations came from former Huskies who had lost lawsuits against the UW, including two who had been kicked off the team for improper behavior.

In mid-December, the Pac-10 Conference officially notified Washington that it was opening up a formal investigation of its football program. Don James was growing weary of the daily questions from the media about Billy Joe Hobert. He even swore at an ESPN reporter named Mark Schwarz, who had tried to goad James into responding to President William Gerberding's statement that Husky football was embarrassing him with its negative headlines.

• • •

One would think that any Rose Bowl appearance would be a momentous occasion. However, on January 1, 1993, the sixth and final Rose Bowl of Don James' career got underway to relatively little fanfare. For the fourth time, he would be facing Michigan in Pasadena. The Huskies took a 21-17 lead into halftime, thanks in part to a deep, magnificent touchdown throw from Mark Brunell to freshman receiver Jason Shelley. But Michigan tailback Tyrone Wheatley opened up the second half by busting loose on an 88-yard touchdown gallop, and would finish the day with 235 yards on a mere 15 carries. Husky quarterback Mark Brunell led the team with his 308 yards passing, but with Washington struggling mightily to run the football, it wasn't enough. Michigan beat Washington 38-31. As the game ended, Wolverine quarterback Elvis Grbac raised his arms in triumph as he jogged toward the enthusiastic Michigan fans. The Wolverines had denied Washington a three-peat.

Some Huskies fumed afterward. "That loss hurt because we were in position to make history, to win three Rose Bowls in a row," recalled fullback Darius Turner years later. "(Offensive Coordinator) Jeff Woodruff called a crap game. He was in love with the option. Running wide was just not working. We players just wanted to smash it right up the middle. But he kept running us wide, and it wasn't working. There is no way we should have lost that game. We were a better team than Michigan. After the game, me and Mark Brunell ran to the locker room, and we were saying, 'Let's get these fucking uniforms off!' We were so pissed."

Six months later, the Pacific-10 Conference charged the University of Washington with 24 allegations of varying degree. They provided the media with a 100-page dossier of alleged wrong-doings, mainly involving Billy Joe Hobert, Husky boosters and manipulated expense reports by student hosts. The bulk of the allegations stemmed from the five former players interviewed by the *Los Angeles Times.*

"I'll be frank," said Don James to *Bitter Roses* author Sam Farmer in July 1993. "I read this and was very disturbed by the first part. Then when I read the responses of the people that were named, I felt much better."

On August 9th through 11th, officials from the University of Washington traveled to San Francisco to meet with the Pac-10 Compliance and Enforcement Committee. The committee then passed along its recommendations to the Conference Council of Athletic Administrators, who voted on penalties and what corrective action to take. Finally, the Presidents and chief executive officers at each of the other nine Pac-10 schools voted on whether to ratify the judgment. The decision was going to be announced eleven days later.

By the morning of Sunday, August 22, 1993, the media, fans and Husky players believed that Washington would be hit with a one-year penalty. *The Seattle Times'* Blaine Newnham speculated on what might have caused the investigation in the first place, by citing a study by economists at George Mason University. The economists suggested that the NCAA uses investigations and penalties as a way of maintaining the status quo, for benefiting the powerful schools at the expense of their rivals. Their study indicated that college programs are more likely to be investigated if they dramatically improve, thus threatening the balance of power and cash flow. Wrote Newnham: "Washington, winning three straight Rose Bowl berths and a national title while accumulating a surplus of $20 million, did that. And why the Los Angeles Times started investigating Washington is not certain. But it is known that former USC Athletic Director Mike McGee was the UW's most outspoken critic in Pac-10 circles... No matter its origin, the investigations did find the Huskies guilty of poor management of their boosters and basically sloppy accounting procedures. In the end they gained a competitive advantage. The Pac-10 could have buried Washington, but apparently has chosen not to."

But the Pac-10 did decide to bury Washington. The Pac-10 crippled the Huskies with two years of probation, a two-year ban on bowl game appearances, a loss of $1.4 million in television revenue, a loss of ten scholarships for both the '94 and '95 recruiting seasons, and a 50% reduction in paid recruiting visits for the next two seasons. These represented the most severe penalties ever handed out by the Pac-10 toward one of its member teams. The Pac-10 would also allow the Huskies to appear on television for the 1993 season, but deny all profits to the University of Washington, as generated by those TV appearances.

Everyone along the west coast was stunned by the news. Jim O'Fallon and Jerry Kingston, the Pac-10 council's two chief inspectors, met with the media to discuss the severe sanctions they were handing down. While it was determined that Billy Joe Hobert's $50,000 loan was inappropriate because it was predicated on forecasted NFL riches, O'Fallon said it was "inconclusive" whether Husky coaches and officials should have been aware of the loan's existence. However, the investigation did uncover numerous smaller infractions. These predominantly involved Los Angeles-based booster Jim Kenyon. *Sports Washington* founder Jim Heckman was cleared by the council of any major infractions.

The report went on to conclude: "Had the athletics department and, in particular, the members of the football coaching staff made even the most cursory examination of that jobs program during the 10 years of its operation, they would have discovered the violations... At the same time the Los Angeles program was operating without controls, the athletics department staff was operating a fairly well-controlled program in the Seattle area. Violations arising out of the Seattle program were generally isolated and few in number. Since a significant number of football student-athletes were recruited from the Los Angeles area each year and many of them were employed by one representative of the university's athletics interests, the university's monitoring program should have been extended to that area despite the distance from the institution's campus."

A little later that Sunday morning, KOMO-TV's Bob Rondeau suddenly dropped the second bomb of the day. Facing the camera with a glum expression, Rondeau broke the news that Don James was resigning as coach of the Washington Huskies. A press conference was hastily scheduled for that afternoon at the University of Washington. Athletic Director Barbara Hedges and Defensive Coordinator Jim Lambright soon sat side-by-side under the bright lights, gazing upon the assemblage of media. Hedges, looking weary with strain, announced that she had just promoted Lambright to interim Head Coach. She then read from a prepared statement by Don James, which concluded by saying: "I have decided I can no longer coach in a conference that treats its members, its coaches and their players so unfairly. We have suffered for nearly ten months from media character assassination. By looking at the penalties, it appears we are all guilty, based in large part upon statements of questionable witnesses."

The news of the sanctions and of James' resignation quickly became a national story. Two days later, the *Seattle P-I* simultaneously ran contrary opinions from John Owen and Art Thiel. John Owen defended the Washington program, stating: "I'm no Sherlock Holmes. I can't even solve the mystery in the *Naked Gun*. Here's my problem: I not only haven't discovered the smoking gun, I can't even find the corpse. Are you sure there has been a murder? The conference report released yesterday said UW coaches and officials were ignorant of (Hobert's) loans. They said `*it is inconclusive whether they should have known*.' Then what did the Pac-10 council conclude from its lengthy investigation into Husky sports? Among other things they said was that the UW Athletic Department `*is not an outlaw*.' The school was `*entirely forthcoming and supportive*' of the investigation. And there was `*no evidence the University of Washington set out to achieve a competitive advantage*' over other Pac-10 schools by illegal means."

Owen went on to point out that there was no evidence that any

Husky coach willfully violated a major NCAA sanction. There were no cases of sports cars being given to blue chip recruits, no bogus grades to keep players eligible, and no under-the-table payments to players or their parents.

Concluded Owen: "Do you know what charge they hung on the Huskies? Failing to keep accurate records of the chump change players are allowed to spend while entertaining visiting athletes... Husky rivals know that James is not a cheat. But that's the label the Pac-10 pinned on him yesterday."

Art Thiel had a different take. He called James a quitter. "No matter his high-sounding rationale," said Thiel, "James committed an act of cowardice he would not respect in any of his players or assistants... It is not the first time James has missed the cruel facts of college sports. Those who have talked to him say he has refused to believe nearly all of the Pac-10 charges. For James to believe any of them would mean someone in whom he bestowed trust betrayed him. To James' way of thinking, that is almost a mortal blow. It is also a mistake in his judgment.

"For (his players), James nailed himself to the cross," said Thiel. "Dying for the sins of the Pac-10, and maybe somehow saving their souls. I wish he had left the soul-saving to a higher authority. The players could have used him on the field. Instead, he quit to make a point that will be little understood and not well-remembered."

Hundreds of fans sent letters during the week to the editors of the *Seattle Times* and *Seattle P-I*. One of them was written by Larry Michael—the back-up tight end who caught the winning two-point conversion to beat Michigan in 1983. "Something seriously wrong happened last Sunday," wrote Michael. "A fine man and a great football program was rendered a tremendous injustice, and I'm having a hard time accepting it. It was an honor and a privilege to play for Coach James, a man of integrity, wisdom and honesty. The ideals he installed in me about life I hold dear to this day. I feel sorry for the guys who will never get the chance that I did."

A man named Mark Thompson wrote: "Although I live in Seattle, I remain a diehard Oregon State fan. I have rooted for the Huskies in recent years, except when they play OSU. They have done much good for the Pac-10. I have never been ashamed of the Pac-10 until today."

From an AP story coming out of Ames, Iowa, Don James' old rival-- former Washington State Cougar Coach Jim Walden-- expressed his thoughts. "When a conference can beat you up that bad, it's like eating your young," Walden said. "It's almost like police brutality that the Pac-10 Conference would go beyond the law... Look what they did to this man. They hung this man. They put the death penalty on Don James, one of the most highly respected people in our profession. They made him look like a slithering thief. They beat that guy up that badly for what he's done for that conference, and you have people say he should stay and fight. My question to you is, how much crap would you take?"

• • •

All that week, under a deluge of interview requests, James granted only three. The first was to play-play announcer Bob Rondeau, the second to *Husky Highlights* host Keith Shipman, and the third to John Owen of the *Seattle P-I*. "The Rose Bowl itself isn't the issue," said James in his interview with Owen. "It's denying us the opportunity to compete for a championship. The conference's decision stripped our players of the chance to compete for a championship this year through hard work and sacrifice. Right now, our players are going through two-a-days. They're doing weight training. It's an unbelievable amount of work and sacrifice. The thought they might be deprived of the chance to compete for a championship really upset me. And then we got a two year bowl ban! I couldn't accept that."

James was also galled by an "informed source" on the Pac-10 council who suggested that the penalties meted out to Washington were exceedingly harsh because of the Huskies' reputation for arrogance.

"That really frustrates me," said James. "I am not an arrogant person. You've read (inflammatory) quotes from opposing coaches and players before and after they have played our teams. I don't think you've ever heard that kind of talk from our coaches or players. It's something we have continually stressed. Our teams play with confidence. But they're not arrogant."

John Owen noted that during the interview, James only hesitated once—when James was asked if Gerberding could have done more to help the team and the program.

"I don't think I want to go into all that," said James.

• • •

Now with the season-opener against Stanford only ten days away, newly-appointed Head Coach Jim Lambright had work to do. He arrived at the Graves building and walked into his office—to find it empty. He discovered that Don and Carol James had already cleaned out the Head Coach's office—and Lambright's staffers had transferred his stuff. "Along with everything else," said Lambright to a reporter, "I come in and the office is different."

That afternoon, the grunts and thwacking of shoulder pads echoed through Husky Stadium during practice. Lambright wandered from drill to drill, keeping an eye on the proceedings. Across the field along the far sideline, Don James's tower stood empty and silent.

Chapter 46

The Past is not Dead

IT WAS ON OCTOBER 7, 1995 that the Seattle sports scene tilted on its axis. That was the afternoon at Husky Stadium that Washington led Notre Dame 21-14 with 3:00 left. But Washington punter John Wales muffed a deep snap and the Fighting Irish recovered and quickly scored a touchdown. Then, as Notre Dame lined up for the go-ahead two point conversion, the Husky defense failed to cover Irish wide receiver Derrick Mayes. Quarterback Ron Powlus spotted this, and made the easy toss to Mayes. Washington mounted one last drive, but Notre Dame's Allen Rossum returned a Damon Huard interception for another score, and the Irish escaped Seattle with a 29-21 victory.

For the Husky Nation, the loss decimated the team's mighty aura. In shocking fashion, Washington had choked away a big game at Husky Stadium. After all, the Dawgs had won 24 of their previous 25 games at home, often by huge margins. *This wouldn't have happened if Don James was here,* shell-shocked fans were heard to mutter, as they filed out of the stadium. But just a few hours later and a few miles south at the old Kingdome, glum would turn to glee. Seattle Mariner Edgar Martinez stepped into the batter's box in a confrontation with the ace closer of the New York Yankees, John Wetteland. It was the eighth inning of Game 4 of the American League Division Series. Seattle had the bases loaded, with the game knotted at 6-6. Martinez worked the count to 2 balls and 2 strikes. Then Wetteland went into the stretch, and came in with a fat pitch over the heart of the plate. Martinez pounced on it like a cat, and blasted the ball deep into center field. As Martinez dropped his bat and began running up the first base line, he watched the ball descend and disappear over the wall into the deepest reaches of the ballpark. He rounded the bases with a clenched fist raised high, as the moment was celebrated by the frenzied cheering of 55,000 delirious fans. The Mariners would win that contest, and the next day's game too, in equally dramatic fashion, to beat the dreaded Yanks 3 games to 2.

The choke job against Notre Dame and that one swing of Edgar Martinez's bat made two things incontrovertibly clear: First, the Seattle Mariners had just supplanted the Washington Huskies as the #1 love in the hearts of Puget Sound sports fans. And second, Jim Lambright, regardless of his strengths or weaknesses as a head coach, would never be able to escape the long shadow of expectations cast by the Don James Era.

In subsequent years, it was as if Don James was the keeper of some sort of old-time religion. James' last three UW teams went to Rose Bowls, and *that* was the measuring stick by which Husky fans judged all future seasons. People tended to underestimate the heavy toll that sanctions took upon the program. But Lambright's fire-from-the-hip coaching mentality periodically angered rivals and embarrassed Tyee boosters. In turn, those boosters would apply continuous pressure to Athletic Director Barbara Hedges. And as the years went by, the embarrassing losses mounted. The Huskies were humiliated twice on national TV—the first a 54-20 drubbing by Notre Dame in 1996, and the second a 55-7 thrashing by Nebraska in 1998. But even worse, was the series of excruciating losses to the up-and-coming Oregon Ducks. Whether he realized it or not, Lambright was skating upon thin ice.

A blowout loss to Air Force, in Hawaii's 1998 Oa'hu Bowl, proved to be the breaking point. Three days later, Hedges summoned Lambright into her office. They loathed each other, and the meeting was terse.

Lambright's firing lasted only five minutes. After thirty years as a player, assistant coach and head coach at Washington, Lambright was told to clean out his office and turn in his keys. He is remembered most for keeping the program together during the probation years, and for overseeing a great moment in Washington history, the so-called "Whammy in Miami." That was in 1994, when the Huskies dominated the Hurricanes 38-20, and ending Miami's NCAA-record 58-game home winning streak.

When Barbara Hedges announced the surprise hiring of Rick Neuheisel in January 1999, as the next Husky football coach, she beamed almost uncontrollably at the press conference. Neuheisel was hip and glib, and boasted openly of transforming Washington into "the Florida State of the West." Provisionally, he succeeded. He guided the Huskies through a series of inexplicable comeback wins in 2000 and won the Rose Bowl over Purdue.

But by 2002, Husky football was floundering. Neuheisel's reputation was starting to catch up with him, involving a myriad of minor recruiting infractions. The upperclassmen like Jerramy Stevens and Willie Hurst complained bitterly in private that the new recruits Neuheisel was bringing in lacked the discipline and talent of past Husky classes. And by November 2nd, immediately following an embarrassing home loss to UCLA, the team was 4-5. The Dawgs were also dead last in the Pac-10 in rushing offense, at 79 paltry yards per game. Once again came forth the familiar cry from the multitudes: *This never would have happened under Don James.* This disillusionment was on display following the UCLA game, at the post-game tailgate known as the 5th Quarter. Neuheisel entered the Dempsey Indoor Center and made his way to the stage. He was greeted by sporadic clapping and a handful of boos. His usual glibness was as absent as Washington's running game. Neuheisel's face carried the expression of just having witnessed a horrific accident. Microphone in hand, he pleaded with the crowd to not give up on him. He pledged that the Huskies would once again play tough defense and rush the ball with authority. He left the stage and exited the Dempsey Indoor to smattering applause.

Seven months later, Neuheisel was gone. Barbara Hedges, looking distraught beneath the glare of media lights, announced the firing of Neuheisel for lying to NCAA investigators, and wagering thousands of dollars in a NCAA basketball pool. Neuheisel would subsequently file and win a lawsuit against the University of Washington. He garnered a hefty financial settlement, but his days as Washington's coach were over.

Transitions are always difficult, but the situation that offensive coordinator Keith Gilbertson was thrust into was damn near impossible. He had inherited the job by default, a mere three months before the season-opener against national champion Ohio State. Many Husky players rebelled or would not conform, as they were used to Neuheisel's country club atmosphere rather than the toughness Gilbertson was trying to instill.

By October 30, 2004, the deteriorating situation had Gilbertson overwhelmed. The losses were piling up like fallen timber from the Mt. Saint Helens explosion, and the landscape of Husky football was scarred and barren much the same. Gilbertson was coming undone—exploding at his players, reporters and assistant coaches, and storming out of meetings. In the latest pratfall, Washington had just been dumped by Oregon 31-6 in Eugene, in which the Huskies committed seven turnovers. What made it worse, Duck fans weren't much reveling in the win. It had come so easily. On Oregon's post-game radio show, the anxiety-ridden fans were *complaining* about how putrid the Ducks had played. It spoke to a surreal truth. For almost a century, the Ducks had been the little brother that the Huskies kicked around. But now, Washington didn't even have Oregon's respect.

Gilbertson slumped against a concrete wall in the visitor's dressing room of the newly-expanded and refurbished Autzen Stadium. "It's a nightmare that we keep reliving," he sighed.

Two days later, Gilbertson choked back tears at a press conference, announcing that he was stepping down. But everyone knew that it was only to avoid being fired by new UW Athletic Director Todd Turner. Turner had replaced Barbara Hedges. Hedges had been forced out by boosters, who decried her incompetence and unwillingness to emphasize and invest fully in football. When the 2004 season finally and mercifully ended, Gilbertson packed up his office. He told a reporter, "I love Husky football. I grew up going to Husky Stadium. This 1-10 season is something I will have to live with for the rest of my life."

• • •

That same year, I was researching an article for *Sports Washington* about former Husky Coach Jim Owens. I interviewed one of Owens's former players—the legendarily tough running back Don McKeta, who led the Huskies to back-to-back Rose Bowl Championships in the early 1960s. At one point, McKeta and I lamented the current downward spiral of Husky football. In a little more than a decade, Washington had gone from 12-0 to 1-10. McKeta's voice grew bitter.

"When the team was put on probation and Don James walked away from it -- the program has suffered tremendously ever since then," said McKeta. "You name me another coach who walked out on his team two weeks before the season began. A lot of people feel the same way as I do. At least Lambright had some credibility, but Neuheisel had zero credibility. There are a lot of things that have to change and heal around here before we can get the good players again."

I felt disheartened that the legacy of Don James was tarnished. Through the years since his retirement, James had kept a relatively low profile, but continued to attend Husky games and support the team. I yearned to know exactly what had occurred in August 1993. Awhile after the McKeta interview, I talked to a prominent UW Tyee booster and told him of McKeta's comments. "He's been going around saying that stuff for awhile," said the booster. "And let me tell you--that act is starting to wear thin with Don James." I asked the booster if James would now want to finally tell his side of the story. "No, I wouldn't go anywhere near that with him," said the booster. "That whole sanctions thing is still a sore spot with Don. That would be a big mistake. I don't see any reason to risk getting him upset with you."

After mulling it over, I decided to ask. I called Don James, and he graciously agreed to meet me at Husky Stadium for a ninety-minute interview. I had no idea what would happen. I had interviewed him twice before, but on the phone. Come the morning of the interview, I stood at a window inside the dimly-lit Don James Center, looking out into an empty Husky Stadium. I glanced at my watch, and just as it became 8:00 AM, I heard the doors open behind me. In walked a smiling Don and Carol James. We shook hands and sat down at a table by a window. I turned on my tape recorder and started asking questions.

That interview and subsequent muckraking unearthed the real story. Don James wasn't the gutless quitter that many people accused him of being. And while it was true that the Pac-10 maliciously hamstrung the Huskies with severe sanctions, the damage couldn't have been inflicted without aid from an enemy within. It pointed to an immutable fact of life. *To protect the sheep, you've got to catch the wolf-- and it takes a wolf to catch a wolf.* Mike Lude, with all his power and connections throughout the NCAA, would have been the protective wolf for Husky Football. But he was gone. He had been unceremoniously fired and replaced by the inexperienced Barbara Hedges. And Hedges proved to be a sheep protecting sheep. The Pac-10, sensing their opportunity to level the playing field, closed in for the easy kill.

The real story behind this downfall could be foreshadowed back to the mid-1980s. That's when the President of the United States, Ronald

Reagan, came to Seattle with the request that Don James introduce him at a fund raiser. James did just that, providing Reagan with a signed football in the process. A month later, Vice President George H.W. Bush made the same request, in a visit to West Seattle. Don James fulfilled that request, and that was when the Seattle media became inflamed. Immediately thereafter, callers besieged James's office for days on end.

Meanwhile, behind closed doors, University of Washington President William Gerberding was furious. He stalked back and forth, screaming obscenities about Don James and Mike Lude. Gerberding already felt that the nation's universities should not be providing mass entertainment to the American public. Some of his viewpoints made perfect sense. But the trouble was that he also seethed over Lude's power, influence and visibility, as related to his own. Gerberding was the head figure of a liberal academic institution. He had, after all, once issued an official apology to Communist sympathizers who were allegedly persecuted by the UW in the years following World War II. So to hear news that his university's football coach introduced a Republican President was, for him, an abomination.

Those were the reasons why Gerberding began tightening the noose around Lude's neck, sabotaging the athletic department in petty little ways; like demanding that no prayers take place in the Husky locker room, and forcing out beloved basketball coach Marv Harshman, and pressuring Lude to donate some of the athletic department's $20 million surplus to the University of Washington. Ultimately, Gerberding forced Lude out too and replaced him with an inexperienced woman who didn't view football as a priority. In the final analysis, Gerberding's idealistic hard stance and bloated sense of self-importance would be why Don James saw no alternative but to step down as head coach of the Washington Huskies.

Chapter 47

The Roses of Wrath

A Decade after Sanctions, Former Washington Coach Don James Opens Up

Sports Washington magazine, October 2004

IT WAS IN AUGUST 1993, a Sunday afternoon in Issaquah, that I was driving down a tree-lined street dappled in sunlight, listening to the Mariner game, when announcer Dave Niehaus became aghast and made the incredulous announcement. "Well, for crying out loud," stated Niehaus in his rich baritone voice. "Over at the University of Washington, they have just announced that Husky coach Don James has resigned in protest of the sanctions levied by the Pacific-10 conference." Then he said slowly, almost painfully, "My.. Oh... My."

Earlier that day, Washington players were involved with fall camp and had congregated for a standard team meeting. When Don James entered into the room, several players picked up that something was wrong; James seemed uncharacteristically somber. He proceeded to tell them that the Pac-10 Conference had put Washington on a two-year probation. For the '93 and '94 seasons, there would be no hopes for a bowl game. The Pac-10 would also be confiscating $1.4 million of TV revenue for the first year, and the Huskies would be docked 20 scholarships. The Washington Football Program, in the throes of three consecutive Rose Bowl berths and deemed by all to be the colossus of the Pac-10 Conference, was having its legs cut out from under it.

Then James announced to his players that he was resigning in protest. The room fell deathly silent.

Recently one quiet morning I interviewed Don James at Husky Stadium. At one point our discussion revolved around the sanctions period, and I asked him what it was like to address the team on that August day in 1993.

"It was terrible," James said quietly. "I knew what I was going to do and they didn't. And the hardest part was to tell them that we got a two-year hit. And I told them that I was going to resign and recommend Jim Lambright as head coach. It was tough. There were a lot of tears shed."

A subsequent news conference was held, featuring then-Athletic Director Barbara Hedges, newly appointed head coach Jim Lambright and four Husky captains. One Husky co-captain, center Jim Nevelle, summed up the youthful sentiments of the Washington squad: "It was probably the saddest thing I have gone through in a long time. Coach James has been like a father figure to all of us. I want everyone to know that whoever went out and took this man out of office, tomorrow morning I want them to wake up and look in the mirror and realize what they did."

For 18 years Don James had stood stoically along the Washington sideline. He was a symbol of integrity, discipline, principle— and most importantly to fickle fans, an icon of tough defense and consistent victories. In the years following that traumatic time, due to his conservative and private nature, Don James has never publicly gone into detail of his perspective of what happened.

Prior to the Pac-10's announcement, Husky fans felt that some sort of minor penalty was inevitable. But when the media announced the severe nature of the sanctions, and the subsequent resignation of James, thousands of Husky fans were stunned and plunged into mourning. The sanctions were enough to arouse anger and disbelief, but losing Don James so abruptly was like suffering a death in the family. The end of his career came without ceremony or a sense of complete closure.

In the time leading up to his resignation, then athletic director Barbara Hedges received a list of the proposed sanction penalties from the Pac-10. The University of Washington would have ten days to appeal them. Don James goes on to describe his final days as Husky coach.

"I had the sanctions in my hand for a week," he recalled. "Barbara got them from the Pac-10, and we had a week to appeal these sanctions and they were not bad at all. We lost some recruiting visits, which was no big deal because we never needed all the recruiting visits. They were going to take scholarships away; well everyone across the country was losing 5 scholarships. The big one was that they weren't going to give us TV revenue (about $2.8 million.) They wanted our money. We'd made this league so damn much money. They didn't want to take us off TV. They wanted that money.

"I went before the players each day, I had the sanctions in my pocket, and I'd say to them: "They're going to take visits, does that bother you? They're going to take scholarships, does that bother you? They're going to take TV money, do YOU get any of that TV money? Does that bother you?"

At this point James' voice lowers further, to a near whisper: "I said to the players; now... they may not let us compete for a championship. I said, you know, we've been to three straight Rose Bowls. But in eleven games this thing is all over, life goes on. That would be the harshest thing they could do."

"So I sat in a meeting in Barbara Hedges' office with some upper campus people, and we talked about the appeal," said James. "My argument was, while we're appealing it, let's let these players compete for a championship. Because there are no coaches' sanctions."

Don James left that meeting with the understanding that the University of Washington would be appealing the ban on bowl games, and thus forgo the two years of TV money. It made sense too, even from a financial standpoint, since it was Washington's football program that had generated the athletic department's $20 million surplus. Keeping it healthy would keep the whole athletic department healthy over the long haul. But when Washington officials went down to San Francisco to meet with Pac-10 officials, something else occurred.

Don James was at his son's house Saturday evening of that week. The phone rang; Barbara Hedges was calling. It was when James picked up the receiver that he learned he had been betrayed. The agreement that he believed had been struck with the four-member committee from the University of Washington had been reneged upon; the UW reps had gone to San Francisco with a different agenda.

"Well they go down and appeal TV revenue," said James. "And I couldn't get this out of anybody on our campus, but I got this from other people who sat in those meetings. And the appeal from our university was, if you take our TV money, it's going to impact non-revenue sports or women's activities. If you're sitting in that meeting, with all these PhDs sitting there, it's wonderful, we'll just give you back half the TV money and instead give you two years probation (for the football team). And so when Barbara called me Saturday night at my son's house, I told her, Barbara, if they don't change that, I'm done. The NCAA had nothing to do with that penalty; it was all our university and the Pac-10."

Before the penalties could be finalized, they needed to be ratified by a vote of the University Presidents from around the league, including University of Washington President Bill Gerberding. But stated Don

James, "I understand that Dr. Gerberding didn't even go to that meeting, he voted by phone or something.

"I have not gotten anyone from our university to admit what I just told you," said James. "I said, 'If this university isn't going to support us any better than that, after all the money these players have made for them, then I'm not going to work here anymore.'"

Former Husky All-American lineman and 11-year NFL veteran Lincoln Kennedy spoke candidly to me in November 2003. "I was greatly disappointed by the University of Washington for the way they turned their back on the players and Coach James. It was like they said, 'Here you go NCAA, you have someone (James) who can take the blame for what occurred, and they accepted his resignation.'

"During the investigation, I came under scrutiny as being a person who took an active role in recruiting", said Kennedy. "The investigators claimed that I was buying things for recruits. But I was never doing anything improper. And I know that I turned in my receipts. But the (Pac-10) investigators claimed that I didn't. They fabricated charges, and it really bothered me. They needed to level the playing field. But there was never a time when the University of Washington stood by its athletes. These athletes are the people out there working hard and representing the university. There was no attempt to offer a protective shield to us."

Kennedy continued: "It left a bad taste, and I'm not close to the program because of it. I'm still bothered by it. Gilby (current Husky Coach Keith Gilbertson) has told me to just let it go and come back into the fold, but I can't. That's why when there is a BYE week with the Raiders I don't go up there to games... I felt like the university turned its back on me, so I will turn my back on them."

Don James leaned forward and looked at me intently.

"I could have coached eleven more games and then resigned, and made $300,000 more money, with all my radio and TV contracts and endorsements. But if I did that, then I figured all my staff probably would have been let go, so I wanted to save the staff and give (newly-appointed successor) Jim Lambright a chance."

But it wasn't just Washington's roll over defense that Don James found most disappointing. The Pacific-10 Conference also discouraged him.

"The thing that frustrates me the most was that Carol and I's alma mater, the University of Miami, was going through similar problems. And the commissioner of their conference came out and said the University of Miami is like part of the family, they're one of us. We're going to work through this, we're going get this over. We're going to do everything we can to not hurt any of the programs.

"And I didn't hear that from the Pac-10", said James. "Why, since we had done so much for this league, why didn't they try to help? It seemed like they were out to get us because we were so good, rather than helping us get through this with the least amount of problems."

Former Washington Athletic Director Mike Lude was asked how he would have dealt with the sanctions had he still been at the helm: "I would have fought it very fiercely," he said. Instead, under the watch of Lude's successor Barbara Hedges, Washington made a series of conciliatory moves that compounded its downfall. On December 18, 1992, President Gerberding hired a Kansas City law firm to come in and investigate. Gerberding instructed them to not leave any stone unturned. Twelve days later, Washington agreed to join investigations with the Pac-10 and share all information.

Eight months later, during the news conference which was in the wake of Don James' resignation, Barbara Hedges sat before the cameras acting anxiously, and protested resolutely: "We believe the penalties are too harsh and unwarranted. We are shocked and stunned. We feel that this sets a precedent at a higher standard that is almost unheard of in the NCAA." Then answering a reporter's question about Don James, she said: "I don't think we realized how difficult this was for him. I believe the second year of the bowl ban did it."

The next day, University of Washington President William Gerberding issued the following statement:

"Neither the university's investigation nor that of the Pac-10 Conference found any instance of willful misconduct by any university employee. Whether one considers the penalties imposed by the conference to be appropriate or fair is a matter of individual judgment. I do not."

Hedges' and Gerberding's actions and comments are contradictory and hypocritical, when contrasted to what Don James describes of that fateful Saturday night phone call he received from Hedges—prior to the announcement to the media: "I mentioned to Barbara to tell Dr. Gerberding that if they go through with this, they're going to need a new coach here. But he wasn't even there at the meeting... And I never heard from Gerberding. I still haven't."

Our interview was drawing to a close, and I asked Coach James whom he blamed for what happened.

"Well for starters, I think its *The Seattle Times,*" said James. "I live in this community and I watch them beat up everybody, not just the football program. I've watched them beat up on Boeing and Nordstrom and all the great industries and businesses in this community. They all get beat up by the local press. Maybe that happens everywhere. But I have lived in a lot of places and I haven't seen it elsewhere.

"But overall I was so disgusted with what had taken place. I really didn't know whom to blame, I still don't. I blame myself I guess, I don't know. You can call Barbara & Gerberding and get their side." Seated at his side, his wife Carol added: "They may not be absolutely honest with what happened." To that James quickly stated, "No, they don't want to take the blame for this."

In conclusion, I asked Don James if he was still bitter about what had occurred a decade ago.

"No, not at all," he said resolutely, and almost as if he was surprised by my question. "We profess to be Christians, and you can't go through life judging others. These are just the things as I perceive them to have happened, but it is over."

Then he paused, glancing out into an empty Husky Stadium, before looking back toward me and quietly adding: "Any time we go through trials in life, we come out as better people, better Christians."

Chapter 48

A Letter from former UW President, Dr. William Gerberding

IN A 1995 INTERVIEW with the UW alumni magazine Columns, *retiring University of Washington President William Gerberding was asked about the sanctions period. He was asked to comment on the blame some people placed on him for being "less than aggressive in representing the university's case."*

"Well, there were even nastier charges than that," said Gerberding. "There was a ... I mean, the most bizarre suggestion was that I was not only ineffective, but that I had somehow conspired to have it happen. I don't suppose there were many people who believed that but it really was ugly out there. And there was a death threat. It just got crazy around here for a while. But if anybody would really like to know what happened in the Pac-10 session on the subject, I would be happy to provide them with the minutes. I didn't write the minutes. They show me very vigorously protesting the proposed sanctions."

• • •

Dr. Gerberding declined my requests for an interview regarding the sanctions period. In August 2006, he wrote the following letter for inclusion in this book. It is shown in its entirety.

—— Original Message ——

From: William Gerberding

To: Derek Johnson

Sent: Thursday, August 17, 2006 4:13 PM

Subject: Re: interview request

Mr. Johnson,

The penalties imposed on the UW football program by the Pac 10 in 1993 were grossly unfair, entirely disproportionate, and a disgrace to the conference.

In the summer of 1993, the Pac 10 office informed us of an array of proposed penalties that would soon be acted upon by the Pac 10 Council, a group consisting of the Athletic Directors and Faculty Representatives of the ten institutions. We regarded those initial proposed penalties as excessive and made it clear in advance to all concerned that this was our view.

During that meeting, our representatives proposed a softening of the proposed penalties. As is customary, our representatives then left the meeting and awaited the decisions of their peers. After the meeting adjourned and the participants had departed, our people were informed that television penalties had been reduced, as we had requested, but that a second year of exclusion from post-season games had been added. This stunning turn of events was devastating to all of us and there was no immediate appeal available. (It is noteworthy, by the way, that the Pac 10 recognized later that this procedure was unfair and it is now part of the regulations that if proposed penalties are altered, then the institution has a right to appeal the changes.)

I was out of town when the Council's decision was made but was, of course, in close touch with UW officials. I learned that because of the imposition of a second year of exclusion from post-season games Don James had indicated that he intended to resign. I called him immediately and urged him to reconsider, but he said his mind was made up. I thought it was a cordial conversation and I understood his anger and bitterness. I shared those sentiments.

In matters of this gravity, Pac 10 Council decisions have to be ratified by the Presidents and Chancellors. Accordingly, shortly thereafter a telephone conference call was set up. In accordance with standard practice, the affected institution was permitted to speak first. I explained as clearly and as forcefully as I could why we regarded the penalties, especially the last-minute ban of a second season of post-season play, as unfair and entirely out of line with previous Pac 10 and NCAA sanctions in cases like ours. Again in accordance with standard practice, I was then required to leave the call.

The Presidents and Chancellors rarely if ever reject a Council decision and they did not do so this time. I can't remember whether the vote was 8 to 1 or 9 to 0 but it was overwhelming.

I had been active in Pac 10 affairs for fourteen years but I was so outraged by these actions that I stopped going to Pac 10 meetings. The only one I attended thereafter was in the spring of 1995 when, at the urging of some Pac 10 officials and some UW associates, I agreed to make a token appearance at the end of one of their sessions and to make a few farewell remarks. Many friendships among my Pac 10 peers were broken or damaged during this terrible time.

Our only recourse thereafter, if it existed at all, was to petition the NCAA to soften the penalties at the hearing of their Enforcement Committee to be held later on. Our strong delegation to that hearing consisted of two UW Regents, our AD, our Faculty Rep, and me. Professor of Law Ron Aronson, our Faculty Rep, had prepared a chart that compared our penalties with those imposed by the NCAA in similar cases in recent years. (The Pac 10 is the only conference that imposes penalties on its own members prior to NCAA action.) It showed in a powerful manner how out of line our penalties were, especially the second year of post-season exclusion. We had prepared extensively and all of the members of our delegation were allowed to speak. Our efforts to have the second post-season ban revoked were in vain. (Interestingly, subsequent to our case the NCAA instituted an appeals process, and overly harsh penalties have since been overturned by the new Infractions Appeals Committee in a number of cases.)

Don James was, of course, a great football coach. He was also a gentleman and a fine representative of the University of Washington for 18 years. During the fourteen years that he and I were together at the UW, I praised him frequently in public and private and I did so with enthusiasm and conviction.

It is always difficult to see into the hearts and minds of other people, but it was and still is difficult not to believe that the Pac 10's treatment of our football program was in good measure a result of jealousy and pettiness. The football team had just been to three consecutive Rose Bowls, and had shared the national championship in one of those years. Some small minds and people seized the opportunity to punish our coach, our team, and our university. It was and remains a bitter experience.

William P. Gerberding
UW President, 1979-1995

Chapter 49

Saying Goodbye

September 4, 1993
Husky Stadium - Washington vs. Stanford

THIS LAST CHAPTER DEPICTS Don James' final hours as Husky Coach, and concludes twelve days later at Husky Stadium, on an emotionally-charged afternoon that my Dad and I will never forget.

Don James went into the other room to take the call from Athletic Director Barbara Hedges. It was that fateful Saturday night of August 20, 1993. Don and his wife Carol were at their son's house, along with Dave Cohn, who was a friend and regent. Don and Carol had been high school sweethearts, married over forty years. Carol knew her husband's idiosyncrasies like nobody else. So when he reentered the room several minutes later, she knew in a millisecond that the worst had occurred; she saw the pursed lips, and the ever-stoic face that now radiated fury.

James believed that the University of Washington had lied to him. They had been telling him that in conversations with the Pac-10, there would be, at worst, a one-year ban on bowl games, and a loss of $2.8 million in TV revenue. Barbara Hedges, however, had just told him on the phone that there would be a devastating two-year ban on bowl games. Behind his back, the university had worked out a different deal with the Pac-10. James heard through sources that the university was concerned that losing revenue would hurt their women's programs and non-revenue sports. So in the phone call James told Hedges to tell President Gerberding that if he didn't change his stance on this, he would quit immediately as head coach at Washington. "Football generates 87% of the athletic department's revenue," James told Hedges. "So for them to say that is ridiculous."

Hedges responded that she was having an emergency meeting with Gerberding the next morning. Meanwhile, Don and Carol returned to their home in Bellevue, for the long night that lay ahead.

In an upstairs office loft, working through intermittent periods of silence, they toiled on two separate media releases. Don would write a draft and then read to Carol for her feedback. Four or five times, the ringing phone shattered the quiet. Dave Cohn was calling repeatedly with pleas for Coach James to reconsider.

"We did not know which press release we would use," Carol James later recalled. "We had no idea what was going to happen. Don said his mind was made up. I asked if he was sure that this is what he wanted to do. Was he sure in his heart that this was it? He said, 'Carol, this is the only thing I can do.' After everything that the team had done for the school and the Pac-10, he wanted to make a very strong statement."

The next morning, Don and Carol James drove across the floating bridge to the University of Washington. The assistant coaches were already there and working. Two-a-days had finished, and the season opener against Stanford was less than two weeks away. The assistant coaches saw Carol, and privately wondered what the coach's wife was doing there. They resumed working. After awhile, the call came from Barbara Hedges. Hedges told Don James that Gerberding never showed up for the emergency meeting. This was a tipping point in Husky football history. Don told Carol to call their kids, and tell them what was happening. Then he gathered his assistant coaches and told them that he was quitting, effective immediately. The assistants were ashen-faced. James then spoke privately with defensive coordinator Jim Lambright for a couple of minutes, before heading over to the meeting room to address the players, who were blithely waiting to be told of the penalties.

The Assembly Room is located halfway up the tunnel into Husky Stadium, containing theatre-style seating, with a gentle downward slope looking upon a podium. For a standard meeting, the offense and defense were usually segregated; but on this day they sat co-mingled. Coach James had been preparing them emotionally all week for receiving the penalties. He had told them that the worst-case scenario was a one-year bowl ban. James was so meticulous with his planning, that the players were always prepared and rarely were surprised by anything. The side door opened and Don and Carol James entered the room. While Don James proceeded to the podium with his head slightly bowed, Carol quietly made her way past the players to take a seat in the back of the room. Carol's presence confused several in the room. For the players up front, confusion swiftly advanced to alarm, as they could see the reddened and moistened eyes of their somber-looking head coach. Don James proceeded to inform the team of his decision to resign in the same manner that he had always conducted meetings; time-conscious, precise and devoid of sentimentality.

"Don started things out, by talking about the penalties," said Carol. "He said that he was disgusted with how the Pac-10 had treated the coaches and players, after all we had done for the conference. Then he said that in protest, he was resigning as of that moment, as head coach at the University of Washington. And it was like the air had been sucked out of the room, just stunned silence."

After a moment, utter silence gave way to shouts from twenty to thirty players at once. "NO COACH! YOU CAN'T DO THIS! THIS ISN'T FAIR!" Carol James stood up and worked her way back toward her husband. Near the front of the room, one of the seniors stood up and told James that the team would not accept his decision. Some players like fullback Leif Johnson, felt anger and betrayal toward James. Others, like lineman Stephen Hoffmann, understood why their coach would do this.

"Don responded that his decision was made," said Carol. "And he told them that he had asked Jim Lambright to take over the rest of this meeting. And that was it. He said a final goodbye, and he and I walked out of the room."

Don and Carol exited the side door and entered the Husky Stadium tunnel. The door closed behind them as they made their way up toward the coaches' offices in the Tubby Graves building. Then they heard that door re-open forcefully, as fifteen or twenty players spilled out into the tunnel and jogged after them, calling out in desperation.

"Don told them, 'No, your place is back with the team now,'" said Carol.

All of the players returned to the meeting room and were seated. Jim Lambright would address the agitated room for several more minutes, stressing the importance of team unity.

Don and Carol James retreated to his office, and embraced each other as they staved off their surging anguish. In a matter of minutes, several players were streaming through the office door, nearly frantic. They met with Don James, pleading with him.

While this raged on, the phone rang out front. Carol answered. It was President Gerberding, calling to talk to her husband. Carol was cold, told him that she wasn't going to interrupt things. She said that some emotional things were going on in the office. As she hung up, more players appeared, flooding the hallway, many of them sobbing. Carol hugged several of them, crying along with them. This went on for a couple of hours, before the raw emotions wore themselves out, like a dissipating tornado. Don James left one of his prepared statements with the Athletic Department to issue to the media the next day. Then he and Carol got in their car and drove back home. Their daughter Jil was there, soon to be joined by their son Jeff.

It was that evening, while watching ESPN that they saw the first report of rumors coming out of Seattle. Their phone started ringing like crazy. Don and Carol didn't answer. Soon, Carol looked out her window and saw radio and TV people gathered outside in the street.

The next day, as Don James was emptying his office, he encountered a couple of freshmen players in the hallway who said they were thinking of transferring to another school. James promptly walked into Barbara Hedges' office and suggested to her that Jim Lambright be named as the permanent head coach. At about the same time, the four senior Husky co-captains went to Hedges and told her that the team would refuse to practice unless the "interim" label was stripped from Lambright's title. Soon after, it was announced to the public that Jim Lambright had been signed to a multi-year deal as Head Coach at the University of Washington.

Meanwhile, over in Bellevue, a florist truck pulled up in front of the James residence. They were there to unload a dozen roses for every Husky victory in Don James' career—one hundred and fifty-three in all. These had been sent by a group of boosters and friends. The roses crammed the driveway. The mailbox was stuffed daily with cards and letters, thousands of them, most expressing personal anguish and blessings.

Members of the Tyee Board asked Don and Carol to attend the first kickoff luncheon, but they declined. "We said 'No, this is Jim Lambright's time,' said Carol. "Don really wanted to stay back because it wasn't about him anymore. It was really an emotional time because everything happened so quickly over that couple of weeks. There was a lot of trauma. But there was no question that we would go to the Stanford game, along with our kids."

In his eighteen years as Washington's coach, Don James had often heard of the fun the fans had in traveling to the Husky football games by boat. A booster quickly invited them to join him on his boat, and Don and Carol accepted. While out upon the gently sloshing blue water of Lake Washington, they enjoyed the ride—despite the trauma they had endured. On this sunny Saturday morning, slowly motoring toward Husky Stadium, a first of two surprises awaited them.

"It was an emotional day to begin with," said Carol. "But what really set it off was that a lot of people had found out that Don was on the boat. When we got onto the dock to walk up to the stadium, it was lined with people cheering all the way to the stadium. It was hard to get through it emotionally, but it was also a great feeling."

When Don and Carol reached the box high above the stadium, a university official quietly told Carol to make sure that her husband was looking to the tunnel as the team came running out. Carol said OK, but didn't grasp what was about to happen.

At that moment, unseen to the eyes of the stadium crowd, the three-time defending Pac-10 Champion Washington Huskies were filing out of their locker room. Normally, as they marched down the dimly-lit passageway and toward the field, the Huskies would be right behind the opposing team, chanting and barking as they followed down through the tunnel. But on this day, the Huskies moved forward in silence, in rows of four, holding hands, walking toward the entryway of daylight ahead. The massive dull rumble of the fired-up crowd was growing louder as the players drew closer to the field.

Stanford preceded them and exited the tunnel, running onto the field. It wasn't hard to notice that their head coach, the legendary Bill Walsh, was surrounded by thirteen security guards in black shirts. Earlier that year, at a Cardinal Alumni luncheon, he had publicly called the Husky players 'mercenaries.' The Washington players heard the lustful booing as Walsh and his Stanford team reached the opposite sideline. Now it was Washington's turn. The first few rows of Husky players reached the mouth of the tunnel and became visible to the 73,000 fans in attendance, as well a national TV audience. The crowd erupted with a massive roar. Washington's gleaming gold helmets shone brilliantly in the September sun.

"As I heard the crowd starting to cheer I looked out and saw that the players were standing in the tunnel," said Carol. "Don was standing in the back of the box talking to our son Jeff. I said to him, 'Oh Don, someone said you should be here to see the team come out of the tunnel.'"

Don moved over next to Carol and they were confused at first whether it was actually the Huskies or some other team. The players were slowly walking out of the tunnel, in rows of four, holding hands and raising them above their helmets. The Husky Stadium crowd realized what was happening; the crescendo shook the foundation of Husky Football existence like an earthquake.

"The players then walked out and at mid-field got down on a knee, and pointed up toward Don," said Carol. "It was an emotional time. It was emotional for a lot of people. We had a lot of people in the stands that day say that there wasn't a dry eye around them."

As the team knelt in a cluster at mid-field and pointed skyward, the home crowd's cathartic roar continued unabated. The Stanford players felt hemmed in amid the ceaseless din. Husky running back Napoleon Kaufman thought to himself, "Dang, Coach James has been here eighteen years. This is his stadium." Don and Carol James, as well their son Jeff, began to cry. Don James would say later, "I've never felt anything like that before."

Coach Jim Lambright said that he and his team captains decided to display a tribute to Don James. "We wanted the beginning of the game's focus on Don and what he had meant to the program for so many years," he said. "We wanted to send a powerful signal that everyone would know that this is special."

With the game about to start, a whirlwind of thoughts and emotions churned through Jim Lambright's psyche as he stood on the Husky Stadium sideline as a head coach for the first time.

"It was everything that someone would imagine, for a person who had played there, coached there for 24 years, and then within two weeks, you're suddenly the head coach out there on the field," said Lambright. "No word is strong enough to describe what that was like. It's an honor and a privilege, and yet you're also just out there doing your job.

"We had had a lot of work to do, just settling the team down, maintaining confidence without Don James," he said. "We were sanctioned not by the NCAA, but by the Pac-10, our own people... And they put us in the *deepest* dungeon. That was triple hard, whereas conference teams usually look out for each other, rallying around a team (that is experiencing challenges), and being protective of each other." After a pause, he chuckled. "That was certainly NOT the case in our situation."

The year before, Washington had buried Stanford 41-7 and knocked their quarterback Steve Stenstrom, out of the game. Now, early in the first quarter, Husky linebacker Andy Mason studied Stenstrom, and knew it was over. "After the first series, I could see it in his eyes. 'Here we go, the same thing all over again.'"

A tight and hard-fought first half opened up for the Huskies in the second half. Husky QB Damon Huard hit tight end Mark Bruener for a 66-yard touchdown pass down the middle of the field. Napoleon Kaufman had picked up a blitzing cornerback and Stanford's young safety failed to cover Bruener on a go route. This play created a psychological chasm between the teams. A few minutes later, Husky tight end Ernie Conwell got into the act, hauling in a 26-yard touchdown pass, to extend the lead to 24-7. With 5:07 left in the game, Damon Huard scored on a keeper from two yards out, and the Huskies led 31-7.

Stanford tallied a TD in the game's final minute, to close the gap to the final score of 31-14. Suddenly appearing along the Washington sideline was President William Gerberding. He was moving among the players and congratulating them on the victory. The response from the players was cordial, but nothing more. As the clock ran out, the Huskies ran out onto the field, chanting DJ! DJ! DJ!, and pointing again skyward.

Washington had rolled up 500 yards of offense, and effectively utilized the tight ends in scoring three touchdowns with them. Running back Napoleon Kaufman racked up 195 yards rushing on 24 carries. Damon Huard threw for 174 yards and 3 TDs. The Cardinal offense was held to a mere 35 yards rushing

Washington's post-game locker room was a scene of raucous appreciation. The Husky players gathered around their new head coach and chanted "Lambo! Lambo! Lambo!" It was one of the great points of Jim Lambright's life. "It's a moment in time as a coach," said Lambright. "But more importantly, it's about a team pulling together. Trying to build as a team."

With the game finished, Don James spent an hour talking to fans on a post-game radio show. Then, feeling drained, he and Carol headed home to begin a new chapter in their lives. Husky Football in the Don James Era was officially over.

"From then on, we felt a part of it, but we really weren't," said Carol. "Unless you're actually on the field you can't be. But in part of our hearts it is really deep, and we'll always have that feeling. Because Husky football was such an important part of our lives for so many years. But we had no regrets. As much as it hurt and as emotional as it was, when Don resigned, we left it all behind us."

THE END

Husky Football in the Don James Era

18 Seasons (153-57-2) (.726)

1975 (6-5)

Pacific-8 - 3rd, Tie

Co-Captains: Ray Pinney, John Whitacre, Dan Lloyd, Al Burleson

12	at Arizona State	35
10	Texas	28
14	Navy	13
27	at Oregon	17
0	at Alabama	52
21	Stanford	24
35	Oregon State	7
17	at UCLA	13
24	at California	27
8	USC	7
28	Washington State	27
196		250

1976 (5-6)

Pacific-8 - 4th, Tie

Co-Captains: Robin Earl, Scott Phillips, Charles Jackson, Mike Baldassin

38	Virginia	17
7	Colorado	21
13	Indiana	20
38	Minnesota	7
24	at Oregon State	12
28	at Stanford	34
14	Oregon	7
21	UCLA	30
0	California	7
3	at USC	7
51	at Washington State	32
237		207

1977 (10-2)

Pacific-8 - 1st

Co-Captains: Warren Moon, Blair Bush, Mike Rohrbach, Dave Browning

18	Mississippi State *	27
24	San Jose State	3
20	at Syracuse	22
17	at Minnesota	19
54	at Oregon	0
45	Stanford	21
14	Oregon State	6
12	UCLA *	20
50	at California	31
28	USC	10
35	Washington State	15
27	Michigan (Rose Bowl)	20
344		194

* forfeit - used ineligible player

1978 (7-4)

Pacific-10 - 2nd, Tie

Co-Captains: Michael Jackson, Jeff Toews, Nesby Glasgow, Scott Greenwood

7	UCLA	10
31	Kansas	2
7	at Indiana	14
34	at Oregon State	0
17	Alabama	20
34	at Stanford	31
20	Oregon	14
41	Arizona State	7
31	Arizona	21
10	at USC	28
38	at Washington State	8
270		155

1979 (10-2)

Pacific-10 - 2nd

Co-Captains: Phil Foreman, Doug Martin, Antowaine Richardson, Joe Steele

38	Wyoming	2
41	Utah	7
21	at Oregon	17
49	Fresno State	14
41	Oregon State	0
7	at Arizona State *	12
14	Pittsburgh	26
34	at UCLA	14
28	at California	24
17	USC	24
17	Washington State	7
14	Texas (**Sun Bowl**)	7
321		154

* forfeit - used ineligible player

1980 (9-3)

Pacific-10 - 1st

Co-Captains: Tom Flick, Randy Van Divier, Rusty Olsen, Ken Gardner

50	Air Force	7
45	Northwestern	7
10	Oregon	34
24	at Oklahoma State	18
41	at Oregon State	6
27	at Stanford	24
10	Navy	24
25	Arizona State	0
45	Arizona	22
20	at USC	10
30	at Washington State	23
6	Michigan (Rose Bowl)	23
333		198

1981 (10-2)

Pacific-10 - 1st

Co-Captains: James Carter, Vince Coby, Fletcher Jenkins, Mark Jerue

34	Pacific	14
20	Kansas State	3
17	at Oregon	3
7	Arizona State	26
27	at California	26
56	Oregon State	17
14	at Texas Tech	7
42	Stanford	31
0	at UCLA	31
13	USC	3
23	Washington State	10
28	Iowa (**Rose Bowl**)	0
281		171

1982 (10-2)

Pacific-10 - 2nd
Co-Captains: Anthony Allen, Ken Driscoll, Paul Skansi, Mark Stewart

55	Texas-El Paso	0
20	at Arizona	13
37	Oregon	21
46	San Diego State	25
50	California	7
34	at Oregon State	17
10	Texas Tech	3
31	at Stanford	43
10	UCLA	7
17	at Arizona State	13
20	at Washington State	24
21	Maryland (**Aloha Bowl**)	20
354		193

1983 (8-4)

Pacific-10 - 2nd
Co-Captains: Steve Pelluer, Rick Mallory, Stewart Hill, Dean Browning

34	at Northwestern	0
25	Michigan	24
14	at Louisiana State	40
27	Navy	10
34	Oregon State	7
32	Stanford	15
32	at Oregon	3
24	at UCLA	27
23	at Arizona	22
24	USC	0
6	Washington State	17
10	Penn State (**Aloha Bowl**)	13
285		178

1984 (11-1)

Pacific-10 - 2nd

Co-Captains: Dan Eernissee, Jim Rodgers, Danny Greene, Tim Meamber

26	Northwestern	0
20	at Michigan	11
35	Houston	7
53	Miami (Ohio)	7
19	at Oregon State	7
37	at Stanford	15
17	Oregon	10
28	Arizona	12
44	California	14
7	at USC	16
38	at Washington State	29
28	Oklahoma (Orange Bowl)	17
352		145

1985 (7-5)

Pacific-10 - 4th, Tie

Co-Captains: Joe Kelly, Vestee Jackson, Hugh Millen, Dennis Soldat

17	Oklahoma State	31
3	at BYU	31
29	at Houston	12
21	UCLA	14
19	at Oregon	13
28	at California	12
20	Oregon State	21
34	Stanford	0
7	at Arizona State	36
20	USC	17
20	Washington State	21
20	Colorado (**Freedom Bowl**)	17
238		225

1986 (8-3-1)

Pacific-10 - 2nd, Tie

Co-Captains: Kevin Gogan, Rod Jones, Rick Fenney, Steve Alford, Reggie Rogers, Tim Peoples

40	Ohio State	7
52	BYU	21
10	at USC	20
50	California	18
24	at Stanford	14
48	Bowling Green	0
38	Oregon	3
21	at Arizona State	34
28	at Oregon State	12
17	UCLA	17
44	at Washington State	23
6	Alabama (**Sun Bowl**)	28
378		197

1987 (7-4-1)

Pacific-10 - 3rd

Co-Captains: Chris Chandler, Darryl Franklin, Brian Habib, David Rill

31	Stanford	21
28	Purdue	10
12	at Texas A&M	29
31	Pacific	3
22	at Oregon	29
27	Arizona State	14
23	USC	37
28	Oregon State	12
21	at Arizona	21
14	at UCLA	47
34	Washington State	19
24	Tulane (**Independence Bowl**)	12
295		254

* forfeit - used ineligible player

1988 (6-5)

Pacific-10 - 6th

Co-Captains: Ricky Andrews, Darryl Hall, Aaron Jenkins, Mike Zandofsky

20	at Purdue	6
31	Army	17
35	San Jose State	31
17	UCLA	24
10	at Arizona State	0
27	at USC	28
14	at Oregon	17
28	Stanford	25
13	Arizona	16
28	California	27
31	at Washington State	32
254		223

1989 (8-4)

Pacific-10 - 2nd, Tie

Co-Captains: Dennis Brown, Cary Conklin, Martin Harrison, Andre Riley

19	Texas A&M	6
38	Purdue	9
17	at Arizona	20
28	Colorado	45
16	at USC	24
20	Oregon	14
29	at California	16
28	UCLA	27
32	Arizona State	34
51	at Oregon State	14
20	Washington State	9
34	Florida (**Freedom Bowl**)	7
281		171

1990 (10-2)

Pacific-10 - 1st

Co-Captains: Eric Briscoe, Dean Kirkland, Greg Lewis, Travis Richardson

20	San Jose State	17
20	at Purdue	14
31	USC	0
14	at Colorado	20
42	at Arizona State	14
38	Oregon	17
52	at Stanford	16
46	California	7
54	Arizona	10
22	UCLA	25
55	at Washington State	10
46	Iowa (**Rose Bowl**)	34
440		184

1991 (12-0)

Pacific-10 - 1st

Co-Captains: Mario Bailey, Brett Collins, Ed Cunningham, Donald Jones

42	at Stanford	7
36	at Nebraska	21
56	Kansas State	3
54	Arizona	0
48	Toledo	0
24	at California	17
29	Oregon	7
44	Arizona State	16
14	at USC	3
58	at Oregon State	6
56	Washington State	21
34	Michigan (**Rose Bowl**)	14
495		115

1992 (9-3)

Pacific-10 - 1st

Co-Captains: Mark Brunell, Dave Hoffmann, Lincoln Kennedy, Shane Pahukoa

31	at Arizona State	7
27	Wisconsin	10
29	Nebraska	14
17	USC	10
35	California	16
24	at Oregon	3
31	Pacific	7
41	Stanford	7
3	at Arizona	16
45	Oregon State	16
23	at Washington State	42
31	Michigan (**Rose Bowl**)	38
337		186